WILL ROGERS' WORLD

WILL ROGERS' WORLD

America's Foremost Political Humorist Comments on the Twenties and Thirties —and Eighties and Nineties

Bryan B. Sterling *and* Frances N. Sterling

M. EVANS AND COMPANY • NEW YORK

Library of Congress Cataloging-in-Publication
Data

Rogers, Will, 1879–1935.
    Will Rogers' world : America's foremost
political humorist comments on the
twenties and thirties—and eighties and
nineties / [edited by] Bryan B. Sterling
and Frances N. Sterling.
        p.   cm.
    Includes index.
    ISBN 0-87131-564-5
    1. United States—Civilization—20th
century—Humor.   2. United States—
Social conditions—20th century—
Humor.   3. United States—Politics and
government—20th century—
Humor.   4. American wit and
humor.   5. Rogers, Will, 1879–
1935.   6. Humorists, American—
Biography.   I. Sterling, Bryan
B.   II. Sterling, Frances N.
III. Title.
PN6161.R664425   1989   89-1129
818'.5202—dc19

M. Evans and Company, Inc.
216 East 49 Street
New York, New York 10017

Design by Cynthia Dunne

Manufactured in the United States of America

9 8 7 6 5 4 3 2 1

CONTENTS

I use only one set method in my little gags,
and that is to try to keep to the truth. Of course you
can exaggerate it, but what you say must be based
on truth. Personally I don't like the jokes that get the
biggest laughs, as they are generally as broad as a
house and require no thought at all. I like one where,
if you are with a friend, and hear it, it makes you
think, and you nudge your friend and say, "He's
right about that."

I would rather have you do that than to have you
laugh—and then forget the next minute what it was
you laughed at.

WILL ROGERS, 1879–1935

Chapter I

INTRODUCTION

C lement Vann Rogers, Will's father, was a well-to-do rancher. He controlled about sixty thousand acres of grazing land along the fertile Verdigris River near the small town of Oologah in the Indian Territory. In 1907 this land was to become a part of the state of Oklahoma, with Clement Vann Rogers one of the leaders of the state constitutional convention.

Uncle Clem, as he was known, had fought in the War between the States as a cavalry officer under General Stand Watie, "but you couldn't get much war news out of Papa. I sho didn't inherit this continuous flow of blathering around from him." Uncle Clem came back to the Verdigris valley to rebuild his prewar wealth. While he was away, fighting for the Confederacy, Northern marauders had destroyed his old home and driven off his cattle. Starting anew, he laboriously increased his holdings and influence. For his growing family he constructed a fine two-story part-log, part-frame building. The "White House on the Verdigris," as the Rogers family home was known in neighboring states, offered many a traveler between Texas, Kansas, or Nebraska good food and friendly hospitality.

On Tuesday, November 4, 1879, William Penn Adair Rogers was born. Just before her delivery, Mary America Rogers asked that she be taken to the log part of the house. There she gave birth to her last

1

surviving child. As Will would tell it afterward, "My mother had just read the life of Lincoln; so I got the log house end of it o.k. All I need now is his other qualifications." His ancestry was Cherokee, on both parents' sides; also Irish, Scottish, and either German or Dutch. When the boy, usually called Willie, was ten years old, his mother died. She had showered Willie, her only surviving son, with great affection and had hoped to see him grow up to be a preacher. Willie was inconsolable over her death. After a year Clem Rogers married again, and the boy was sent to live with his much older married sister Sallie McSpadden, in nearby Chelsea.

Will was never happier than when he had a horse to ride and a rope to spin. He learned to use a lariat from Dan Walker, a black man who worked for Clem Rogers. Wherever Will went, he usually had a rope in his hands, practicing and trying to learn new and more difficult tricks.

For the next few years Willie attended several of the best schools in the area, rarely staying very long at any of them. Finally, Clem Rogers sent his son to the Kemper Military School at Boonville, Missouri. "I have my hard-to-manage son in a military school," he told a friend. Will stayed there less than two years—"One year in the guard house, the other in the fourth reader; one was about as bad as the other," was the way he put it.

Will Rogers was probably the greatest practical joker Kemper had ever admitted. His pranks, ranging from roping the commandant to dousing fellow students in the middle of the night, pretending it was a fire drill, earned him admiration from the pupils and demerits from the staff. One night, late in 1898, Will ran away from Kemper and "quit the school business for life." He left behind, so the story goes, 150 demerits; each one called for a full hour's march along a prescribed beat. It was the only obligation Will Rogers never paid.

The next few years were a learning process, with Will the eager student, discovering life firsthand. He worked as a cowboy in Texas, then managed his own cattle in the Indian Territory, near Claremore, the town he was to call his home ("a town in physique, but a city at heart"). He sold the herd and struck out for the Argentine, having to go by way of England. Will had always wanted to see the gauchos. But having to travel this circuitous way he was able to take in other sights. He, like so many other tourists, stood outside Buckingham Palace and watched the changing of the guard. Will even caught a glimpse of King Edward VII, but doubted, as he wrote in a letter home, that "the king recognized me."

His stay in the Argentine was cut short when he ran out of money. There are indications that he must have missed quite a number of meals. Finally he was able to get a job to "chaperon mules and she-cows" on a transport to Durban, Natal. Will was more seasick than the cattle he was tending.

After several jobs, ranging from driving the herd into the interior to breaking horses for the British army, Will Rogers' future was shaped by a chance meeting. Looking for employment in Johannesburg, South Africa, Will met "Texas Jack," the owner and principal star of a Wild West show. Will, who had developed an astonishing dexterity with the lasso, now could put it to good use. Billed as the "Cherokee Kid," he learned the rudiments of show business and was "ruined for life as far as honest work was concerned."

After traveling with the show for a number of months, he left and joined the Wirth Brothers' Circus in Australia. The circus moved on to New Zealand and Will went along. When he decided to return to the United States he had just enough money left to book third-class passage. He arrived back home broke.

But Will Rogers had savored show business, and it kept beckoning him. The year 1904 found him at the St. Louis World's Fair with Colonel Zack Mulhall's Wild West show. The following year he appeared with the same group at New York's Madison Square Garden, as part of the annual Horse Fair.

When the Colonel and his troupe returned to its base in the Indian Territory, Will Rogers stayed behind in New York. He was determined to break into vaudeville. His act was quite unusual. He employed a horse and rider and proceeded to demonstrate his superior artistry with the lariat, catching either horse or rider—or both—with a variety of loops. The act was "dumb." Will never spoke, but simply demonstrated the various catches, one after another. Audiences liked what they saw, but Will's effortless performance made them unaware of the skill involved. Finally, fellow performers suggested that Will introduce each "catch." At first Will was reluctant to speak to the audience, especially when there was laughter at his shy, embarrassed Western twang. But eventually he learned to encourage that laughter and to demonstrate the difficulty of his performance by an occasional missed toss—mostly on purpose. He had "ad libs" prepared for such occasions. "Well, I got all my feet through but one!" he would say as he retrieved the rope. Or, "Swinging a rope is all right, provided your neck ain't in it!"

Will was booked along the various vaudeville circuits, with their three or four performances a day, and he traveled across the country, forming friendships with other acts. He became known for his great ability with the lasso and also for his wit, though as yet he used it sparingly in his act. Little by little, he began to insert humorous comments about other acts on the bill. Then, between performances, during the long waits before it was time to go on stage again, Will would learn from some of the other acts. From a fine bicycle performer named Chester Johnstone he picked up the knack of riding a unicycle, a trick he occasionally included in his roping act. He learned to juggle and even to imitate voices.

On November 25, 1908, Will Rogers married Betty Blake in her hometown, Rogers, Arkansas. He had courted her for years, mostly by mail, ever since he first saw her in Oologah. Betty had come there to visit her sister, who had married the local railroad agent. Will and Betty's honeymoon started in New York City and extended all along the vaudeville circuit. "When I roped her," he would say of Betty, "that was the star performance of my life."

In October 1911, Will, Jr., was born. Life changed, as Betty would no longer accompany her husband. Home was now New York City, while Will was on tour. Two years later Mary was born. Will Rogers was an established vaudevillian, well known, but he was not satisfied. Little seemed to change in his career, and the children were growing up while he was away from home. There were several brief Broadway appearances in short-lived musicals. Will Rogers received fine reviews in the newspapers, but he always had to return to vaudeville. Will had long ago given up the horse and rider for his roping tricks; he now used far more talk, and the rope had become incidental. People came to listen to the Westerner, with his humorous points of view, far more than to see him throw his lasso.

In 1915 another child, Jimmy, joined the family, and fate stepped in. Gene Buck, lyricist and author who also scouted for Theatrical producer Florenz Ziegfeld, had caught Will Rogers' act in one of the revues and hired him for the *Midnight Frolic.*

The *Midnight Frolic* was, as its advertising proclaimed, the "Aerial Gardens Atop The New Amsterdam Theatre." Nightly at the stroke of midnight, this luxurious cabaret became New York's foremost night-club. The main attraction was a typical Florenz Ziegfeld production, lavish and extravagant. Here affluent people would gather after an evening at the theater, or just for late-night food, drink, and enter-tainment. Many of the guests came several times a week, as one might frequent a favorite bar or restaurant.

When Florenz Ziegfeld first heard that Gene Buck had hired some cowboy to appear in his sophisticated showplace, he wanted no part of it. The fact that this cowboy was a humorist only added fuel to his objections. Ziegfeld was not partial to funny men. "Get rid of him," he was to have said. Buck never acceded.

The show was completely different from and superior to the one seen earlier in the evening at the *Ziegfeld Follies* in the theater on the ground floor. The famed Ziegfeld girls were the prettiest to be found, the costumes the best Lucile (Lady Duff Gordon) could design and money could pay for; it was without a doubt the best show in New York City. Will Rogers, in his cowboy outfit, might have seemed out of place amid the gentlemen in evening wear and the glamorous ladies, both in the show and in the audience; but his plainness merely height-ened the impact of his words.

One thing became immediately apparent to Will Rogers. The finely honed act he had developed along the vaudeville circuit could not be used night after night. Repeat guests would not laugh at the same jokes twice. He would need new material every night. It was Betty who first suggested that, since Will read every newspaper, he should use the day's news as his basis for comments. "Fresh laid jokes," Will would call them. And so, every evening before show time, he would scan the day's newspapers and pick his newest material. Since the audience had read the same news, he did not need to explain the jokes but could simply deliver his comments. What he had to say made sense, and guests came again and again, just to hear what he had to say and laugh with Will Rogers at the follies of big men in and out of government. He was quoted, and newspapers began to pay attention to him.

Even "Flo" Ziegfeld saw the error of his preconception. Seeing how successful Will Rogers was in the *Midnight Frolic*, he now wanted him also to appear regularly in the *Follies*. Will agreed. The *Follies* of 1915, featuring W.C. Fields, Ed Wynn, Ina Clair, Ann Pennington, Bert Williams, Leon Errol, Mae Murray, and George White, lacked a certain cohesion. Ziegfeld hoped that adding this new super attraction from the *Frolic* would help the *Follies*. It did.

The very next year, in the *Ziegfeld Follies* of 1916, Will Rogers already had star billing, just below Fannie Bryce and ahead of W.C. Fields, Bert Williams, Ann Pennington, Ina Clair, and Marion Davies. It was a dramatic rise of a new star.

In 1918 Goldwyn Pictures Corp. signed Will to a one-motion-picture contract. The film was based on a book by Rex Beach, *Laughing Bill Hyde*. The Goldwyn studio was located in Fort Lee, New Jersey. During the day Will Rogers worked for Goldwyn, just across the Hudson River from Manhattan, and on matinees and evenings he appeared for Ziegfeld.

The film was very well received by critics and the public, and so on November 30, 1918, Will Rogers signed a one-year contract with Samuel Goldfish, who had not yet changed his name to Goldwyn. The contract called for Rogers to star in motion pictures in California for one year, starting on the sixteenth of June, 1919. Will's salary was to be $2,250 per week, "during each week of the term thereof." There was a renewal clause for an additional year, at a new salary of $3,000 per week.

The Rogers family moved and settled first in Hollywood, then in Beverly Hills. Will Rogers had become a movie star, albeit a silent one. His biggest asset, his voice, could not yet be put on film. Goldwyn did pick up the option.

Just before the year 1922 closed, Will began an additional, new career: he became a syndicated columnist. He would write these weekly articles, around 1,500 words, until his death in 1935.

When Will's contract with Goldwyn ran out, he produced his own films and learned a costly lesson. There was far more to the film business than simply taking a good story and putting it—well lighted—on celluloid. There were problems with distribution, advertising, and negotiations. Before Will had produced three motion pictures, his assets were gone; only one film survives in its original form, *The Ropin' Fool*. It is a masterpiece, documenting for all time Will Rogers' artistry with the lariat.

Because Will needed money to pay his debts, he went to work for Hal Roach, acting in short comedies at $2,500 per week. Every available dollar went into retiring Will's debts.

While the family stayed in California, Will went back to Broadway and the *Ziegfeld Follies*. Flo received him with open arms. To earn more money Will now accepted speaking engagements. In the next two years he addressed conventions of manufacturers and salesmen of every conceivable item that the American public could very well have done without. Will Rogers became New York's favorite after-dinner speaker. All extra money was sent back to California; it was still not enough to retire the debt.

In 1925, Charles Wagner, successful impresario of concert tours, booked Will Rogers and a famous foursome of male singers, the De Reszke Quartet, on a cross-country tour. It was really a two-act vaudeville show, with the quartet singing some of the songs of the times and Will talking about anything and everything that had made the news. The advantage here was that most of the same act could be used over and over, as the tour played in a different city every night.

Eventually Will no longer carried the quartet, and the show became a lecture tour. Except for a few days at Christmas, Will was on the road from late fall until the end of spring. For four tours, Will traveled every day; he never complained.

In 1926, Will entered a new phase of his writing career. In addition to his weekly syndicated column, he now contracted to write a daily squib, usually no more than two hundred words. At first he filed the column daily, seven times a week; later that was reduced to six. It was this column that gave him the widest readership. In all, he filed over 2,800 such daily articles.

On a trip to Europe that year, Will took along a cameraman and director and filmed a dozen travelogues, starring in them. Later he added the humorous panels that served as narration in those silent days. Will also flew into Russia, a trip that resulted in a series of

Saturday Evening Post articles; they were later published in a book called *There's Not a Bathing Suit in Russia & Other Bare Facts.*

In the years after leaving Hal Roach, Will made several independently produced silent feature films. But it was not until 1929, when Will Rogers signed a contract with Fox Film Corporation, that he made his first sound film. Will was an instant hit. For the first time movie audiences were able to hear his voice, his humor, his guilelessness. Will Rogers was immediately accepted as a star. Fox Film Corporation had taken a great chance. On March 22, 1929, they had signed Will to a four-feature contract, the films to be completed by September 30, 1930, sixteen months later. Will's salary for the four motion pictures was $600,000.

In October 1929, when the stock market crashed, many businesses either folded or were forced to cut back. The measure of Will Rogers' financial value to Fox Film Corporation is best seen by the fact that on October 27, 1930, they signed him to a new contract. Now one year into the Depression, this new contract called for six additional films for a total salary of $1,025,000, or over $170,000 per film. By this time all debts remaining from Will's own film venture had been repaid in full.

Also in 1930, Will Rogers took on yet another task. He signed a contract for a dozen radio broadcasts for E.R. Squibb & Sons. This, too, proved highly successful. It led later to further broadcasts sponsored by Gulf Oil Company. Between his newspaper articles and his radio addresses, Will reached 40 million Americans a week. This was at a time when the entire population of the United States—men, women, and children—numbered 120 million. It is not surprising that he was such an influential personality, eagerly sought by politicians, whether presidents or local sheriffs. With a single line in his daily squib, he could show the inanity in a bill pending in Congress or explode the myth behind a policy touted as "world-saving." He kidded the great and the near-great, but he never hurt anyone. He threw velvet-tipped harpoons at sacred cows, yet never left a wound or scar. Untouched by political party affiliation, Will never showed partisanship. Thus he had more power to influence the thinking of America than any elected official, even the president of the United States. Such power in the hands of a lesser man, or an ambitious politician, could have created chaos, yet he never once abused it.

Will traveled extensively in this country and abroad. He felt he had to know firsthand what he was writing about. He often chided editorial writers who, from the confines of their "ivory towers," could solve all the problems of the world. He felt that, having been to Italy, or Russia, or Nicaragua, or Cuba, he could perhaps see more clearly the real reasons behind their dissatisfaction.

To save time, Will would fly whenever, and wherever, he could. He was one of the first civilians, if not the first, to fly on a coast-to-coast flight. Will had special permission to fly on mail planes. He not only boosted civilian flying but also military air power. He was a staunch defender of General Billy Mitchell, whose criticisms of interservice rivalry led to his court-martial in 1926.

In motion pictures, from 1933 until his death, Will Rogers was the number one male box-office attraction, leading Clark Gable, Fred Astaire, Wallace Beery, and James Cagney.

In August 1935, having some free time, Will fulfilled a lifelong ambition. He visited Alaska. With pilot Wiley Post, who had circled the world twice, he flew to Juneau, visited Dawson, Aklavik in the Yukon, Fairbanks, and Anchorage. Then, on August fifteenth, it was off to Barrow.

Eleven miles short of their goal, lost in fog and overcast, Post set the plane down on a lagoon to get directions. After about ten minutes on the water the seaplane took off, climbing steeply; the engine stalled at a height of only 200 feet. The tiny plane fell nose first into the lagoon. Both men were killed.

When the report of Will Rogers' death reached the outside world, a pall settled over the land. For decades afterward people would remember where they were and what they were doing at the moment they heard the news. It was a tragedy nobody believed, for no one wanted to believe it.

Will Rogers had not been some unapproachable, distant movie star; he was a familiar voice who called Sundays, on the radio, and who spoke to millions in darkened movie houses; he was a friend—no, more than that, he was a father image, the kindly uncle everyone wished to have. To an American in the midst of the worst depression of its history, he had been a calming voice that seemed to know the answers, that reassured, that brought sanity and laughter to a world gone broke.

It was left to the famous Irish tenor, John McCormack, to describe a country without Will Rogers: "A smile has disappeared from the lips of America and her eyes are suffused with tears."

Chapter II

AMERICA

"Will Rogers was," as the great journalist Damon Runyon wrote, "America's most complete document." Part Indian, part cowboy, born in the rugged Indian Territory, he was equally at ease roping calves on a roundup and performing in New York's Carnegie Hall; he had little trouble sleeping "on the back of his neck" on a plane or spending a night in Lincoln's bedroom in the White House in Washington, D.C., under President Calvin Coolidge and later under Franklin D. Roosevelt; he could talk away an afternoon with the cowboys in the bunkhouse at Muleshoe, Texas, or with the Prince of Wales at York House, London; he was the top male box-office attraction in American films, yet he would feel hurt if he was not asked to play a benefit— for free; he was wealthy, yet lived quietly and gave away more money than he kept; if help was needed anywhere, Will Rogers—so it was said—would beat the Red Cross to the disaster site. When a raging Mississippi River flooded, causing millions of dollars in damage, Will Rogers financed his own benefit tour, raising huge sums. Wherever he appeared, he would start the collection for the needy with his own hefty offering. Will Rogers was himself, and his inherent instincts dictated the right thing to do.

He loved his own country passionately, but not blindly. He could see and comment on every blemish, every smudge, but it did not affect his love. He could take America to task for her many imperfections, yet he would—as a father with an errant child—grasp her with both arms and draw her close. Will never wrapped himself in the flag, though he had dual citizenship in his nation. He was an American —as a quarter-blood Cherokee, more so than most of his countrymen. He had the self-assurance and inner strength of both his heritages, European and indigenous. He was fiercely proud of his Cherokee ancestry at a time when Indians in some Western states still were forced to step off the sidewalk to let the white man pass. He saw the heartless inequities minorities suffered, and he attacked them. He saw riches and poverty, privileges and deprivations, happiness and desolation, and he addressed them all. His writings reflect a mirror image of his times, the good and the bad. They are a history of the roaring twenties and the terrible thirties. It is an era seen through the eyes of a most astute, unbiased humorist, reported not in the hues of dejected analysis, but with compassion; for Will Rogers not only lived it but, as President Roosevelt was to say, "made it bearable."

Despite his love for America—a few have even called him an isolationist—Will Rogers never subscribed to a movement—America First!—that was then gaining converts. He took his stand, deriding it in his own way:

> Now, of course you all have read about Mayor Bill Thompson's society, "America First," that he is forming. He has asked all the mayors of the country to join, and as soon as he gets them in, he will go after some prominent people, and it looks like it might develop into quite a thing. Well, of course, getting my idea from him, I go ahead and form me one "America Only."
>
> There has been a terrible lot of various societies formed to try and instill Americanism into our lagging patriots. If you have never formed a society in your life and don't know what to form one about, why, don't let that worry you in the least. Just start to sponsor "Better Citizenship," or "100 percent Americanism," "America for Americans" or any of these original ideas. There has been quite an epidemic of these, especially since the war.
>
> It seems that before the war come along we were really sorter lax in our duty toward declaring just what we were.

The war come along and about all we could do was to muster up five or six million men of every breed and color that ever been invented. . . . They thought that as long as they paid their taxes, tended to their own business, went to their own churches, kept kinder within the law, that that was all they was supposed to do. You see, we was a backward nation and dident know it.

What we had to learn was to be better Americans. . . . So when the war come along and we found out that all everybody would do was to die, or suffer, or get rich (or whatever the circumstances called for) for his country, why we saw right away that something was needed to instill patriotism. So hence the forming of all these various societies. . . .

Now I have looked over all these clubs and none of them seem to have enough scope, so I want to get this society "America Only" going. "America First" is all right, but it allows somebody else to be second. . . .

I am getting a lot of applications already, real red-blooded go-gettum Americans that have seen this country trampled under foreign feet enough, and they are right out in the open. Why, I figure the patriotism in my organization when I get it formed will run around 165 or 170 percent American. It will make a sucker out of these little 100 percent organizations. It's not too late to send your $20 yet. Remember when you belong to "America Only" you are the last word in organizations.*

Few men had such impact on their age as Will Rogers did.

Certainly none of them provided as detailed an account of what he found—and left.

AMERICA

You can diplomat America out of almost everything she has, but don't try to bluff her.

Europe has got a thing that America always falls for, and that's when they tell us they want our moral leadership!

It's almost like telling an old man that he's got sex appeal.

---

*Syndicated weekly article, published November 13, 1927.

Your own country always looks like they are the only ones doing the wrong thing.

It will take America fifteen years of steady taking care of our own business and letting everybody else's alone, to get us back to where everybody speaks to us again.

We'll show the world we are prosperous, even if we have to go broke to do it.

If you want to really know one of the major things that's wrong with us, read an article in the *Saturday Evening Post*. Then go out, and before you buy the baby a rattle, your sweetheart a toothbrush, your wife a pair of rubber boots, ask if they are "Made in America."

We are getting to be a nation that can't read anymore. If the thing hasn't got a picture of it, why, we are sunk. That's why the Bible is not read more than it is. If they could see a picture of David in his training quarters getting ready to slay Goliath with the jawbone of a Senator, why, people would stop to glance at it.

De Mille in a moving picture parted the Red Sea, and more people have seen it in the picture than ever heard of it outside of pictures. I have had more people ask me where De Mille got that idea, and they say it certainly was original.

To us progress is to work ourselves up to a six-cylinder Buick, have a dinner jacket, belong to six luncheon clubs and wear knee breeches on Sunday when we play golf.

Then we go out and tell the whole world how the standard of living has raised. And start telling the whole world: We are the ones with the right idea.

The greatest thing that the Petrified Forest has demonstrated to the world is that there is nothing that the American tourist won't carry off. The whole wayside is strewn with cars that tried to get out with too much.

President Roosevelt just created the F.E.R.A. (Federal Emergency Relief Association) and the A.A.A. (Agricultural Adjustment Administration) and the P.W.A. (Public Works Administration), so the F.E.R.A. and the A.A.A. and the P.W.A. are to work in conjunction with the N.R.A. (National Recovery Administration) with the financial help of the R.F.C.* who will pay the C.O.D.s of the C.C.C. (Citizens Conservation Camps) and take in return money loaned out to all these initials' I.O.U.s.

Never was a country in the throes of more capital letters than the old U.S.A. But we still haven't sent out the S.O.S.

That's the trouble with most of us, we gab too much. We write too much, we do everything too much. Everybody getting lots of education, but nobody don't know much—but any country that is seriously debating paying a man as much to not work, as to work—why, we are unique, anyhow.

I think we are the most fortunate people in the world. Perhaps we are not the most humorous people in the world, but the provocation to humor is greater in this country than anywhere else.

There is not a minute goes by that there's not some of us doing something seriously that brings smiles to everybody else.

Europe is disgusted with America because she won't say exactly what the dollar is worth. We say our dollar is worth whatever they are worth to you. They may go to ten cents abroad, but they are still worth a dollar to us.

I imagine it has been said before, and I don't claim this as an entirely new observation, but radio is a great thing. I believe it's our greatest invention, far greater than the automobile, for it don't kill anybody. It don't cost us millions for roads.

When you are too lazy, or too old, to do anything else, we can still listen in.

All you got to do in America to enjoy life is to "Don't let your next payment worry you!"

The nearest the street cars ever came to being on time was the day they turned the clock back one hour.

Cities are full of country folks and all the city folks are trying to get little places in the country.

---

*Reconstruction Finance Corporation, a federal agency created in 1932. Originally designed to facilitate economic activity in the Depression by making loans.

No wonder American people are filling the roads, trains and air. There is so much to see. What we lack in reading we make up in looking.

There is an awful lot of these nudist colonies. Seems like even the law can't get clothes on 'em. I'm just waiting for the first frost and see what happened. That will bust up an awful exhilarating pastime, I'll tell you that.

Americans are the greatest people in the world who want to talk big and go to big things. They will go to the biggest hotel—regardless of service, the biggest theatre—regardless of performance, the biggest funeral—regardless of whether they knew the corpse.

Everything is a slogan and of all the bunk things in America, the slogan is the champ. You can't form a club or manufacture a new article unless it has a catchy slogan. The merits of a thing have nothing to do with it.

The preacher says: "Let no man put asunder," and two thirds of the married world is asunder in less than three months.

"It's cheaper to buy than to rent!" And half the people of the United States are living off interest paid by people who will never get the last mortgage paid out.

American people get tired of anything awful quick. We just jump from one extreme to another. We are much more apt to make a whole change than we ever are a partial change.

If a giant is all the rage this year, next year it won't be an ordinary-sized man. No, we will jump right from the giant to a midget.

It takes years in this country to tell whether anybody is right or wrong. It's kinder of a case of just how far ahead you can see.

The fellow that can only see a week ahead, is always the popular fellow, for he's looking with the crowd. But the one that can see years ahead, he has a telescope but he can't make anybody believe he has it.

This country is not where it is today on account of any one man. It is here on account of the real common sense of the big normal majority.

A sixteen-year-old Will (seated) with two friends, Gordon Lindsay and John Phillips, at Scarrett College, Neosho, Missouri. It was said that most mothers of local young ladies disdained Will's friends as "too wild and liable to drink hard liquor at times." 1896. (Courtesy UCLA)

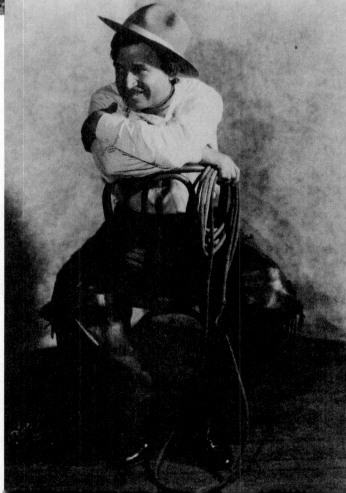

Publicity photo for a rapidly rising Ziegfeld star, c. 1916.

Will's family pays a visit to the Goldwyn studio. From left, Jimmy, Will, Jr., Mary, and Betty, c. 1919.

Will's earliest known film poster, advertising his first silent motion picture, Laughing Bill Hyde, 1918. (Courtesy Charles Banks Wilson)

February 1920. At the Mission San Juan Capistrano, California, Will with author Eugene Manlove Rhodes (West is West, Say Now Shibboleth); author Vicente Blasco Ibáñez (The Four Horsemen of the Apocalypse; Blood and Sand), and Charles F. Lummis, Americanist, author. (Photo courtesy The Southwest Museum, Los Angeles)

Now if there is one thing that we Americans do worse than any other nation, it is try and manage somebody else's affairs.

In Europe I saw forests, the most beautiful forests, all out in a row. Every time they cut down a tree, it looks like they plant two in its place. Every time we cut one down, the fellow that cuts it down, sits down to have a smoke and celebrate. He throws his cigarette away and burns up the rest of the forest.

You know, we're always talking about pioneers and what great folks the pioneers were. Well, I think if we stopped and looked history in the face, the pioneer wasn't a thing in the world but a guy that wanted something for nothing. He was a guy that wanted to live off everything that nature had done. He wanted to cut a tree down that didn't cost him anything, but he never did plant one. He wanted to plow up the land that should have been left to grass. We are just now learning that we can rob from nature the same way as we can rob from an individual. That pioneer thought he was living off nature, but it was really future generations he was living off of.

We are known as the wealthiest nation of all time. Well, in the first place we are not. The difference between our rich and our poor grows greater every year. Our distribution of wealth is getting more uneven all the time. We are always reading "how many men paid over a million dollars income tax."

But we never read about "how many there is that are not eating regular."

ARMED FORCES

The United States entered the Great War—"The War to End All Wars"—in April 1917. Will Rogers was thirty-seven years old, married, and had three children. He was an established *Ziegfeld Follies* star and, though too old to be drafted, there were things he wanted to contribute. He entertained the troops, helped to sell war bonds, and pledged to the Red Cross the substantial sum of one hundred dollars per week for the duration of the war.

After the armistice in November 1918, the return of the more than one million men in the AEF (American Expeditionary Force) was slow. While other participating nations demobilized their soldiers, America's force was used as an army of occupation in Germany. When at last American soldiers were brought back, Will Rogers kidded, "We would have brought them back sooner, but two of our men hadn't yet married over there."

The returning "Dough-Boys" did not exactly find the better world they had expected. Quipped Rogers, "They left singing 'Over There!' and came back singing 'I'm Always Chasing Rainbows!' "

Though America had been caught in 1917 without a mobile army, Congress reduced America's defense force to 125,000 soldiers. The twenties roared in the rarefied air of Prohibition. The decade of fast automobiles, speakeasies, bathtub gin, radios, electric refrigerators, and installment buying with "a dollar down and a dollar a week" ended with the stock market crash, followed by unemployment, hunger, and despair. Congress had promised the returning soldiers a bonus, over the vetoes of both presidents Harding and Coolidge. Now, in 1932, the desperate veterans wanted payment earlier than agreed. Thousands congregated in Washington, calling themselves the BEF, the "Bonus Expeditionary Force."

Will Rogers took his stand with the soldiers:

> Just been reading in the Literary Digest what both sides have to say for and against the Soldiers' Bonus. My opinion on this question is not issued after first taking the opinions of any constituents and stringing with the majority. . . . We promised them everything if they would go to war, and all they got was $1.25 a day and some knitted sweaters and sox.
>
> As to the Soldiers' Bonus, you promised them everything but the kitchen stove. . . . I never met 10 who were not injured in some minor way, to say nothing of the dissatisfaction. I claim we owe them everything we have got, and if they will settle for the Bonus, we are lucky.

Will advocated a strong army and a powerful army air force. When America's rose-colored slogan was "Prosperity is just around the corner," Will Rogers' realistic estimate was "War is closer around the corner than prosperity!"

Will, as so often, was right.

You don't have to be war-like to get a real kick out of our greatest army post Schofield Barracks and the navy at Pearl Harbor. If war was declared with some Pacific nation, we would lose the Philippines before lunch, but if we lost these, it would be our own fault.

You can have all the advanced war methods you want, but, after all, nobody has ever invented a war that you didn't have to have somebody in the guise of soldiers to stop the bullets.

If we really wanted to honor our Boys, why don't we let them sit on the reviewing stands and make the people march by?

We are the only nation in the world that waits till we get into a war before we start getting ready for it.

We can't go back in those native mountains and jungles, so what's the use sicking Marines on somebody away off in those bush league countries, where, if we lose one Marine, we are losers more—even if we captured their leader.

We ought to have the greatest air defense in the world, we got more air.

If the rest of the world knew that we had the greatest Air Force in the world, we wouldn't have to be worrying over any disarmament conferences and a thousand and one other things that we get mixed up in now.

All we would have to do is just sit here and take care of our own business, and you can bet no one would ever have any idea of coming over and pouncing on us.

We can't possibly get into a war without going from 3 to 7 thousand miles to find it, and when you have to go that far, why, it just ain't hardly worth the trip.

We better start doing something about our defense. All we got to go by is history, and history don't record that "Economy" ever won a war. So I believe I would save some money somewhere else, even if I had to work a little shorter-handed around the Capitol there in Washington.

I see where the Senate voted three new cruisers. We had to have them to deliver our Marines around to various battle fronts.

There is only one unpardonable thing you can say in the navy, army or in politics, and that is to propose to cut down expenditure. You can accuse them of negligence and even laziness, but to suggest spending less money!

I am glad for once in our lives we got our Marines back home. I know they are laying off, waiting for some war somewhere. There is one in Afghanistan, but we got nobody in Washington that knows where it is.

We have every kind of week in the world; there's Apple Week; Don't Blame Your Congressman Week; Do Your Christmas Shopping Early Week.

Let's add one sensible one to 'em all: Remember Our Heroes Week. You would be surprised how many we got that have been forgotten.

If you haven't bought a poppy this morning as you read this, go right now and do so. The soldier boys in the hospitals make 'em and it's for a great charity.

The further we get in years away from war, the less we think of it; but that's not these fellow's fault. They never thought so much of it, even at the time.

At one time our Marines were enforcing American diplomacy from the Yangtze River in China to the headwaters of Lake Managua, in Nicaragua. We had no trouble getting soldiers to enlist, but we had to draft ambassadors to go to any foreign country.

You see, by this time we have helped so many people out in wars that it is just a mania with us. We will send Marines anywhere that can get ten signers to a petition that says they want us. We are in the humanity business, and we are going to do it right.

The British were there protecting their interest with a fleet, as is usual. I even read where a Portuguese gun boat was away out in Canton, China. The world is coming to a fine point where lesser nations have to emigrate to another country before shooting each other without interference.

Even America is stealing their stuff. You can't pick up a paper without seeing the Marines were landed to keep some nations from shooting each other, and if necessary we will shoot them to keep them from shooting each other.

Didn't we invent the airplanes and then think after we had invented them that that was all you was supposed to do with them? European nations might not have our foresight for amassing the dollar, but they know what altitude of the elements the next war will be held in.

CRIME

Chicago and its suburbs were considered the official crime capital of the United States. In 1929, for example, statistics show that Chicago had 498 reported murders, while New York City, next in line, had 401. In the twenties and thirties, Chicago crime bosses constantly made the news. There were gun battles in broad daylight, the St. Valentine's Day Massacre, gangster funerals with garish floral-car corteges several blocks long, holdups of lucrative liquor and beer deliveries, kidnappings, and just plain, ordinary rub-outs. Prohibition and the relative affluence of the twenties made crime highly profitable, while the hunger and deprivations of the thirties often made it tempting.

But while Chicago cornered most of the headlines, crime in America at large, too, was excessive. The names of criminals like John Dillinger, "Pretty Boy" Floyd, Al Capone, Bonnie (Parker) and Clyde (Barrow), Fred and "Ma" Barker, "Legs" Diamond, "Bugs" Moran, Charles "Lucky" Luciano, George "Machine-gun" Kelley, and "Dutch" Schultz were as familiar to newspaper readers as were the names of local baseball players.

Perhaps no crime of the period so shocked America, and the world, as the kidnapping and murder of the baby son of Charles A. Lindbergh, the man who had completed the first solo transatlantic flight in May 1927. Abducted during the night of March 1, 1932, at Hopewell, New Jersey, Charles Augustus Lindbergh, Jr., was found buried in a shallow grave nearby on May 12.

Will Rogers learned about the abduction within hours at his ranch home in Pacific Palisades, California.

> I was awakened out of my sleep about 2:30 in the morning by a phone call.
>
> I am half asleep and nervously grabbed the telephone and it was young Bill Hearst from New York. I had just been up to his father's ranch [San Simeon] about half way between Frisco and here, and I thought maybe I did something up there that I shouldn't. Maybe some of the silver is missing. Maybe there is an old William, the Conquerer, tapestry misplaced.
>
> Then when he says, "The Lindbergh baby has been kidnapped!" it was just one of those things that hit you right between the eyes.

Only days earlier, while in the East, Will and Betty Rogers had visited at Anne Morrow Lindbergh's family home in New Jersey, where Charles and Anne were staying. And on March 2, 1932, Will told about the baby in his daily column:

> Mrs. Rogers and I spent the day with them. The whole family interest centered around him. He had his father's blond hair, even more so than his dad's. It's almost golden and all in little curls. His face is more of his mother's. He has her eyes exactly.
>
> His mother sat on the floor in the sun parlor among all of us and played blocks with him for hours. His dad was pitching a soft sofa pillow at him as he was toddling around. The weight of it would knock him over. I asked Lindy if he was rehearsing him for forced landings.
>
> After about the fourth time of being knocked over he did the cutest thing. He dropped of his own accord when he saw it coming. He was just stumbling and jabbering around like any kid 20 months old.
>
> He crawled up in the back of the Morrow automobile

that was going to take us home, and he howled like an
Indian when they dragged him out.
    I wish we had taken him home with us and kept him.

No doubt Will and Betty Rogers saw in little Charles Lindbergh
their own son Freddie, who had died when he, too, was just twenty
months old.

Racketeering is America's biggest industry, and their funerals is "big
business."

I interviewed Al Capone once, but I never did write the story. There
was no way I could write it and not make a hero out of him.
    What is the matter with us when our biggest gangster is our greatest
national interest?

Headline in the paper says: "Thieves get 2,000 dollars worth of liquor."
At today's prices they must have taken two bottles.

I see where they are going to be more strict with these robbers; when
they catch 'em from now on, they're going to publish their names.

Here in London, there was a famous case being tried where a fellow
had swindled (through fake stock transactions) the people out of ten
million dollars. They just give him fourteen years so fast it took all
the Americans' breath away, and all they have talked about is English
justice compared to ours. It's the consensus of opinion of all of them
here that if it had been at home, that fellow would have gone into
show business, or the Senate.
    None of that habeas corpusing and suspended sentences, or ap-
pealing it when you commit a crime over here. You just wake up,
surrounded by a small space. Some delegation ought to come over
here studying British justice. Our battleships are not harming us near
as much as our court delays, corruption and shyster lawyers.

In Sing Sing a few weeks ago there were three young fellows electrocuted, and there were over two thousand applications to the warden
to see them go to their deaths. Imagine, if you can, people who want
to see somebody else killed!
    Anybody whose pleasure it is watching somebody else die, is about
as little use to humanity as the person being electrocuted.

Last week we had quite an unusual murder out here (and it's getting very hard to put on anything unusual in the way of murder).

A well-known politician was killed and at first they could find no reason. Then it was discovered that he was on the verge of financing a preacher in establishing a radio broadcasting station. So now the murderer will surrender and show that his deed was to save the public and he will be acquitted with honors, and his services will be in demand everywhere.

The regret is that this hero didn't start his life's work earlier.

A policeman used to have a beat to walk, and he was watching all the time for some crooked business. But you haven't seen a policeman walking on the sidewalk since Henry Ford perfected his first carburetor.

Policemen used to carry a billy club that they used to crack over crooks' head. Now they have discarded that and they have a whistle. That's why there is so much crime. Whistling at a crook is not near as effective as to crack him on the bean with a hickory stick.

Crime looks like it's making money, but it isn't. Statistics show that very few of the present day criminals wind up with much. When you pay your lawyer and have to retain him by the year, whether you are robbing or not, and then pay the bondsman, and hand out hundreds among the various police forces, then the late hours, and with the present price of ammunition, and the inconvenience of getting a pistol—sometimes you have to walk a whole block—it just in the end figures out to a fair living.

Business depression has caused this wave of robberies. The poor robbers have to rob more people nowadays to make their quota than they used to. Give us good times again, and the robber will get what he needs that day out of the first man he robs.

See where they convicted Al Capone on five counts of silk underwear and four others. Now comes the "out-on-bail, new trial, change of venue, habeas corpus, stay of execution" and twenty-one other things that the law has invented to hinder justice.

Do you know what has been the cause of the big increase in murders? It's been the manufacture of the automatic pistol. The automatic pistol is as much more dangerous and destructive than the old six-shooter, as poison gas is over perfume. There is no skill required in using it.

They should advertise those guns: "Killing made easy! Just hold the trigger down and we guarantee you somebody!"

And the more drunk or drugged a man is, the more he will hit.

If it's a small crime nowadays, say robbery, we fine 'em; and if it's confessed murder, why, they plead insanity. We go on the theory that if you confess, you must be insane.

This gun thing is getting pretty serious here around New York. A gun is now considered standard equipment with every tough kid. Everybody that hasn't got a gun is being shot by somebody.

They pinch a thousand people a day for parking 5 minutes too long, but I have yet to read where a policeman ever searched a bunch of toughs hanging around a place to see if any carried concealed weapons. They could start searching everybody and in one day they would get enough pistols to dam up the Hudson River.

You see, lots of people think that racketeering and corruption is just a fly-by-night business. Well, you were never more wrong in your life. People are going to use dope and somebody has to supply it. People are going to gamble, and somebody has to prepare them a place to do it. It was originally a small business but it grew and grew far beyond even the expectations of its most optimistic boosters, till today it's no longer a business, it's an industry.

So you see, it's not a fly-by-night industry; meanness has always been better organized and conducted than righteousness.

WOMEN

I doubt if a charging elephant, or a rhino, is as determined or hard to check as a socially ambitious mother.

At the Democratic Convention, a band of women hailed me and wanted me to write something about helping them get "Equal Rights."

So I told them that I thought myself that they had too many and it was mighty nice of them to want to split some of them with the men.

They forget that when women enter politics, their prayers don't mean any more to the Lord than men's.

At the disarmament conference in Geneva, our feminine delegate Dr. Mary E. Wooley, president of Mount Holyoke College, is the outstanding novelty.

It's no joking matter getting the world to disarm. Maybe a woman can do it. It's a cinch men can't.

The female of the human race has retained her beauty, but the male has been a throw-back. He has retained none of the springy movement and the grace and beauty of form and skin. Our only salvation is to raise just females.

You see short dresses was made for certain figures, but fashion decrees that everybody be fashionable, so that means there is going to be folks try and keep up with fashions that while they might be financially able, are physically unfit—their purse is good, but their build is bad.

I'm so glad you ladies lengthened your dresses. Concealment has led more men to the altar than exposure has.

Today's news highlight: Some woman married her fifth naval officer.
    One more naval disarmament conference and she will have to start marrying a few civilians.

Headline says: "Society women of New York smoking pipes!"
    The only way to break 'em from it is not to watch 'em do it.

I tell you, them old Bolsheviks is just plumb smart. They sure have found out how to handle women—doggone. Any time a woman hollers for liberty over there, they just give her a spade and tell her to go out and dig some liberty.
    All along the Trans-Siberian railway, the women would be harvesting the crops, and the men would come down to watch the train come in.

Democrats, tell the women that we are the party that will observe the sanctity of the home. If we discover a husband that says he is going "away on business" we will look into his business! Let us make promises to the women. Let us promise them Cabinet positions. Why should the Republicans be the ones that have a monopoly of lying to the women?

What is holding women back nowadays is that they stop to powder their noses. And why should a mirror always accompany the calcimining operation? With all the practice they get, any woman that can't find her nose without a mirror should not be allowed to have a nose. Suppose the men of the specie (who is usually more dumb than the female) had to take out a mirror to find his nose every time he wanted to blow it. Suppose he had lost the mirror. His nose would have to go blowless.

Besides, why you want your nose, which has a natural tendency to be red, to be changed to white, while your cheeks, which are naturally white, to be red, I also don't know.

Tammany Hall is just a bunch banded together under a constitution which says: "Get these jobs and stay with 'em, and if the time ever does come when you have to give it up, give it up to another Tammany man!"

Well, they had a meeting to elect a leader, why, the women came in and wanted to vote. Well, they had never considered that, they had forgot about the Nineteenth Amendment—giving women the vote—on account of being so busy thinking of the Eighteenth—Prohibition.

Well, nobody knew what to do with these women. Then somebody thought of the idea of adjourning. When a meeting ain't running right, why, the thing to do is to adjourn, reorganize and meet some time when the ones that are against you don't know when you are going to meet.

Anyhow, women are getting into more things that are embarrassing to the men. You see, the first idea of giving them the vote was just to use the vote. But the women, contrary like they are, they wasn't satisfied with that. They started to take this equality thing serious.

The women figured that "while we may not be as good as a man, we are at least as good as a politician." So they commenced to want to get in on the loot. As soon as they found out that a political job took no experience to hold, that it only took experience to get, why, they commenced to making themselves rather embarrassing around the political employment bureau.

It was all right with the men when the women took the little committee assignments where there was no salary connected, but when they started to want to put their powdered noses into the feed trough, why, that brought on complications. Now they are wondering: "Was the women's vote worth what they are asking for it?"

To us fellows that are not in politics, we are tickled to death to see the women folks dealing such misery to the politicians. And in the long run it's good for humanity. Every job a woman can grab off, it just drives another politician to either work or the poor house.

And this next Congress, did you notice the amount of crepe de chine and lingerie there is mixed up in it? Why, pretty near every prominent man we ever had in politics has got a daughter entered in that Congress. Course, that's another trouble with politics, it breeds politics! So that makes it pretty hard to stamp out. The only way to do it is we got to get birth control among politicians.

I wouldn't be a bit surprised that it won't be no time till some woman will become so desperate politically, and just lose all prospects of right and wrong, and maybe go from bad to worse, and finally wind up in the Senate.

Now you know that no father or mother ever had any idea that the offspring would ever darken a Senate door. Course, up to now there has been no need for anything resembling a woman in the Senate—especially an old woman—for there is more old women in there already than there is in the old ladies home. But they are awful nice old fellows and they don't do any particular harm; course they don't do any great good, either.

DUST BOWL

I've been reading a lot about these dust storms, and that's how every civilization since time began has been covered up. It's been this dust. It's a terrible thing to happen to those people that are out there in the middle-west, but on the other hand it's a great tribute to feel that the Lord feels that you have a civilization that is so advanced that it's the first place to be buried under. I didn't think at first that we was that smart in Oklahoma, in Kansas, in Texas and eastern Colorado, but our Almighty must know.

Now that it would ever cover up California for the same reason, I've got my doubts.

I remember once we wanted to raise commodity prices, so somebody had a plan to plow under every third acre of wheat—and the wind came along and blew out the other two acres.

If history has shown the Lord does bury each succeeding civilization in accordance to the advancement of the people in that neighborhood, I feel proud that I come from that particular Middle West belt. . . . If a civilization had to be buried as it becomes advanced enough, we feel proud that we are the ones to be plowed under first, that's all. In years to come, the archaeologists—I hope I've got that word right—the archaeologists will dig and find Claremore, Oklahoma, and people will come to the ruins and dig down and say: "Here lied a civilization!"

And later, eventually, Washington is covered up—on account of it's being the least civilized, it will be the last place to be covered up. They will excavate in there, and they'll come from the four corners of the earth to see what queer race lived there. And they'll find places called Banks, where the money changers were—men who in those ancient days lived by interest alone.

EDUCATION

Education never helped morals. The smarter the guy, the bigger the rascal.

The public don't care how you got to college. It's how you are going to get from the forty yard line over the goal line that they are worrying about.

Say, any of you that have kids in schools, either grammar, high or college, it don't make any difference, but can any of you parents get head or tail of what they are doing? None of 'em can write so you can read it, none of 'em can spell, figure or tell you even what bounds Korea.

Some of these days they are going to remove so much of the "hooey" and the thousands of things the schools have become clogged up with, and we will find that we can educate our broods for about one-tenth of the price and learn 'em something they might accidentally use after they escape.

They call Domestic Science a course now. In the old days you learned that at home. You had to be good at it, for you had to eat it.

I think you can learn the same at all schools, outside of football.

In the old days boys wanted an education. They even had reading, writing and arithmetic, instead of football. Up to then boys had gone there for their heads and not their shoulders.

When ignorance gets started, it knows no bounds.

Villains are getting as thick as college degrees—and sometimes on the same fellow.

My daughter was graduated yesterday at a girls preparatory school. They read off what course each girl had taken. When they said "Mary

Rogers, Diploma in English," I had to laugh at that. One of my children studying English—why, it's just inherited! You don't have to study that in our family.

Doug Fairbanks had a niece graduating, Wallace Beery had a relation, Frank Lloyd, the great director, a daughter, and all four of us sat there and purred like four old tomcats, basking in a little reflected sunshine and secretly congratulating ourselves on choosing a profession where education played no part.

Nicholas Murray Butler, president of Columbia University, deserves a lot of credit. He has taken a college that didn't amount to much right in the heart of New York City, a place where you would think would be the last place to get anybody interested in education, and he has built it up just by making rich men think that by leaving something to a school, it would help the rest of America forget how some of them got the money.

I've been reading some of the addresses delivered to the graduating classes. Any man that's made mistakes is being asked to address the boys somewhere, and tell 'em how to go through life. And they tell 'em that they are living in a time of great changes, and that they must prepare themselves for the new civilization that's coming.

I bet you there hasn't been a class graduated in the last hundred years that hasn't been told the same old gag.

INDIANS

Every man in our history that killed the most Indians has got a statue built for him.

"Status Quo Ante" it's an old Cherokee word that means: This thing has gone far enough—let's go back to where we started and next time we will watch each other closer.

Our record with the Indians is going down in history. It is going to make us mighty proud of it in the future when our children of ten more generations read of what we did to them.

When the white folks come in and took Oklahoma from us Indians, they spoiled a happy hunting ground. Now there is a good deal in the papers about giving my native state of Oklahoma back to the Indians.

Now I am a Cherokee, and very proud of it, but I doubt if you can get the Indians to accept it—not in its present condition.

Thanksgiving was started by the Pilgrims, who would give thanks every time they killed an Indian and took more of his land. As years went by and they had all of his land, they changed it into a day to give thanks for the bountiful harvest, when the boll weevil and the protective tariff didn't remove all cause for thanks.

Back in my old home state of Oklahoma I got more and better kin folks than anybody. I believe Injun families stick a little closer together than Yonakers do (That's Cherokee for "white man.")

There ain't nothing to life but satisfaction. If you want to ship fat beef cattle at the end of their existence, you got to have 'em satisfied on the range.

Indians and primitive races were the highest civilized, because they were more satisfied, and they depended less on each other, and took less from each other.

We couldn't live a day without depending on everybody, so our civilization has given us no liberty or independence.

Well, all I know is just what I read in the papers and what I see as I soar over these United States. It does look like after flying over as much of it as I have lately, and seeing the millions of acres that we don't use anyway, as I say, it does look like America was big enough that they could have staked off, say, at least a fourth, or a fifth, of it and given it to the Indians for all time to come.

Then I wouldn't have seen General Custer's battleground and hundreds of other graves in all those lonely old western forts. The Indians woulda never bothered a soul if we had split the country, even 80–20 with them.

HOLIDAYS

This is Mother's Day. My own mother died when I was ten years old. My folks have told me that what little humor I have comes from her. I can't remember her humor but I can remember her love and understanding of me.

Of course, the mother I know the most about is the mother of our little group. She has been for twenty-two years trying to raise to maturity four children, three by birth and one by marriage. While she hasn't done a good job, the poor soul has done all that mortal human could do with the material she has had to work with.

This being Mother's Day, I wanted to tell you that a mother is the only thing that is so constituted that they possess eternal love under any and all circumstances. I was telling that to my wife and I said, you know, Betty, a mother and a dog is the only things that has eternal love, no matter how you treat them—and my wife made me cut the dog out.

So I can't use the dog, but my wife runs this outfit.

July Fourth, 1776, that's when we tore ourselves loose from England and it's a question of who it was a better deal for.

And the tax in those days, that we fought to do away with, why, it must have been at least five percent of what it is today.

After reading the casualty list every fifth of July morning, one learns that we have killed more people celebrating our independence than we lost fighting for it.

An American ambassador to England has really only two duties. One is to introduce daughters of prominent Americans at court, and the other one is to make a speech on the Fourth of July that will make England think we are not celebrating us licking them on that date.

Charley Dawes, our present ambassador, did mighty fine. His speech really made it look like England won.

Every holiday ought to be named "Labor Day." If we could ever get vacations down to where you wasn't any more tired on the day one was over than on a regular work day, it would be wonderful.

By the way, a good stiff sales tax on hamburgers today would have paid our national debt.

The Columbus Day celebration has rather an added significance to Los Angeles, as they want to celebrate the good fortune of his landing on the Atlantic instead of the Pacific side, because if he had landed out here in California, he never would have gone back to tell the queen.

He would have stayed right here and nobody would have ever known about America, but him.

Being an Indian, I don't mind telling you, personally I am sorry Christopher Columbus ever found us. The discovery has been of no material benefit to us, outside of losing our land. I am proud to say that I have never yet seen a statue to him in Oklahoma.

Spain and Italy are having an argument over which country Christopher Columbus really come from. Spain claims that he might have been born in Italy, but it was without his consent. Then Italy claims that when Columbus died, Spain buried him in their country, but without his consent.

The Mayflower either brought a million, or the few thousand it did bring were very prolific.

Thanksgiving Day. In the days of our founders, they were willing to give thanks for mighty little, for mighty little was all they expected. But now, neither government or nature can give enough but what we think it's too little. Those old boys in the fall of the year, if they could gather in a few pumpkins, potatoes and some corn for the winter, they was in a thanking mood.

But if we can't gather in a new Buick, a new radio, a tuxedo and some government relief, why, we feel like the world is against us.

I referred to the Pilgrims landing on Plymouth Rock. Oh, boy! You should have heard what I got from New England.

It seems there's a town up there called Provincetown, and they have adopted a slogan which says: Don't be misled by history, or any other unreliable source, here's the official landing place where the Pilgrims landed. This is by unanimous vote of the Chamber of Commerce of Provincetown. Any Pilgrim landing in any other place, was not official.

Well, Thanksgiving is over. With all our boasted prosperity I don't see that we are any better off. The old turkey hash showed up as usual today and will be with us the next few days, just the same as it did when we were poor.

While we are merging everything in the world that has no relation to each other, why not merge Fourth of July, Ground Hog Day, Thanksgiving, Labor Day, Halloween, New Year's, and April's Fool, all into one glorious day that would give everybody a chance to get some work done during the year.

And look at the speeches, sermons and turkey it would save.

SPORTS

In the summer of 1926, Will Rogers appeared in Charles Cochran's *Revue* at the Pavilion Theatre in London. As had been his habit in the *Ziegfeld Follies*, he would, while "blathering," walk about the stage and introduce famous personalities in the audience. One night he introduced two men who were sitting together. They had much in common; both had the given name "Thomas," and both were identified with favored libations. Lord Thomas Dewar manufactured scotch in Perth, Scotland, while Sir Thomas Lipton packaged tea. A lot of entertaining banter went on between the stage and those two men in the audience.

Lord Dewar was a well-known sportsman who raised horses and dogs. As a token of his affection for Rogers, he sent him one of his Sealyham terriers, called Jock, stating that it was the best of its breed. The Rogers children loved and spoiled the dog. Will, who could sum up a volume in one sentence, wrote, "If this dog knew how well bred he was he wouldn't speak to any of us."

As a lark, the Rogers family entered him in a dog show and Jock won second place. The family was pleased and proud, but Will could not suppress his jesting. He wired Lord Dewar: "DOG WON SECOND. IF YOU HAD GIVEN ME A GOOD ONE HE WOULD HAVE WON FIRST."

Will and Sir Thomas Lipton had met many times, and Will became very fond of the older man. Sir Thomas had a great sense of humor and was an accomplished raconteur. He had hobnobbed with the rich and idle, and with the poor and active, as he had worked his way up from great poverty.

What had made Sir Thomas a household name in the United States was his persevering pursuit of the America's Cup. He would always be the British challenger, and with a series of specially built boats he would come to American waters and—lose. It was Will's friendship with the tea king, and his sense of fairness, which usually made him root for the underdog. And while that may have been the emotional way to cheer, it was not the way to bet. Lipton's boats, always called *Shamrock*, carried an ascending number, such as *Shamrock I, Shamrock II*, and so on. Faithfully, Sir Thomas would come again and again, only to go home once more without the trophy.

It must have been the mental image of the hapless Sir Thomas going home once again without the hoped-for prize that prompted Will to write an article about his friend, "The World's Best Loser." Then he had an idea. He started a nationwide campaign to collect pennies from sports fans and then present Sir Thomas Lipton with a gold cup in lieu of the elusive America's Cup.

The response was surprising. The stock market had collapsed, and still contributions rolled in. Utah residents, for example, subscribed fifty pounds of silver for the base. In just a few months, by October 18, 1930, the fund had amassed $5,290, which was more than enough to purchase what *The New York Times* called a "handsome gold cup mounted on a sterling silver base."

The dedication read:

> A voluntary outpouring of love, admiration and esteem to the greatest loser in the world of sports. In the name of the hundreds of thousands of Americans and well-wishers of Sir Thomas Johnston Lipton, Bart, K.C.V.O.

When the cup was presented with Mayor Jimmy Walker of New York City attending, Will Rogers, who had started it all, could not be there. He sent a telegram:

> SURE SORRY I CAN'T BE WITH YOU AND THE MAYOR BUT, SIR THOMAS, IF YOU EVER TRIED TO EARN A LIVING UNDER A REPUBLICAN ADMIN- ISTRATION, YOU WOULD KNOW YOU HAVEN'T GOT ANY TIME TO BE GADDING ABOUT. YOU THINK THIS IS A FINE CUP? SAY, THIS IS NOTHING TO THE ONE WE ARE GOING TO GIVE YOU WHEN YOU LOSE NEXT TIME. I AM ALREADY STARTING IN ON IT. I LOVE YOU, SIR THOMAS, BUT I WON'T DRINK THAT DAMNED TEA. COME WEST, YOUNG MAN.

Presenting the cup, Mr. Hector Fuller censored Will's writing and omitted the line about the tea.

They call polo a gentleman's game for the same reason they call a tall man "Shorty."

Golf is the only game, outside of solitaire, where you play alone. What you do with your ball hasn't got anything to do with what the other fellow does with his. I can play you a game, and I can play in the morning and you can play a month from then. It's solitaire, only much quieter.

Golf, it's wonderful exercise. You stand on your feet for hours watching somebody else putt. It's just the old-fashioned pool hall moved outdoors, but with no chairs around the wall.

Would you believe there is 3,500 miniature golf courses in the city of Los Angeles? Half of America is bent over. In two more generations our children will grow upward as far as the hips, then they will turn off at right angles and with their arms hanging down, mankind will be right back where we started from.
   Darwin was right!

It was the women's golf championship of America. We used to think going to see women play golf would be like going to see men crochet, but say, there is nothing effeminate about this golf thing as played by these championship women.
   They just lay that innocent little ball down, grit their teeth and swing like a woodchopper, and it takes one of our modern men in mighty good physical condition to even walk to where that ball goes.
   I would hate to beat one of these women to a parking space.

You let the poor all get to playing golf and you watch the rich give it up. Americans don't like common things.

Went down last night to a world's champion wrestling match. Us movie actors are advised to go there by our producers, so we can learn how to act.
   It was a fine show, everybody enjoyed it, but wrestling management are overlooking an extra big revenue, for folks would pay even more to see them rehearse with each other before the match.

I see where American women are swimming the English channel again. Crowds of men are standing on the shore, waiting for a smooth sea to cross it in a boat.

This swimming has not only called for a new definition in the dictionary describing which is the weaker sex, but it has demonstrated just how close together England and France are. Neither one of them wants to be that close to the other.

Everybody will start reading the papers now that the baseball season has opened. I was able to be at the opening in Philadelphia. They had three umpires; one to correct the other two.

Well, it's just as well to get the baseball season over with, for the boys that are working their way through football are all ready to break a leg for big gate receipts.

The trouble with football is, you can't carry your cheerleaders with you through life.

The Ohio State football coach just showed me their new stadium seating 100,000, built by hard study and excellent scholarship. They lost to Michigan by a kick after touchdown. He has 400 students practicing day and night in relays to kick field goals.

I suggest they practice making another touchdown, then they wouldn't have to worry about the goal kicking.

The stadium where Notre Dame played seats about an eighth of a million—why, I paid $10 just for a space to hear it over the radio.

You have all seen these modern football players that can't kick a goal from the twenty yard line. Well, our old friend Jim Thorpe, the greatest athlete this country ever produced, was telling me that he went out last fall, and he is 46 years old, and gave exhibitions kicking goals from 15 yards past the center of the field. He says he drop-kicked a goal over 70 yards, that's further than the modern player punts. Jim says he one time punted from ten yards behind his own goal line and it rolled out on the other team's three yard line.

Jim is a Sac and Fox Indian. When he plays football he is more Fox than Sac.

Do you know I used to play football? I used to play me a pretty good End, that is, a substitute End. The rough way they was playing in those days, that didn't hurt my feelings any, not getting in there often.

I played, what you might call a "Wide End." I would play out so far that the other 21 would be pretty well piled up before I could possibly reach 'em. You see, when I picked this "Deep End" job, I kinder figured that I would arrive a little late for most of the festivities. That's why to this very day I don't carry any football scars or bruises.

I was a pretty fast runner. Down in the Indian Territory they used to call me "Rabbit." I could never figure out if that referred to my speed, or my heart.

In those days, you either played, or you didn't play. You wasn't allowed to run in and out like a bellhop.

The Humane Society stops all cruelty to animals. Well, why don't they do something in this football situation by making it an unlawful offense for a western college to assault, maim and disfigure the inmates of eastern universities?

Just flew down to Pimlico, Maryland, to see the great Preakness race. Bucked a headwind but not as strong a one as the horse I bet on bucked.

Jack Dempsey, the former heavyweight champion of the world, told me tonight he would fight champion Gene Tunney in September if he got enough money for it.

I told Jack, I would fight Tunney myself, if they gave me enough money.

CITIES

There is just three towns in the whole of America that are different and distinct, New Orleans, Frisco and San Antonio. They each got something that even the most persistent Chamber of Commerce can't standardize.

I went into Boston. But I wasn't smart enough to understand anything there. Everything was over my head. All I could hear was "Mayflower" and "traditions." I talked to the editor of the *Boston Globe*. Then I wanted to get in and talk to the *Transcript*, but the office boy said: "What year?"

I said: "What do you mean 'what year'?"

He replied: "Why, what year did you come out of Harvard?"

I had to tell him I had never even come *by* Harvard; that I was so ignorant that I had never quite finished Yale. I tried to tell him that

I was Roger Williams, and had reversed my name to protect it when I went on the lecture platform.

But one thing they got here in Boston, and that's the old fighting ship *Constitution*, the only ship that has withstood every disarmament conference.

We are up here at this beautiful Lake Tahoe, near Reno, Nevada, working on a picture and today a fellow come up and wanted me to help him into a soft job in the movies. I asked him what he was doing. He said, "I am a house detective in the big hotel in Reno, where all the divorcees live."

I said, "Brother, you must be hard to please. John Barrymore is not doing as well as you. Why, go back to work and don't envy anybody. But if you are going to give the job up, consult me. I'll change with you."

I am in St. Paul. Glad to see the Mississippi River before Kansas City and St. Louis get a chance to dirty it all up. This is the town where no one can remember whether it is in Wisconsin or Minnesota, and it acts more like North Dakota. Climatically it's the capitol of Siberia. Somebody with a sense of humor built it and Minneapolis right close together, and then moved away to watch the fun. If either city could find the fellow that did it, his life wouldn't be worth as much as a bank messenger's in Chicago.

They were born the "Twin Cities" but since birth they have grown together. Now they are locked. One can't do anything without interfering with the other. If one dances the other wants to sit down, and if one wants to sit down, the other one wants to dance. What one eats don't agree with the other one. The Mississippi River is between them, but Lord, that don't stop 'em from cussing each other. The Pacific Ocean should separate them.

Winston-Salem, two towns that went together to see if they could amount to anything.

Indianapolis is all agog, they found two councilmen that they hope will be honest.

Did you ever see the Bay of Naples that you have heard and read so much about? Did you ever see the harbor in San Francisco? Well, it makes the Bay of Naples look like the Chicago Drainage Canal, and mind you, I am from Los Angeles.

Frisco is to California what the Cherokee Nation is to Oklahoma—
it's the aristocracy of the Commonwealth.

San Francisco children are taught two things; one is to love the Lord
and the other is to hate Los Angeles.

You can't explain Frisco. It's just the Greta Garbo of the West.

San Jose, California, is the prune town of the world. I was reported
to the police this morning for ordering grapefruit.

Up here, attending the beautiful Santa Barbara fiesta, showing the life
in California before Ford, movie salaries and realtors made a Coney
Island out of the state.

Los Angeles, the city of the Lost Angels, the exclusive home of the
Eighth Art, the home of the performer and the reformer.

Headlines in all the Los Angeles papers say: "Asylum Break! Authorities
Having Trouble Rounding Up Twelve Escaped Lunatics!"
    I guess the main trouble is recognizing 'em. I bet they get a different
twelve back.

Hollywood may not keep you young, but it sure keeps you marrying.

We had a big flood out here in California. For about 36 hours the
old heavens just opened up and give us both barrels. You never saw
so much water in your life. All a fellow needed was an Ark, for old
Hollywood would have been a great place to get two of every kind of
animal in it.

I am in my mayor's office in Beverly Hills. As long as they keep their
paving and light and water taxes paid, why, I don't worry much about
how my constituents live. I have found out that it don't pay to interfere
with any kind of sex problems. I just figure if both sides are not slick
enough not to get caught, they are too commonplace for me to waste
my official time on.
    My constituents, I don't claim that they are all good, but most of
them is at least slick.

Just passed through Jefferson City, Missouri, the home of the State
Prison and the State Capitol. The worst in the state is sent there. The

Sheriff was on the train and he had two men who had escaped and he was taking them back to the Legislature.

Every guy thinks the first time he sees anything, that that is the first time it ever existed. I will never forget the first time I went to St. Louis. I thought sure I was the first one to find it.

A headline says: "13 Bankers in Detroit Indicted!"
You would think Detroit was a bigger town than that.

I always wanted to see South Bend, Indiana. I wanted to see what it was the "South Bend" of. There is something crooked—even in the name.
This is the home of Notre Dame, where they have never allowed either learning or religion to interfere with football.

We got a new police chief in New York and he has arrested most of the population and over half the police force. He has the cops so scared that they are arresting traffic instead of directing it. It would be a good joke on this town if he did clean it up.

Here I am in Carnegie Hall. Whew! In Carnegie Hall! That's the great musical center of New York. I don't know what we're doing in here. I am just as much at a loss to be in here as these musicians in the orchestra are. They don't know why they're here, either.

I knew the Ku Klux Klan wouldn't be a success in New York—not enough clean white sheets there for 'em. Besides, they are against the Catholics, the colored folks and the Jewish people, and no organization can get along on 2 percent of the population.

They have an exhibit here in New York, representing Progress, showing how much faster we cross the street compared with what we used to. Now it's a run, and if you don't make it—and the probabilities are you won't—they show you how much quicker they can get you to a hospital, so you can die there, instead of en route, as you used to.
It shows how years ago they had street cars pulled by horses, but they were up on the level of the ground and were very unsanitary— bad air and everything. Now it shows how you can be in a nice tunnel under the ground where the air is good. You know it's good because there have been hundreds using it before you got a hold of it.

I spent the morning at Tuskegee, Alabama, that living monument to Booker T. Washington. They have a great idea there that some of our schools are copying. They teach the pupils that they are going to have to work when they get out, and how to work. Our old mode of college education was teach 'em so they think they won't have to work.

Here we are at Newport, Rhode Island. They won't let an actor bathe at Bailey's Beach. I just come to show 'em that actors didn't need to bathe at Bailey's Beach. Keep the place for them that need it.
    Yours, in Newport, but out of place.

Just passed through Chicago. It's not a boast, it's an achievement. The snow was so deep today, the crooks could only shoot a tall man. To try and diminish crime, they laid off six hundred cops. Chicago has no tax money, all their influential men are engaged in tax exempt occupations. What they got to do is tax murder. Put such a stiff tax on it that only the higher class gangsters can afford it. It's the riff-raff that makes any business disreputable.

Congratulations to the other cowboy mayor, Bill Thompson of Chicago! They was trying to beat Bill with the better element vote.
    The trouble with Chicago is there ain't much "better element."

STATES

The Governors of all the states are gathered together in Connecticut, to show how far apart they are.

Everything is in California, all the great sights of Nature, and along with all these wonders, we have out here the world's greatest collection of freak humans on earth.
    We maintain more freak religions and cults than all the rest of the world combined. Just start anything out here and if it's cuckoo enough, you will get followers.

The other day our California state legislature repealed a law, where when you wanted to get married, you used to have to give three day's notice—you know, give intention of marrying. Well, they did away with that now. It was longer than most of the marriages in California was lasting.
    Now you don't have to file any intention of marrying at all; in fact,

you don't even have to give your right name—you just pay a small amusement tax, is all.

I am back here in California among the orange squeezers, and say, speaking of oranges, did you know that juice in a big hotel is fifty cents a glass? That runs about 150 dollars a barrel.

You can have it, or oil, both cost the same. And the price of steaks! My wife and I had one each and I could have gone home to Oklahoma and bought a good, off-colored dry cow for that.

Everything out here in California that is not an apartment, is a "ranch." If you have 20 feet in your back yard, it's a "ranch." If you got an old avocado bush (no matter if it bears or not), why, it's an "avocado ranch."

I never saw California looking so beautiful—the tremendous rains out here have washed away all the real estate signs.

I am shaking the dust of California's little heralded climate from my feet and am slowly trudging my way across the burning sands to New York City.

I am leaving California, this land of perpetual publicity, where a lot on the corner is worth two in the middle. I do leave with great regret. I know that I am exchanging the sub-division for the subway, and one single California flea for a billion Long Island mosquitos. I am leaving a city where English is the dominant tongue, to return to a city where it is seldom heard and never understood. I leave from the land where the movies are made to return to the land where the bills are paid.

Don't miss seeing Boulder Dam. . . . The dam is entirely between Nevada and Arizona. All California gets out of it is the water.

Am down in Old Virginia, the mother of Presidents, when we thought Presidents had to be aristocrats. Since we got wise to the limitations of aristocrats, Virginia has featured their ham over their Presidential timber.

Texas is a great state. It's the "Old Man River" of states. No matter who runs it, or what happens to it politically, it just keeps rolling along.

I been flying, railroading, automobiling, horseback and buggy riding over Texas for 33 years and I'll swear I have not seen a tenth of it.

What has the size of a state got to do with how good it is? I heard of a fellow that was satisfied with Rhode Island—and part of his garage lopped over into Connecticut, and half his yard was in Massachusetts.

Vermont is, what you would call a "hard-boiled" state. The principal ingredients are granite, rock salt and Republicans. The last being the hardest of the three.

There ought to be a law passed in Congress that no one was allowed to receive a passport to leave this country till they had visited New Mexico and Arizona. If Europe had them, they would fence them off and charge admission and get enough to pay off their national debt.

There is nothing like it anywhere. Hawaii might at first suggest nothing but sunburn and surf boarding, ukuleles and coconuts. But when you pull up to the dock, they start giving you those beautiful leis, then the wonderful Hawaiian band plays a great welcome. From the hotel you look right down onto the beautiful ocean and Waikiki Beach.

    Guess I am the only person ever went to Honolulu and didn't take a whirl at the ocean, but I couldn't ride one of those ironing boards.

The State of Louisiana, without any blare of trumpets, is doing the biggest thing being done in our land today. They are teaching over a hundred thousand to read and write, mostly older people.

    They are going to wipe out illiteracy in two years with both whites and blacks. That beats all your luncheon clubs and your advertising campaigns. That is like learning the cripple to walk and the blind to see. One hundred thousand happy citizens will bring your state more dividends than one hundred thousand miles of bonded concrete roads will.

Introducing an Oklahoma Governor is kinder a tough job. You never know before you get through speaking but what he has been impeached while you were singing his praises.

Some of the governors we have had in Oklahoma couldn't send their laundry out and be sure they would be there when it come back.

No wonder comedians come from Oklahoma. Did you ever read our Constitution? It says: "A Governor is to be duly elected and seated and serve till duly found out and unseated."

    It's the one state where a Lieutenant Governor always gets a break, if you can call it that.

Starring in Fruits of Faith, *one of three silent films Will Rogers produced; though critically acclaimed, it lost money because Will had no means for national distribution, 1922.*

Jimmy, Will, Jr., Mary, Will, and Betty Rogers with "Lord Jock Dewar," called "Jock" for short. The Sealyham Terrier was given to the Rogers children by Sir Thomas Dewar in 1926.

"Formally" attired in pin-striped suit on the veranda of the family's Beverly Hills home, 1927.

My native Oklahoma has an all-year-round climate. Our people don't move with the seasons, our climate changes with our seasons. Why, we throw away more climate that we don't need in one year than Florida or California have charged their customers for.

We don't sell climate; it goes with the purchase of the land, just as the darkness or the light.

WASHINGTON, D.C.

Everybody that comes to Washington either has a kick or a wish, and he is just as big a pest no matter which one he is there on.

In Washington they just generally figure that one hatred offsets the other, and they are both even.

It's not the humidity in Washington, it's the humiliation of having to meet who you do.

I don't want to get mixed up in any argument in Washington. No person has ever convinced another. People's minds are changed through observation and not through argument.

George Washington really took the job as first President so he could locate the Capitol in Washington. At one time it was on Wall Street and George was inaugurated there and he had to stand up all during the ceremony for they wanted $50 for a seat on the Exchange and he said it wasn't worth it and he moved the Capitol to Washington, where you can sit down for nothing. In fact, that is the principal industry there, sitting down.

MISCELLANEOUS

They make beer nowadays so light that you have to take a glass of it for a chaser after drinking water.

There is a lot more common folks than will admit to it.

Things in our country are not ever fixed, they just wear themselves out.

America has been just muscle bound from holding a steering wheel. The only callus place on an American was the bottom of his driving toe.

As high priced as it is to live in, I don't see anybody leaving the country.

We are the first nation to starve to death in a storehouse that's overfilled with everything we want.

There ain't nothing that breaks up homes, country and nations like somebody publishing their memoirs.

America isn't as bad off as it might seem. The young are not drinking themselves to death and the old are not worrying themselves to death over whether the young are drinking or not.

Somebody is always quoting figures to prove that the country is prosperous, but the only real, bona fide indication of it was in the paper today: Divorces in Reno have increased over 105 percent in the last year!

Now that's prosperity, for you can't be broke and get a divorce. That's why the poor have to live with each other.

American people like to have you repent; then they are generous.

What is Society? Society is any band of folks that kinder throw in with each other and mess around together for each other's discomfort. The ones with the more money have more to eat and drink at their affairs, so that's called "High Society." Now the morals and personal behavior of its members have nothing to do with it. The oftener they can crash the front page, the solider they are in their fraternity. And it's sorter hereditary. No matter who you raise up in your family zoo, why, they inherit your space in the "Social Register."

We ought to set by a day of thanksgiving, blessing the Atlantic and Pacific Oceans for their splendid judgment in locating where they did.

It's a great country, if you got the influence.

Chapter III

CONGRESS

W ill Rogers' favorite subject for his comments was Congress. He showed no partiality to either the House of Representatives or the Senate; nor did he make a distinction whether Democrats or Republicans were in control. He had many personal friends among members of Congress, but as a group, he recognized no individual friendships.

Mixing much truth with a little inspired creativity, shaking both well so that no one could tell where one began and the other ended, he could report with a straight face:

> I just got back from Washington, D.C. (Department of Comedy). I had heard that the Congressional Show was to close on June 7th. I don't see why they are closing then. They could bring that same show with the original cast they have to New York, and it would run for years.
>
> I am to go into Ziegfeld's new Follies, and I have no act. So I thought I will run down to Washington and get some material. Most people and actors appearing on the stage have some writers to write their material—but I don't do that. Congress is good enough for me. They have been writing my material for years and I am not ashamed of the material I have had. I am going to stick to them.
>
> Why should I go and pay some famous author, or even

47

myself, sit down all day trying to dope out something funny
to say on the stage? No sir; I have found that there is nothing
as funny as things that have happened, and that people
know that have happened. So I just have them mail me
every day the Congressional Record. It is to me what the
Police Gazette used to be to the fellow who was waiting for
a haircut. In other words, it is a life saver.

So wrote Will Rogers in his nationally syndicated weekly article
published June 8, 1924. It is not only funny but perfectly true. Almost
daily Congress would indeed furnish Rogers with both events and funny
lines. Of course, in 1924, Rogers had not yet the means to be completely topical. The weekly column had a lead time of two weeks,
which meant that anything he wrote would not appear in print until
at least two weeks later. Thus the front-page news he would cite was
already old news if not, indeed, forgotten. In his writing of these weekly
articles, he would often place the time properly for his readers; alluding
to an event of the moment, he would fix it as "a couple of weeks
ago. . . ."

Only after late 1926, when Will Rogers began his daily squib, would
he have the means to comment on any current event. There was the
headline news across the top of the page, and close to it was Will
Rogers' humorous commentary on it. As James A. Farley* revealed:
"President Roosevelt would listen to Will—everybody else did. Or
most people who read *The New York Times*,** the first thing they did
was to look for his observation that day. Regardless whether it was
good or bad for us, there was always a laugh in it."

When Will Rogers began to broadcast, his Sunday radio monologues
made it possible for millions to hear his summary of the week's news;
of course, it was delivered in Rogers' own style, from his unique point
of view.

After his broadcast of May 5, 1935, during which he unfolded a
gigantic national lottery plan to raise money, interest, and—most
assuredly—prestige in our national elections, Will received a telegram

---

*Farley was President Franklin D. Roosevelt's campaign manager in 1932 and 1936, and
   postmaster general from 1933 to 1940. [Interview October 30, 1975]
**Will Rogers' daily column appeared on the first page of the second section of *The New York
   Times*.

from a congressman who wanted to read a copy of that "plan" into the *Congressional Record*. The following week, May 12, Will feigned great pride:

> I feel pretty good about that; that's the highest praise that a humorist can have is to get your stuff into the Congressional Record. Just think, my name will be right in there along side of Huey Long's and all those other big humorists.
>
> You see, ordinarily you got to work your way up as a humorist and first get into Congress. Then you work your way up into the Senate, and then, if your stuff is funny enough it goes into the Congressional Record. But for an outsider to get in there as a humorist without having served his apprenticeship in either the House or the Senate, why, mind you, I'm not bragging, but by golly I feel pretty big about it.
>
> Did I ever tell you about the first time I ever had any stuff in that daily? Well, I'd written some fool thing, and it pertained to the bill that they were arguing—or that they were kidding about, rather—at the time in the Senate. So some Senator read my little article, and as it was during his speech, it naturally went into the Congressional Record. So another Senator rose and said, you know how they always do, if you ever seen 'em. "Does the gentleman yield?" They always say "gentleman" in there. But the tone—the tone that they put on the word, it would be more appropriate— you know the way they can say "gentleman"—it would sound right if they come right out and said "Does the coyote from Maine yield?" You know what I mean; that's about the way it sounds. So the coyote from Maine says, "I yield to the polecat from Oregon," for if he don't, the other guy will keep on talking anyhow. You know he don't say "polecat," but he says "gentleman" in such a way that it's almost like polecat. They are very polite in there.
>
> Well, I must get back to my story. When this Senator read my offering, the other Senator said, after all the yielding was over: I object! I object to the remarks of a professional joke maker being put into the Congressional Record! You know, meaning me. See? Taking a dig at me. They didn't want any outside fellow contributing. Well, he had me all wrong. Compared to them I'm an amateur, and the thing about my jokes is they don't hurt anybody. You can take

'em or leave 'em. You know what I mean? You know, you can say, well, they're funny, or they're terrible, or they're good, or whatever, but they don't do any harm. You can just pass them by. But with Congress, every time they make a joke it's a law! And every time they make a law, it's a joke.

Will considered Congress his private hunting preserve. It was his "Joke Factory," located on "Handicap Hill." Despite the ribbing its members received from Will Rogers, he was lionized any time he appeared in the Capitol, and congressmen thought it an honor to be included in his monologues. Being photographed or seen with Will bestowed a mantle of importance. Having one's name mentioned in his articles was a distinction to be treasured.

In 1933, after a number of broadcasts for Gulf Oil, Will announced that he would quit his weekly broadcasts. To his surprise seventy-four senators and the sergeant-at-arms signed a petition, asking that he remain on the air. Will was touched—and laid off Congress for a whole day.

SENATE

If we took Congress serious, we would be worrying all the time.

Our Senate always opens with a prayer, followed by an investigation.

Congress was behaving itself for a short period, and that hurt the news—course it helped the country.

The importance of a Senate job is mighty overrated. They can only do us little temporary damages, so it really don't matter much who is in there.

I read where the Republic of Ireland was about to do away with their Senate. Let us ask our Redeemer to not let us act too hastily in following Ireland's example.

Thou Almighty, who seest all things, must know that as disciples there is not a Saint Peter in the Senate, and as for prophets, there is not a Moses in a car-load. They seest not, but neither do the ones who sent 'em there see, so let's be charitable. But, Lord, if Ireland should be right, help us to see the light immediately!

I have often said that with all our kidding and cussing our public elected officials, that they are a good deal better than we, who elected 'em.

It's hard to get money out of the Senate for anything but for politics.

Senators and Congressmen don't get such tremendous salaries, but when you figure that there is hundreds and hundreds of them, I tell you, it runs into heavy jack. And all in the world they have to do is to shut up, both sides, and let the people vote on it.

I knock Congress, but I like 'em, and I understand 'em. I know they do wrong sometimes, but they mean well. They just don't know any better.

The Senate was arguing on some country called Latvia. Well, if you had locked that whole Senate membership up and said: "Not a soul can leave this room until you can tell me where Latvia is," why, in years to come they would point out the Senate chamber as the place where 96 men perished through starvation.

You see, in Washington they have two of these bodies, Senate and the House of Representatives. That is for the convenience of visitors. If there is nothing funny happening in one, there is sure to be in the other, and in case one body passes a good bill, why, the other can see it in time and kill it.

Say, did anybody ever see a United States Senator in his home state after the night he is elected? I have met 'em all over the world when Congress was not in session, but I never saw one at home. They are always making speeches about "My Fine People Back Home" but they never want to go see 'em.

I hereby start a movement to create another week, like Apple Week and Prune Week. It's "Meet Your Own Senator Week"! Let's make him come home, no matter what happens to him.

I wanted to have the home folks meet their Senator. Now that sounded practical, but you would be surprised at the amount of resentment that has come to my roll-top desk.

They all claim they don't want to see their Senator. That's why they elected him—to get rid of him. If they had wanted him at home, they would have kept him at home!

You let a Senator get some million dollar contributions behind him and you can't tell me that he wouldn't command some respect and that is what we have got to get back in our Senate that has been lost —respect!

I am a strong advocate for selling the Senate seats to the highest bidder; they do it on the Stock Exchange and it has proven successful.

Don't run for the Senate, you would be sunk in there! They wouldn't listen to Abraham Lincoln his first ten years in there if he was to come back and be elected to it.

You would think that a Senate resolution meant something, but they carry no more authority than a Chamber of Commerce one does.

In the old days, when Senators were Senators, why, the state legislature picked out the ones that were to run. Nowadays there is no qualification outside of an intention necessary.

I see where Mrs. Morrow* has been offered her husband's seat in the Senate if she wants it. Now in most cases those positions are offered widows just out of courtesy, but Mrs. Morrow is just about as unusual a woman as her husband was.
    If she goes in there she will know what the Senate is all about. Well, of course, not exactly, but as near as it can be found out.

I like to make little jokes and kid about the Senators, those rascals. When you meet 'em face to face and know 'em, they are mighty nice fellows. It must be something in the office that makes 'em so ornery sometimes.

We finally got the real low-down on the intelligence of the Senate. The Capitol building put in dial telephones and only two knew how to work 'em. And both these members were men who had been defeated at the last election, showing they knew entirely too much to be in there.
    So they are going to have those telephones taken out. There is

---

*Mrs. Elizabeth C. Morrow, poet, educator; widow of Dwight W. Morrow, Republican, U.S. senator from New Jersey.

nobody to put the blame on but yourself if you get a wrong number. They want nothing connected with the Senate in any way where the responsibility can't be shifted.

I called at the Capitol to see what our hired help were doing. It is almost superfluous to tell you they were doing nothing. I wish we could get them interested in something. I have often thought a book wouldn't be bad, or do you think we could get them to read it?

It sure did kick up some excitement in the Senate when Senator George Moses of New Hampshire called the other Senators "sons of wild jackasses!"
   Well, if you think it made the Senators hot, you wait till you see what happens when the jackasses hear how they have been slandered.

Most of the letters I get claim they couldn't get hold of a Senator or a Congressman. Well, that's been the trouble with all of us, we couldn't lay our hands on a Senator or lawmaker. If we could lay our hands on 'em, they wouldn't today constitute one of our menaces.

I have been interested in the scheme of my old friend Jack Garner of Texas. Jack wants to divide up the great state of Texas into five states. Why he wants to stop at five, nobody knows.
   The paper states that Texas would make 220 states the size of Rhode Island, and 54 the size of Connecticut, and that it's six times bigger than the whole of New England.
   Jack wants more Senators to offset that mess from the East. Well, let's make some Rhode Islands out of Texas and that will give us— 220 times bigger—that's 440 Senators!
   Now that ought to satisfy anybody, even if you are fond of Senators.

The way our Congressional business is carried on nowadays, being a Senator or a Congressman is not much, it just really consists in receiving telegrams.

You ought to see this ranch I'm on here in Texas—300,000 acres. If it was back East, eight senators and twenty-four congressmen would have to live off it.

Some Senator says that no man should be allowed to earn over $75,000. They forget that a man that earns that much, or more, works for a different kind of employer from the one Senators work for.
   Suppose you got $100,000 a year for working for a firm and you

spent $200 billion of their money that you didn't have and you didn't know where you was going to get it, how long would you be working for that firm?

The scene is laid in the United States Senate, the most dignified and deliberate Legislative Body in the world, as that is what they call themselves.

Well, there is the first laugh right there, even before they open their mouths. Then as these Professional Law Makers are starting to operate at the advanced salary that they so reluctantly voted themselves last fall, why, there is also another scene being enacted at the opposite end from this exhaust end of the Capitol corridor. It's the Amateur Branch of our Lawgivers Association.

Festivities opened with a prayer as usual in both theaters. The Chaplains of both places began their hopeless supplication for guidance and knowledge.

HOUSE OF REPRESENTATIVES

In August 1927, Will Rogers was in Washington, D.C., filming *A Texas Steer*. He was just recovering from a serious operation for the removal of gallstones, which had been reported by almost every newspaper in the country. *A Texas Steer* had a scene in which Will's character, a newly elected congressman, had to gallop up the steps of Congress. Will's scars had hardly healed, making it necessary for the famous cowboy to have a double do the actual riding. That, too, had been duly reported in the papers. *A Texas Steer* had been a much-traveled play, and was well known. As Will explained the plot:

> It is the movie of the old stage play by Charles Hale Hoyt. It was the story of a Texas cowman elected to Congress on bought votes. We brought it up to date by not changing it at all. In the stage version he didn't know what to do when he got to Congress. That part is allowed to remain as it was.
> The cattleman-Congressman used to play poker more than legislate, and that's left in the movie. There was a little drinking among the members at the time. For correct detail in our modern version, that has been allowed to remain in.

On August 27, Mr. and Mrs. Will Rogers were invited by the National Press Club to the Washington Auditorium. Attending the reception were Secretary of Commerce Herbert Hoover and Mrs. Hoover; Commissioner of Internal Revenue D.H. Blair; General John J. Pershing; chairman of the Democratic Congressional Committee, Representative William A. Oldfield; Senator Alben W. Barkley of Kentucky; and Senator Duncan U. Fletcher of Florida.

In the Rogers party were Sam E. Roark, the producer of A *Texas Steer*, and Mrs. Roark; Richard Wallace, the director of the film, and Mrs. Wallace; and Douglas Fairbanks, Jr., who played the juvenile lead, and his mother.

Presenting a scroll, Louis Ludlow, president of the National Press Club, explained that lawyers of the Club had studied the Constitution of the United States and had determined that "all powers not expressly reserved to the Federal Government are to be exercised by the National Press Club." With that slightly contorted logic, the Press Club had usurped the power to bestow upon one Will Rogers the title of "Congressman-at-Large." As Mr. Ludlow explained:

> We set about to find a job for him. Our first thought was to back him for the Vice-Presidential nomination on a Coolidge-Rogers ticket. Our idea was that Will would represent noise and the President would stand for silence. The President could throw the lariat and Will could throw the bull and it would be a well-balanced ticket. Just when we had that all arranged the President "chose" to renege, and Will's vice-presidential prospects went blooey.

Will Rogers was not awed. He responded by making it clear that he did not consider his appointment "any honor." He explained the proceedings, as he viewed them: "They took me to a dinner at the Club and then later to a big hall they hired. They had 6,000 people there to see me publicly humiliated and appointed a Congressman. I certainly regret the humiliation. My folks always raised me right and warned me about being a Congressman."

Will also objected to the manner in which this humiliation had been perpetrated: "When a man wants to lower an employee, he calls him into his private office. We don't hire a hall to execute our criminals. They fed me just like they do a condemned man, then marched me to the execution."

Actually, Will was pleased and for a short while signed his daily columns as "Congressman." Then, made ambitious by his esteemed status as Congressman-at-Large, he decided the following year to "run" for the U.S. Presidency on the "Bunkless Party."

Today's session was very congenial. They met, prayed, and adjourned.

That's what a Congressman or Senator is for—to see that too much money don't accumulate in the national Treasury.

Proposing something in a debate is just like writing a letter to your Congressman, nothing ever comes of it.

There is homes in New York that a Congressman would have to disguise himself as a waiter to get into. It's nothing against Congressmen but you are just a bunch of people that haven't been house broke to their ways. If one does happen to crash a swell dinner party, he is there in about the same capacity as an actor, a prize fighter or a channel swimmer—just to be looked at at close range and not through any degree of equality.

Congressmen, if it looks like you can help the farmer, why, do it! When something accidentally comes up that is good for the country, get in there and act like you was working for the taxpayers, instead of exclusively for the Democratic Party and go shame the Republicans into decency.

Now there is another thing, that extra session of Congress. Why call 'em in extra session? Why call 'em in regular session?

Nobody has ever suggested giving Congress a medal. I believe I will have one struck off and give it to Congress for "Endurance in Oratory beyond, and far on the other side of the duties for which they were elected." It might encourage them, because there is times when I think that they feel that they are not appreciated.

Flew into Washington this afternoon to see what the boys who live by the ballot box are doing. Busy as usual passing appropriation bills like hot biscuits at a country farm house.

It takes a man that can think in big numbers to introduce a bill in Congress nowadays. A bill under a hundred million dollars would be so unusual that it wouldn't pass. They would say, We can't spend our time voting on trifles!

As long as we have a mud hole or a gully in this country, there will be a Congressman there to ask for an appropriation to have it widened, or dug deeper.
What they should do is fill 'em all up, and save bridges.

A bunch of Congressmen landed in New York from the Panama Canal where they had been at Government expense to see if it really connected the two oceans, or was it just propaganda.

This is the way our President works Congress. He never scolds 'em, he knows that they are just children at heart. When he wants something done, he just coaxes 'em and the first thing you know, they have voted "yes."
Well, I can't do that. I have to cuss 'em a little sometimes. I like 'em at heart as much as the President, maybe more, but they do vex the very old devil out of me, and all of us, at times.

CONGRESSIONAL RECORD

All I know is just what I read in the Congressional Record. They have had some awful funny articles in there lately. As our government deteriorates, our humor increases.

A foreigner coming here and reading the Congressional Record would say that the President of the United States was elected solely for the purpose of giving Senators somebody to call a horse thief.

The Congressional Record, a Dictionary and a Political Platform is the three least-used things in existence today.

All one has to do to get one's stuff in the Congressional Record is to find a stenographer that can stay awake long enough to take it down. Then you mark in the "Applause" and "Laughter" parts yourself.

This stuff they are talking here in Congress costs the people of the United States $44 a page. That's beside what it costs to ship it to the asylums where it's read.

Me back to reading the Congressional Record, where they ain't supposed to be doing nothing but lying when they say it.

Speaking of Congress, my name was dragged into a discussion that happened on the floor recently. We have had the misfortune to have parts of at least five separate articles read into the Yearly Joke Book (the Congressional Record) beginning with a Bonus Article I wrote a year or so ago, and lately some on airships and battleships and lack of preparedness.

I have engaged counsel and if they ever put any more of my material into that "Record of Inefficiency" I will start suit for deformation of character. I don't want my stuff buried away where nobody reads it. I am willing to give them a raise in salary. But I am not going to lower myself enough to associate with them in a literary way.

PORK BARREL

Will Rogers, the politically astute observer, knew only too well that politicians got reelected by judicious abuse of the pork barrel. Whether a politician was able to better the lot of mankind at large counted little with the folks back home; what did matter was the amount of loot he could pilfer out of the public feed trough for their personal benefit. Though not a politician, Will, too, reached into that bottomless treasure chest—once. Only in this case it was not for himself, but for his adopted hometown of Claremore, Oklahoma.

It seems the new local recreation area included a lake, and Mayor Church and his advisors thought that it would add a nice touch to stock it with fish, especially if that stocking could be done at somebody else's expense. Rather than petition Washington in their own name, it seems they approached their foremost citizen and asked him to do the pleading. Will Rogers wrote:

WILL ROGERS
BEVERLY HILLS CALIFORNIA

DEPARTMENT OF COMMERCE.
FISHERIES DEPARTMENT.

Dear Sirs. I have written and asked for everything in my life, (not the government). They always been the one writing to me to send 'em something. But I tell you this is the first time I ever asked for fish. I don't ask for it at a cafe. I am a kind of meat hound myself, but we have spent all we had in Claremore to build a kind of rodeo ground for fish, and now we haven't got enough left to get the fish with, but we heard that you all had fish that you distributed around to the voters. Course, right after an election is a terrible time to ask a Republican administration for a hand out, even if it's just fish, 'course the Chamber of Commerce with their usual bad judgement ought to have got the fish before the election. Cause I am like George Washington, I can't tell a lie, we voted against you, but we did want your fish. If you fill the boys up with fish for the next four years in good shape, I believe I can make 'em see the light, and sprinkle in a few Republican votes.

We got a lake that a fish would be proud to call home, every fish gets a room and bath. We will take good care of 'em, we won't catch many of 'em, most of our folks are too lazy to fish.

What we want to do is make another Rapidan* out of Claremore. And we want Mr. Hoover to come and catch some of his own fish. We are a broadminded people and outside of election time we treat a Republican the same as any other human. We want to get Coolidge down there too.

So please send us some fish, for Pat Hurley** will be back there, and he will want to fish, so you wouldent keep Pat from fishing, would you?

Let us know when they are coming and we will have the Chamber of Commerce and the band down to meet 'em, we will give these fish a reception like they never had before.

Send 'em before Roosevelt gets in there for he is a deep sea fisherman, and may send the wrong kind.

Despite unorthodox grammar, erratic syntax, and inventive spelling, the name of this letter-writer performed a miracle. At atypical, un-

---

*Rapidan River, in the Blue Ridge Mountains of Northern Virginia, where President Hoover liked to fish.
**Patrick J. Hurley, Oklahoma-born secretary of war under President Hoover.

precedented governmental speed, a mere two weeks after this letter was written, two express carloads of fish arrived in Claremore.

Congress got a dandy comedy; they put it on every year. It's really their yearly bonus, in addition to their salary. It's called "River and Harbors," or "I'll get mine!"

They take billions of dollars of the people's money and they promise to make a home state stream wide enough to fish in.

Congress says, "We are going to divide up, whether there is anything, or not. What do you suppose we are in Congress for, if it ain't to split up the swag? Please pass the gravy."

The height of statesmanship is to come home with a dam, even if you have nowhere to put it.

Congress is getting uneasy to start muddling things up again. Every little one-cylinder Senator and punctured-tire Congressman from all over the country is going to try and put over his little local scheme.

And that's the sad part about politics. These are the men that will get elected every time—the ones that are able to hornswoggle the government out of something for their own district's special benefit.

Massachusetts, through good manipulation of their Senators and Congressmen, got in on the government pork barrel and opened them up the Cape Cod Canal, to allow cod fish who couldn't make it around the Cape, to cut through and exchange courtesies with the cod on the other side. It's been a social success for the cod fish, but financially it hasn't paid the lighthouse keeper.

A gang of government experts was out in Kansas City a few days ago, talking about whether it would be practical to navigate the Mississippi River. It's funny, experts have to come clear out of Washington to see if the Mississippi and the Missouri can be made navigable, when for years and years that's the only way people got around out here.

Now every local Senator and Congressman within drowning distance of these rivers will go back to Washington and start working his head off for an appropriation.

I see by the papers that every appropriation bill is being passed. Too bad you didn't ask for something. You would have gotten it.

Suppose four different groups from four different parts of the country all want something and all trade votes with each other so that everybody gets theirs. What chance has the Treasury got?

There is times when it looks like the Jesse James boys got their robbery reputation on mighty scant evidence.

Congress is working on a new dam. Now dams are pretty much alike. They all work on the same principle. You stop up the creek or river at some point, then the water generally backs up away from it, and how far it backs up denotes approximately how much the American taxpayer overpaid to keep it backed up.

Well, all I know is just what I read in the papers, or what falls under my gaze, and it's going to take an awful lot of letter writing to make up for some of these. The following towns received the following "Doles": Post Office at Huntsville, Alabama, $234,000; Post Office, Waycross, Georgia, $1,350,000 (their representative in Congress is a statesman, not just a Congressman). Now Gainsville, Georgia, only gets $301,500. They are just building practically a shed and shouldn't be allowed in the same state with Waycross.

But get poor old Los Angeles. All she got was $63,000 for a quarantine station. That's a station to dip the people that come in there from the North, or Frisco end of the state. You can build a pretty good dipping vat for $63,000.

New England is still in politics rather heavily. Boston got $3,700,000 for a Parcel Post Building. So you see Massachusetts representatives were not exactly what you would call asleep at the dole bag.

Calais, Maine, did you ever hear of that one? They got $100,000 to build a "Border Station." That's a pretty fancy comfort station just for moose hunters to check in and out of on their way to Canada.

Well, I would write to their Congressman. I don't know his name now, but he will become famous in a very short time, for he will no doubt have the capitol at Washington moved there. So you write and compliment this Congressman, and if his state don't properly appreciates him, Claremore, Oklahoma, hereby makes him an offer. Why, with him as our representative, and a town the size of Claremore, we would have gotten a three-quarter million bucks post shack, a quarantine dipping vat and a two hundred thousand smackers comfort station.

FILIBUSTER

The Senate is having what is called a filibuster. The name is just as silly as the thing itself. It means that a man can get up and talk for 15 or 20 hours at a time, then he is relieved by another, just to keep some bill from coming to a vote, no matter the merit of this particular bill. There is no other body of lawmakers in the world that has a thing like that.

Why, if an inmate did that in an asylum they would put him in solitary confinement. And mind you, if any demented person spoke that long there would be something in that speech you would remember, for he, at least, had to be smart, or he would never have gone crazy. These in the Senate just mumble away on any subject.

Imagine a ball player standing at bat and not letting the other side play, to keep from having the game called against him. Now if someone had read them the Bible, that would have been a good thing for it would have given a lot of them a chance to hear what it says. Instead they just did their own act for 10 or 12 hours each. To imagine how bad this thing is, did you ever attend a dinner and hear a Senator speak for 50 minutes or an hour? If you have, you remember what that did to you! Well, just imagine the same thing only 12 times worse.

LAME DUCK

If you don't know what a "Lame Duck" Congress is, it's the type where nobody is going to try to do anything till another Congress is called.

It's like a troupe of actors getting hissed off the stage, but insisting on staying on there because they had a two weeks contract.

A Lame Duck is a politician who is still alive, but the government paymaster has been notified that he will become totally disabled when Congress convenes.

The Lame Duck Congress has been putting on a mighty inspiring example of just how ornery a Congress can be, if they make up their minds to be ornery. We just got about four more weeks of show and then these boys go into what some writers termed "oblivion." "Oblivion" is a one-way ticket town.

This is what is called "The Short Session." But not short enough. It's also called "The Lame Duck Congress" for there will be a lot of guys in it that made a forced landing during the late storm of votes. Now they ain't going to be wishing anybody much good, especially the voters back home that didn't renew their contract.

Did you read where some Senator from Colorado was giving up his seat to his successor the day after he lost the election? He figured that the folks elected the other fellow and he was the one they wanted in there.

That's almost unheard of in political life. There is a "lame duck" that should have a statue!

LOBBYISTS

If one man with no official connection can change a whole conference, it's not him you want to investigate, it's the guys that he influenced. And it's the same with lobbying in Washington. If we have Senators and Congressmen there that can't protect themselves against these evil temptations of lobbyists, we don't need to change our lobbies, we need to change our representatives.

There is no law against lobbying any more than there is against a man trying to get votes for the Senator when they are running for office. But Washington is going to investigate them and see how they make this living, for it looks like a terribly easy graft.

California had a bill in to investigate lobbying, and the lobbyists bought off all the votes and now they can't even find the bill. Putting a lobbyist out of business is like a hired man trying to fire his boss.

The lobbyists have taken the whole convention. They give you a badge and a drink. Lots of us don't know what to do with the badges.

Any person that can't spot a lobbyist a mile away, must be a person so blind they still think toupees are deceptive, and can't tell a hotel house detective from a guest.

All the lobbies are gathered in Washington to see that taxes are put on somebody else's business, but not on theirs.

INVESTIGATIONS

The United States Senate investigates everything—usually after it's dead.

Everybody wants to hear accusations and nobody wants to hear denials.

We would rather see things not investigated. Then it will be remedied. But anything that is ever investigated, nothing is ever done about it.

Nowadays it's about as big a crime to be dumb, as it is to be dishonest.

From the looks of the various investigations in Washington, rugged individualism got a little too rugged and was caught by the umpire.

There is something about a Democrat that makes 'em awful inquisitive, especially if it's on a Republican, and there is an awful lot to find out about most Republicans.

President Franklin D. Roosevelt gets back tomorrow and I suppose his fishing trip will be followed by an investigation, for the Democrats claim he caught some fish, and the Republicans are equally insistent that he didn't.
    It's like all investigations. It's absolutely necessary. If there is men in this country that claim they caught a fish when they didn't catch one, it should be known by the people of this country—no matter how high up the investigation has to reach.

This investigation has been a fine thing for Washington. The hotels are crowded. Every time a guest registers the clerk asks him, "I suppose you will be here until you testify?"
    If they would all tell the truth the first time they testify they wouldn't have to testify again, like they are doing now. And they would get this thing over a lot quicker. They ought to pass a rule in this country that in any investigation, if a man couldn't tell the truth the first time he shouldn't be allowed to try again.

One good thing about these investigations, they always give a party a chance a second time, so he can explain how he was misunderstood the first one.

A thing that struck me rather odd was that there was no prayer, or benediction, or blessing, or a single thing to start it off. You would have thought that they would have made some plea for Divine guidance. But they seemed to have enough confidence in themselves that they didn't need any help from the Lord.
    However, I think by now they wish they had asked Him to give some small assistance.

Investigations are held just for photographers. They start out so sensational and peter out so quietly.

While the Senate is investigating everything from chewing gum to parking spaces, the poor old House of Representatives can't get a speck of publicity and the members are up to the Senate, laughing at the denials of the witnesses. Why, it beats murder for publicity!

I see where they have investigated some birds in the legislature. It seems that a gang of low principled persons inveigled them into a scheme. Naturally they didn't know what it was; they thought it was some charitable organization.

One bird says that after they got to him and he found out what it was, he pulled right out. I bet you there is a lot of big men in public life that maybe are not as lucky as he was to get out before they could give him any money.

There is things in our affairs that you sometimes think we have no sense of smell at all, or we would certainly smell some of the things that are being put over on us every day.

I think of all the bunch on the witness stand in Washington that lawyers are the worst. You see, a lawyer has so many angles that he is trying to use a little of all of them and he winds up making everybody believe that he didn't tell half he knew, and didn't know half he told.

I wish America could get some of the political bandits that live off this country, to come and give themselves up. Then we would know just what we are paying them to live on, instead of the present system of letting them grab what they can.

This term of Congress will go down in history. It's the most accommodating session I ever saw. They couldn't pass any bills, for everybody was on the stand testifying somewhere. Their slogan is: "Testimony made easy!"

Every newspaper in the United States runs what you say, even if you don't say anything. Look at the President. Every paper was full of what he didn't say.

There is many an investigation going on. I never saw such an eager Senate. I was looking for the airplane investigation and run into the first room I saw, thinking that was it, but this was an investigation on sugar. Went down the hall and butted into another one, and it was on anti-lynching. The next one was "Has the army paid too much for what they bought?"

MISCELLANEOUS

Congress met. I was afraid they would.

The Opera Comique, both ends of it, the Senate and the House.

Papers today stated that President Hoover is going to issue a denunciation of the House and the Senate.
    Denounce 'em? Everybody is surprised he hasn't shot 'em.

You know how Congress is. They'll vote for anything if the thing they vote for will turn around and vote for them. Politics ain't nothing but reciprocity.

Well, the boys are off in Congress again. But if you think that politics is based on patriotism, and not on business, you just watch the press from now on. Five hundred men in the House and another hundred in the Senate will argue on what to do with the taxpayers' money.

Hurray! Congress is to adjourn! Only four more days of Congressional burglary on the Treasury!

The regular session of Congress opened today. The President is not responsible for the holding of this session. Got to blame the founders of the Constitution for it.

They have an unwritten law there in Congress, that a new member is not allowed to say anything when he first gets in, and another unwritten law that whatever he says afterwards is not to amount to anything.

Chapter IV

ELECTIONS

W ill Rogers was born on the first Tuesday in November of 1879, Election Day. "I didn't vote, but they voted my name every year up to 18," Will would later recount. "Women couldn't vote in those days so my mother thought she would do something, so she stayed home and gave birth to me. I decided to get even with the government."

Even though Rogers spoke and wrote on politics in all its forms, he did not get to attend a national nominating convention until fairly late in his life. For the national conventions of 1920, Will Rogers signed a contract with the Newspaper Enterprises Association (NEA) to submit "at least ten jokes a day" for syndication. By this time Rogers was well established as an oft-quoted humorist and movie star, and his incisive, witty observations found a ready market. To report his firsthand impressions, Rogers prepared to attend both the Republican convention in Chicago and the Democratic one in San Francisco. Fate decreed otherwise.

Goldwyn Pictures Corporation had exercised its option to retain Will Rogers' services for the second year of their contract, and on May 28, 1920, he was busy on location, having started the filming of *Honest Hutch*. The Republican convention was scheduled for June 8 to 12. It seems that the front office was not willing to suspend the shooting schedule, with its attendant losses, just to permit Will Rogers' trip to Chicago.

What nobody could foresee was that Will Rogers would have to leave the film crew abruptly and rush six hundred miles by a relay of automobiles to his home in Hollywood. His three sons, Will, Jr., Jimmy, and the very young Freddie, had been stricken with sore throats, thought to be tonsillitis. Because the doctor's diagnosis indicated no danger, Betty Rogers thought it unnecessary to alarm Will. By the time the condition was correctly identified as dreaded diphtheria, it was quite late. Will was immediately notified and he rushed through the night with antitoxin. The two older boys recovered. Twenty-month-old Freddie died June 17.

It was a shattering blow to Will Rogers, and yet he would continue with the filming of *Honest Hutch*. The film was not completed until July 15.

The Democratic convention opened June 28, 1920, in San Francisco, with Will Rogers still working on his current film. Yet he still managed to fulfill his contract with NEA. He pretended that, rather than attend the two conventions, he had gone to Washington, the seat of political command posts, where the power brokers controlled events at both conventions via telephone. His "gags" were in the form of interviews.

Will Rogers attended the 1924, 1928, and 1932 conventions in person, and reported them faithfully. He enjoyed them for what they were—"glorified Mickey Mouse cartoons . . . solely for amusement purposes."

Looking back on the 1928 conventions, Rogers described his experiences:

> A couple of weeks ago after I had foolishly sat for a week in each place and watched and heard men burlesquing political speeches, it kinder made you wonder, "Are we doing all this progressing that we talk about all the time?"
>
> They say that practice makes perfect. But I tell you 'taint so. No nation that was ever invented under the sun, does as much practicing "talking" as we do, and if you think we are perfect at it, you just listen over the radio, or worse still, in person, to the speeches at these conventions.

The most terrible things were the nominating speeches. Every man would talk for half the time about what his state had done. . . .

Mrs. Nellie Ross started her speech with: "As I look into this sea of faces. . . ." So that shows you how far speech-making has advanced. It was Noah that first pulled that one when he looked over the bunch just before pulling in the gang plank. . . .

Maybe in the old days speeches were just as idea-less. But they were only being listened to by the delegates, and the man making the speech only had to appeal to intelligence as high as his own. But nowadays this radio thing has changed all that. People are getting wise to the type of man that is supposed to be saving the country. A speech nowadays is just like bootleg liquor; nobody knows what all the junk is they put in it, but everybody knows that it don't stand up. So let's don't hold another convention till somebody can think of a new speech. *

In Chicago, on June 30, the fourth day of the 1932 Democratic convention, Oklahoma's popular governor, "Alfalfa" Bill Murray, voted his state's twenty-two votes for "that sterling citizen, that wise philosopher, that great heart, that favorite son of Oklahoma, Will Rogers!" The huge assembly roared its approval, but the subject of their affection was fast asleep in the press gallery. One of his fellow reporters poked him in the ribs to tell him of his nomination. Will reported it in his own way to his syndicated readers:

Politics ain't on the level. I was only in 'em for an hour and in that short space of time somebody stole 22 votes from me. I was sitting there in the press stand, asleep and wasn't bothering a soul when they woke me and said Oklahoma had started me on the way to the White House with 22 votes.

I thought to myself, well there is no use going there this late in the morning, so I dropped off to sleep again and that's when somebody touched me for my whole roll, took the whole 22 votes, didn't even leave me a vote to get breakfast on.

---

*Syndicated weekly article, July 15, 1928.

Course I realize now that I should have stayed awake and protected my interest, but it was the only time I had ever entered national politics and I didn't look for the boys to nick me so quick. Course I should have had a manager but the whole thing come on me so sudden and I was so sleepy. I had been taking opiates all night—no man can listen to thirty-five nominating speeches and hold his head up. And I am sure some of these that did the nominating can never hold theirs up again.

Now I don't want you to think that I am belittling the importance of those 22 votes. They was worth something there at that time. Not in money, mind you, for there is not $2.80 in the whole convention. But they buy 'em with promises of offices.

I expect at that minute Roosevelt's bunch would have given me Secretary of State for that 22. And I could have sold 'em to Al Smith for maybe mayor of New York.

Why, I could have taken those votes and run Andy Mellon out of the embassy in England with 'em. I could have got that job with only ten of those votes.

And what do I do? Go to sleep and wake up without even the support of the Virgin Islands. They not only took my votes but they got my hat and my typewriter. I not only lost my 22 delegates but I woke up without even as much as an alternate.

Now what am I? Just another ex-Democratic Presidential candidate. There's thousands of 'em. Well, the whole thing has been a terrible lesson to me and nothing to do but start in and live it down.*

It was the last national convention Will Rogers would attend.

CONVENTION

The convention was billed to start at 10:30 this morning, but it didn't start until 11:15. No one had the nerve to start it.

We got an example of the chairman's methods. The minority was drowned out by the gavel.

---

*Syndicated article, July 1, 1932.

To show you that true democracy will rule the convention, the first thing they did was to throw out two delegates the people had elected.

Political conventions would die standing up if it wasn't for the inventive genius of the boys that make the politicians look "colorful."

It's the only place where our public men can do foolish things, and due to the surroundings they kinder look plausible at the time.

The convention met last night and then adjourned in five minutes. That was the most successful convention the people of the country ever enjoyed.

They met again at 10 this morning, but unfortunately didn't adjourn. It looked like they had, but they hadn't.

Another preacher prayed this morning and he read his prayer. There hasn't been a one that could make an impromptu prayer.

The show was called to order at 12:20 Jefferson time. It took Clem Shaver, the chairman, twenty minutes of steady hammering to get order enough for them to listen to a prayer. They didn't want to listen to a prayer; it was an argument that they wanted to listen to.

Finally some man prayed. I didn't get his name or political faith. But from his earnestness I should say he was a Democrat. He not only asked for guidance, but wisely insinuated for votes in early November. He read his prayer, ending with the Lord's Prayer. He read that too. I am going to keep going to these conventions till I find a preacher that can pray from memory and practice. These that I have seen all act like it was their maiden prayer.

This is the third day of the convention. This is the day the Republicans adjourned. Why, the Democrats haven't done anything yet but meet and pray.

That's one thing about a Democrat. They are never as serious as the Republicans. The Democrats take the whole thing as a joke and the Republicans take it serious, but run it like a joke. So there is not much difference.

I guess there is no profession as "crazy" as politics. It's a profession all its own, with all the "trades" and "deals" and "under-cover happenings" that go on during one of these conventions.

It's a show that no American should miss. It's entertainment and it's enlightening. It gives us a kind of an idea that most men that emerge from it with any spoils were more lucky than competent.

I saw something yesterday that for stupidity, lack of judgment, non-sensicality, unexcitement, uselessness and childishness has anything I've ever seen, beaten. It was the Democratic national convention.
Imagine, if you can, thousands of people gathered in a hall at 10:30 in the morning from all over the Union, forced to sit there from then to 6 in the evening and listen to the very same identical speech, made over and over again by fifty different people.

I have read about this fine acceptance speech, one of his best ones and he's been accepting since he was old enough to hold office. What did he say?
Well, what do they all say?
Did he come out on the leading issues of the day?
He did!
Did he solve them?
He sure did!
How did he solve them?
By promising anything that was needed!

They adjourned till tomorrow for the sake of the hotels. They could have finished this convention in ten minutes today.

Men who yesterday wouldn't allow their names to be associated with the Vice Presidency are today announcing they would consider being drafted.

Illinois had forty delegates and they are all for different candidates and all have to make either nominating speeches, or seconding speeches.
According to the speeches, a candidate is harder to second than he is to nominate.

I have heard so much at this convention about "Getting back to the old Jeffersonian Principles" that, being an amateur, I am wondering as to why they ever left them in the first place.

What a keynote speech by this bird Claude Bowers*, why, you haven't heard the Republicans called anything, till you hear this fellow—

---

*Claude G. Bowers, Democratic politician, author, ambassador to Spain, Chile.

comedy, oratory, facts and sense. He makes the Republicans pretty near as bad as they are. That's how good he is.

The loudspeaker system didn't work and half of 'em couldn't hear the keynote speech. They got mad and got to leaving—but not as quick as those that was sitting near and could hear it.

My press seat was near an exit, just ideal.

Now comes Senator Alben Barkley with the keynote speech. What do you mean "keynote?" This was no "note"; this was in three volumes.

It had to be a long speech, for when you start enumerating the things that the Republicans got away with, you have cut yourself out a job.

If you don't think the Democratic party is a large party, you just sit and count the men in it that are nominated. There was candidates' names presented that the newspaper men had to go back to old United States census reports to find any mention of them. Most of the speeches were not nominations, they were letters of introduction.

The Republicans had to hold their convention either in Chicago or New York this year as no other city was big enough to hold all their candidates.

The President and the Vice-President were both nominated last night. The Presidential candidate early in the evening at the convention, and the Vice-Presidential candidate later at the hotel.

I said: "What makes a delegate change? Don't they stay with their man?"

Senator Penrose said: "The delegates vote the way their people told them on the first ballot. But after that they sell to the highest bidder."

I said: "But that's not honest, is it?"

Penrose said: "No, just politics!"

Times are so hard that the next Democratic convention will be held under the auspices of the Red Cross.

I said to one of the speakers: "There were fewer high-toned phrases and big words in your speech."

He said: "I had to make it very plain. Did you ever get a good look at a delegate?"

The resolutions committee just got a dictionary apiece and found all the possible phrases and words that don't mean anything, then got 'em together and called it a resolution.

It offers no solution but will prolong the argument. The press boys accused me of writing it.

They had to adjourn this afternoon; they had gone as far as they could. Nobody would change their vote for nothing.

Favorite son governors who have been holding their states to the last finally told them: "Boys, leave me and get out and do the best you can, but remember one thing: Don't ever let it be said that our glorious state is cheap."

I entered the hall with William Jennings Bryan. As we entered, everybody stood up. Both of us looked at each other rather embarrassed as we didn't know which one the demonstration was meant for—they were rising to sing the national anthem.

By the way, the Democrats don't know the words any better than the plain people.

The hall was full. It looked kinder like a church; everybody was sleeping.

Some bird from Michigan made such a flowery and glowing tribute to one of his fellow statesmen that it did not look to me as if a soul in Michigan could fill the bill but Henry Ford, but he fooled us by naming their governor.

A lady was the best thing on the program today. She was to introduce Mr. Mondell of Wyoming as the chairman of the convention. She simply walked to the front and said: "Convention, I submit to you Mr. Mondell!"

Now the lady in being so brief was either smart, or else she couldn't think of anything good to say about him.

They nominated today. I wish you could have been here and heard what great men we have in this country. We started out with 16 men for President.

Here is what each of them was: "The only man who can carry the Democratic Party to a glorious victory in November; whose every act has been an inspiration to his fellow men; and not only loved in his home state but in every state!"

Apparently even an honorary mayor cannot please his entire constituency; Los Angeles, March 5, 1927.

To improve strained relations between the U.S. and Mexico, American Ambassador Dwight Morrow invited Will and Charles Lindbergh for an "official" visit. The two celebrities served their country well by making many friends among officials and citizens. Here, in Mexico City, they watch a bull fight, December 1927. (Courtesy National Archives)

With Assistant Secretary of the Navy, David S. Ingalls, after landing at North Island near San Diego, California, November 1930. (Courtesy National Archives)

June 25, 1932. With the customary newspapers in his hand, Will is off on a night trip to Chicago, where the Democratic National Convention will open in two days. With 22 votes, Oklahoma will nominate Rogers as a favorite son; the Convention will settle on Franklin Delano Roosevelt and John Nance Garner.

I thought yesterday when you heard all this unnecessary spouting about each man nominated, what their wives must have thought of all these men that they were married to all these years, and were just finding out how wonderful they were.

The building is literally lined with flags. I could never understand the exact connection between the flag and a bunch of politicians. It's beyond me why a political speaker's platform should be draped in flags, any more than a factory where honest men work.

If they would just eliminate the names Lincoln, Washington, Roosevelt, Jefferson, Jackson and Wilson, why, both conventions could get out three days earlier.

To shorten the time of conventions to almost nothing, the main thing is to make 'em cut the so-called "History of the Party."
  They always start out, "This party has always, since its early birth, been the Party of Right. The other Party has been cockeyed all their life. Noah, when he founded our Party, had both sides to pick from, right and wrong, and he wisely chose Right—and Right we have ever remained. Our great Party had its Birth in Virtue, its Youth in Righteousness, and is spending its Old Age in Holiness."

PLATFORMS

A man read the platform last night. He was perhaps the last man that will ever read it.

They are stalling with the platform, and when it is ready, there is not a wire walker in America that can stand on it.

The Republicans built their platform not only to stand on, but it's in such a shape that they can run on it, hide behind it, run clear around it, or even crawl under it.

They read the platform.
  P.S. It is now six hours later and everybody has forgotten what the platform was.

Talk about economizing and cutting out all the unnecessaries, what's the idea of holding the Republican convention?

As for the platform, it will be the same one they have read for forty years, but have never used.

And the speeches will be the same ones delivered for forty years but never listened to.

CANDIDATES

Even before the 1928 Democratic national convention met, Will Rogers had written a lengthy article for the *Saturday Evening Post** in which he suggested to his friend Al Smith that it might be wise for him to forego the nomination that year. Al Smith was the Catholic, "wet" governor of New York state, and was the front-runner. Will saw the realities of the forthcoming race and was certain that no Democrat could win.

He predicted that if Al Smith stepped aside in 1928, offering the nomination to someone else, he would not only be offered the nomination by acclamation in 1932, but he would win. Will Rogers correctly analyzed the political climate. He tried to reason with Smith:

> It's not that you ain't strong all over the country, Al, for you are; you are the strongest one they got—that is for a Democrat—and if you was running against Democrats you would beat 'em. But unfortunately in the finals of this somebody has to meet a Republican, and when a Democrat meets him next year it's just too bad. Everybody talks about what's wrong with the Democratic Party. Well, if they will be honest with themselves they will admit there is just one thing wrong with it. They haven't got enough voters.

Disguising it in humor, Will continued this most logical prediction of an election which was still thirteen months away:

> You know that your Prohibition stand wouldent be any worse off in four years. It's not going to be an issue this election. Both sides are afraid of it. You watch those platforms and you will see both parties walk around Prohibition like a skunk in the road. If you think this country ain't dry,

---

*"Duck Al! Here's Another Open Letter," October 29, 1927.

you just watch 'em vote; and if you think this country ain't
wet, you just watch 'em drink.

Maintaining that the Republicans were unbeatable in 1928,
Will took an optimistic, Democratic view of 1932:

> By that time the Republicans will have done some fool
> thing. They have gone along now longer than their average;
> they are bound to make up for lost time in the next four
> years . . . The trouble with you politicians is you see, but
> you don't see far. You wear your reading glasses when you
> are looking at the future. You got your putter in your hand
> when you ought to have your driver.

History records that Will's friend, Al Smith, was nominated in 1928,
that he accepted the nomination, and that he lost the election to
Herbert Hoover. Four years later, in 1932, the country was in a deep
depression and the Democrats nominated Franklin Delano Roosevelt.
They did not want to go with Al Smith, a loser.

Now there are the early bird variety of candidates for President. There
will be dozens come in, mostly through starvation and partly through
thinking that the Democrats can win with practically nothing, and
there will be some entering the race that will qualify for "nothing."

Of all the dumb issues that candidates bring up to try and influence
people how to vote, I think "prosperity" takes the cake. How a speaker
can convince a man that he is prosperous when he is broke, or that
he is not prosperous when he is doing well, is beyond me.
   If a voter can't feel in his pocket and see if he is doing well without
having a total stranger tell him, then this government shouldn't be in
the hands of the people.

I look for one of the candidates to have to go out around Iowa, to help
plant some spring wheat. That's the tough part about being a candidate,
your backers won't let you act natural and do the very things that you
have always done. You can't be the man; you must be the candidate.

You see, it don't take near as good a man to be a candidate as it does
to hold office.
   That's why we wisely defeat more than we elect.

Two Democratic contenders made up. Yes, sir, they made up and they decided to bury the hatchet.

They decided to bury it in the Republican President.

The candidates carry on the glorious tradition of their great parties, because they are in favor of motherhood, virtue, the Constitution, and anything that seems to call for a word of praise, including the farmer.

Sunday I got an idea I would see just how religious all the politicians really are, as I had heard that religion might play some part in the fall festivities. So I grab a cab and rush from one church to the other all over town, and not a single candidate was among the worshipers.

Still, you will hear them get up and shout: We must continue to be God-fearing people! Our church is our salvation!

Well, our churches are our salvation, but some of those candidates won't be among those saved.

The candidates are "High Typed Gentlemen" till the contest gets close, then the "Brute" comes out in 'em. What starts out to be a nice fight winds up in a street brawl.

But it all comes under the heading of Democracy, and as bad as it is, it's the best scheme we can think of.

The Democrats can always furnish more candidates than the Republicans. Just after the previous election, well, the next morning after it, every Democrat who had been elected to anything at all the night before, his local paper said: "Jim Jasbo swept all opposition before him at the polls yesterday. He will be the best Justice of the Peace the Democrats ever had in this country, and the U.S. Senate is in his grasp, and the White House is before him!"

And he like a yap believed it.

Why do these candidates go to Omaha, or Denver, or Wildcat Junction, Tennessee, to speak? Do they think that they are paying a big compliment to that particular section?

This thing of meeting your hero and getting acquainted with him is awful liable to make you start hunting another hero.

The Democratic candidate brought up Nicaragua. He said he would protect American lives down there, even if he had to send some there to protect.

If all the charges made against both candidates were laid end to end, it would take 'em over two hours to pass a given point.

And if all the denials were heaped in a pile, Lindbergh couldn't fly over them. You know, the funny thing about a denial, it takes twice as many words to deny it as it did to make the accusation.

CAMPAIGNS

Campaigns have ruined more men than they ever made.

The Democrats should go out and get themselves some slick candidates and not preach too much on their party's honesty in this campaign. Shrewdness in public life all over the world is always honored, while honesty in public men is generally attributed to dumbness and is seldom rewarded.

Corruption is an awful good denouncing subject, but a poor campaign or vote getting subject; it's like a long hit foul ball in baseball.

Democrats, if the Republicans get a slush fund, don't waste all your time criticizing and investigating theirs; get out and get a bigger one yourself. Don't concentrate on the oil scandal. You didn't study human nature, you know the scandal happened six months too early to do you any good as a weapon. Ask any soldier and he will tell you America forgot the war in one year, how are they going to remember the oil scandal for six months? You can't beat an administration by attacking it. You have to show some plan of improving on it.

There is a big demand in this country for a return to "normalcy." But there is not two people that can agree just when normalcy was.

In the mind of the candidates the country is always "on the brink." And your decision on election day will be the deciding factor on whether it goes on over the brink—or if you vote wisely for him, he will grab it just as it's going over and pull it back for you.

Poor old "brink." I don't know of anything we've been on more of than we have it. I am beginning to believe that we wouldn't go over it on a bet.

Now this applies to all Presidents. There is nothing that will send a candidate to bed as drunk and dejected on election night as for him to be endorsed by a President.

Voters just don't like a President butting in.

The less a voter knows about you, the longer he is liable to vote for you.

One candidate took up the hardship of maternity in the early days. He insinuated that under Democratic federal control, motherhood would again become a burden.

I asked, "Can you tell me what the Democrats have agreed on as a campaign issue in Texas for the forthcoming election?"
"The Democrats never agree on anything in Texas. That's why they are Democrats; if they could agree with each other, they would be Republicans."

The "Outs" are attacking and the "Ins" are defending. All the "Outs" have to do is promise what they would do if they got in.
But the "Ins" have to promise what they would do, and then explain why they haven't already done it.

The old campaign is sure getting hot. God help a man out looking for re-election on a night like this.

This country is a thousand times bigger than any two candidates, or any two parties in it. This country has gotten where it is in spite of politics, not by the aid of it. That we have carried as much political bunk as we have and still survived, shows that we are a super-nation.
If by some divine act of Providence we could get rid of both these parties and hire some good men, like any other big business does, we would be sitting pretty.

Well, it's fine for candidates to run their campaigns on a high plane, but it would be like me wanting to conduct this column on a strictly grammatical basis. I would like to, but I just ain't equipped for it, and that's the way they are. With politicians as the tools, you just ain't equipped to conduct anything on a high plane.

They talk about what a great thing the radio has been for politicians and candidates. Why, there has been more people got wise to over the radio than Senate investigations have exposed.
Nothing in the world exposes how little you have to say, as radio.

Conditions win elections, not speeches.

If every radio went off the air from now till election day, it would be a godsend to a suffering public, and no loss to political knowledge.

Well, here goes the radio again: "If I am elected I will pledge myself to relieve the farmer, I will enforce the law and . . ." Oh, applesauce, I will be glad when it's over!

The new way to get in the papers is to bolt your party and jump to the opposing candidate. They always announce that they will take their supporters with them. Their support generally consists of a wife who didn't register, and two children too young to vote.

Personally I am in favor of money spent on election campaigns. The more money the better. If they can get contributions from rich men and distribute them around among the poor and needy, I think it's a good thing. It puts money into circulation that otherwise would be loaned out at a ruinous rate of interest.

I believe that a man should be allowed to spend as much as he can to be elected. No man rises above his surroundings, and if you put a man in that was elected on nothing but campaign speeches, you are going to have nothing but a wind-bag to represent you.

Sundays you get more politics than all the rest of the week combined. That's when the preachers start 'lectioneering.
    They all start out by saying "The Church should not enter into politics, BUT . . ." then they show you in their case it is different; that they are not entering politics, they are just advising, that people are so flighty nowadays that if they are not advised properly, why, they are apt to be led astray by the opposition.

Both candidates are fine men and would perhaps do equally as well, but if you listen to either side you would think that for the opponent to get in would be a return of the whole country to slavery, free silver, "empty dinner pails," long skirts, bustles and suspenders.
    Why, we have got people that are really taking this whole campaigning thing serious. They must think a President has got something to do with running the country.

It's like a campaign promise; it's too good to be true.

PUBLIC OPINION POLLS

Will Rogers scoffed at the accuracy, indeed the usefulness, of "straw voting," as polls were called in the twenties. One of the most prestigious polls was taken and disseminated by *The Literary Digest*, a magazine ascribed Republican leanings:

> It is impossible for the weather department to announce rain on a certain day without the Digest taking a poll on the matter. They have polled every question from "Should the Ku Klux Klan be allowed to inter-marry?" on down.
>
> They had one on the Democratic nominations and wasted enough mail back and forth to have made Sears Roebuck ashamed and they never did guess the right guy. More men have been elected by straw votes, and fewer received a salary. It's like winning on the races in your mind.

The system employed by *The Literary Digest* was to mail out stamped postcards, which were to be filled out by the recipients and returned. Naturally this form of poll was criticized as being too haphazard. In 1924, when the *Digest's* poll showed Coolidge way ahead, the Republican newspapers claimed that the results reflected the true and fair sentiment of the country; the Democrats, on the other side of the aisle, claimed that those questionnaires had only been sent to Republicans, and that Democrats never even saw any cards.

Will drew his own conclusion from these polls:

> Personally I don't think this straw vote demonstrates but one thing; that is that there are more Republicans that can write than there are Democrats.

We are straw voting around again. This straw voting, or polling, is about the lowest form of voting there is. It don't decide much, but it works 'em up while it lasts, but these old boys have got it down pretty fine and the side that loses might try to kid it off as a joke, but at heart they will take it mighty serious.

'Course, who ever wins, it won't mean anything, only another argument.

A fellow in Beverly Hills says *The Literary Digest* poll should be abolished on account of their accuracy. He don't mind polls if they ain't right, but he is agin the true ones. He says people read 'em and then vote with the majority.

But here is what he don't explain. What makes the majority in the opinion poll in the first place?

No mathematician in this country has ever been able to figure out how many hundred straw votes it takes to equal one legitimate vote.

I see where the *New York World* suggests barring *The Literary Digest* from announcing the results of its poll beforehand.

They claim it takes all the life and pep out of the minority party. I would think the election four years previous would do the same thing, so why not bar it too?

Now I get this news from a feller that is doing nothing but taking "hearings" on public opinion. He just holds a clinic over every voter. He writes: "The far South don't even know Hoover is running. If he gets a vote south of the Mason Dixon line, it will be some stray kin folks of his."

Poll voters are mighty unreliable. You got to become a liar before you become a voter.

We will know lots more in a week from now. There is going to be a terrible lot of people fooled. I have always said that voting in a poll is a funny thing, a fellow will lie about the way he'll vote as easy as about a golf score. Every candidate in the race on both sides has had enough promises to elect him unanimously, but you wait till the votes are counted on election day, and it will tell you how many liars there are of legal age.

Everyone is watching the straw vote. It's like a rehearsal for the election every year and in case the straw vote is over before the election, I doubt if they hold the election at all; they will just take this poll and inaugurate the man on that.

Some people can get nourishment out of the most peculiar things.

VOTERS

Us voters are more smart-aleck than we ever were, but we are no smarter. In fact, we don't know any more than we did the year they promised us a "full dinner pail."

No voter in the world ever voted for nothing. He jumps the way his bread looks like it's buttered the thickest.

No voter can remember back a year. What happened in the last six months is as far as his mind can grasp.

Voters go to the polls and if their stomachs are full, they keep the guy that's already in; and if the old stomach is empty, they vote to chuck him out.

In most places it's awful hard to get folks to go and register, but out here in Los Angeles where we do everything "big," why, each qualified voter is allowed to register himself and ten dead friends. If he hasn't got ten dead friends, why, he is allowed to pick out ten live ones, just so they don't live in this state.

The Republicans are kicking on this arrangement, as they claim that system of registration gives the Democrats the best of it, as very few Republicans have ten friends.

Every guy just looks in his own pocket and then votes, and the funny part of it is that it's the last year of an administration that counts. It can have three bad ones and then wind up with everybody having money in the fourth, and the incumbent will win so far he needn't even stay up to hear the returns.

We voters read more and we hear more over the radio, but the stuff we read and the stuff we hear don't make us any smarter. For the people that write it, and the ones that talk over the radio are no smarter than the ones that used to have to hand down the dope for our old forefathers.

Voters go to the polls in an automobile, but they don't carry any more in their heads than the old timer that went there on a mule. So the old bunk that you can't fool the voter is the biggest bunk there is. He has been fooled all his life and he will always be fooled.

ELECTIONS

As Maine goes, so goes New Hampshire.

I want to see elections brought back to the good old days when a man would not only argue with you that you was voting for the wrong man, but he would put up what should be the legitimate end of any argument, and that was the Do, Re, Me.
   I want to see elections made a gamble, and not a ratification.

I hope some of the men who get the most votes will be elected. That is of course not always the case.

Yesterday our municipal elections ran true to form. The sewer was defeated, but the councilman got it.

The minute it's not raining enough and we can't raise anything, or it's raining too much and we raise too much, we throw our President out and get a new one.

It don't mean anything. We been staggering along under every conceivable horse thief that could get into office, and yet, here we are, still going strong.

We have various pestilences every once in a while, but the only advertised and known calamity is our elections. It's just like an operation, the anesthetic is the worst part of it. It's these weeks of putting you under that is the trying part of an election.

As a life member of the Red Cross, we are rushing doctors to Chicago with all speed to have them there when the bombing starts next Tuesday at their primary. We are establishing first-aid stations just about where we figure the voting booths will be blown to.
   I am covering the Chicago election for the Nicaraguan press. As they are putting on their own election in October and are anxious to learn what it will be like.
   The roads are packed with refugees leaving Chicago.

A noisy vote don't do any more than a quiet one does.

Those that are in are trying to stay in and those that are out are trying to get in, and that's about all there is to the game.

They are voting whether to keep a governor two years or four. I think a good, honest governor should get four years, and the others life.

The short memories of the American voters is what keeps our politicians in office.

I've been reading about the primary elections back home. Looks like everybody that remains honest is getting beat.

It takes a great country to stand a thing like elections hitting it every four years. When you figure that you have a system where you make business stand still and people go nutty for three months every four years, why, somebody who concocted the idea of elections certainly figured out a devastating scheme.

The locusts that I saw swarming in the Argentine are houseflies compared to the destruction by a Presidential election.

More men will be elected tonight through good counting than were elected today through voting.
   Yours for reasonable honesty in politics.

POST-ELECTION

Well, the election is finally over. The result was just as big a surprise as the announcement that Xmas was coming in December.

I don't know of any quicker way in the world to be forgotten in this country than to be defeated for President. A man can leave the country and people will remember that he went some place. But if he is defeated for President, they can't remember that he ever did anything.

The campaign lasted only a few months, but it will take two generations to sweep up the dirt.

The Democrats ran on "Honesty" and I told 'em at the time they would never get anywhere. It was too radical for politics. The Republicans ran on "Common Sense" and the returns showed that there were 8 million more people in the United States who had "Common Sense" enough not to believe that there was "Honesty" in politics.

Honesty in politics? If the Democrats had brought back Thomas Jefferson, he couldn't have carried his own precinct on that platform.

We have gone through the most exciting and bitter election. Friends have been turned into enemies, families have been split. Husbands have choked wives, and wives have attempted to murder husbands, all because one wanted one guy to draw a government salary, and the other member wanted the other fellow to live in the White House the next four years.

I attribute Hoover's success to the fact that we have never seen his picture on a golf course. Nothing outside of a senatorial investigation can ruin a man so completely with the general public as golf pictures can.

Chapter V

GOVERNMENT

"*T*axation is about all there is to government," wrote Will Rogers, and he battled long in the belief that "the crime of taxation is not in the taking of it, it is in the way it's spent."

"There is dozens of great humanitarian things that could be done at a very little cost," he maintained, "if the tax money was properly applied. It's the waste in government that gets everybody's goat."

In 1924, just four years after his twenty-month-old son Fred died of diphtheria when serum could not be supplied in time, he ridiculed the government's action—and inaction—on another epidemic: hoof-and-mouth disease. Cases of the dread contagion had occurred in California, and the governments—state and federal—were, as usual, stepping in. Will, having been born and raised in cattle country, was familiar with the nature of the disease. When the government interceded in this case, while remaining passive in related ones, he saw an angle others might have missed. Thinking of his lost son, he chided the government for ineptness and its waste of time and money.

I am writing this out here in California and I don't know whether this will get through or not. We have an encounter out here with the hoof and mouth disease, and they are quarantining about everything that goes out of the state.

Arizona is the worst; they tried to stop an aviator the other day that was flying over the state from California to Texas.

They don't allow passengers that are going through the state to get off the train. They have to carry the disease, if they have it, on into New Mexico. Of course, if they don't care to get off there, they can go on into Kansas or Oklahoma with it. They stopped a shipment of furniture; guess they figured that a cow might have occupied one of the beds at some time or another. You see, a cloven hoofed animal is the only one that gets it. They get it first by breaking out between the slit part of their foot; then they lick it and it infects their mouth. That's where it derives its name, the foot and mouth disease.

Now with animals, when a case breaks out they shoot every animal of that same kind in the state.

You see this disease started a hundred years ago somewhere in Europe and they didn't know what it was; so the veterinarian just shot the cow and as there happened to be another cow standing by this one, and he happened to have two bullets, why, he shot her too.

Well, things went along until finally another case was discovered, and this veterinarian says to himself, "I will not only see them but raise them." So he shot the afflicted cow, then shot all of her friends. So that's the way this disease has drifted just from one shooting to another.

It's the only disease in the world where shooting is the remedy. Instead of developing veterinarians' medical knowledge, it has only developed their marksmanship. The U.S. Government appropriated one and one-half million dollars just for more ammunition to help eradicate the disease. The whole state has been put under federal marksmanship.

They have put an embargo on fruit and vegetables being shipped. Now if there is a man living that can tell me when a cabbage has the foot and mouth disease, and where, I will gladly retract. I don't care if carrots do have it; I hate them anyway.

Now they could find out something about how the disease works, but the minute it breaks out, why, they call a conference and they all get together and decide where the next conference will be. Then the next day they hold another conference.

If doctors of humans held that many conferences, every-

body in the United States would die while they were conferring.

You wire the state or the federal government that your
cow is sick and they will send out experts from Washington
and appropriate money to eradicate the cause. You wire
your government that your baby has the diphtheria or scarlet
fever, and see what they do. All you will do is hire your
own doctor, if you are able.

You can have 5 children down with infantile paralysis,
more deadly 10 times over than any foot and mouth disease,
and see how many doctors they send out from Washington
to help you. . . .

Why can't we get a government to at least do for a child's
protection, what they do for a cow?*

Will was quite serious when he asked that last question. Little Freddie's death was never far from his mind, even though he rarely allowed
anyone a glimpse into his sorrow. He never said it explicitly, but he
must have felt that incisive and concerned government action could
have saved his little boy's life.

GOVERNMENT

People often ask me, "Will, where do you get your jokes?"

I just tell 'em, "Well, I watch the government and report the facts,
that is all I do, and I don't even find it necessary to exaggerate."

Every time our government starts to run something, why, the politicians raise up and howl: "Don't put the U.S. government in business!"

They are always wanting the government to spend the taxpayers'
money to build something, then they don't want 'em to run it.

Say, have you been reading these articles that Mrs. Mabel Willebrandt,
our former Assistant Attorney General, is writing? Mabel tells how
Prohibition is linked with politics. Mr. Coolidge, our former President,
in his last article hopped on the lobbies in Washington.

---

*Syndicated weekly article, published May 11, 1924.

It's too bad our system of etiquette don't allow everybody to speak the truth while they are IN office.

Didn't you see a headline in this morning's paper saying that "Russia is going to extract snow from clouds before those clouds reach Moscow"?

Now that sounds silly, don't it? But then, in the next column it says, "President and Congressional committee propose to reduce government expenditure by 200 million dollars." Well, I bet you the Russians get the snow out of the clouds before the President and Congress get any government employees out of their swivel-chairs.

Always remember this, that as bad as we sometimes think our government is run, it's the best run I've ever seen.

Everybody is on a trip somewhere if they work for the government. I wonder when the taxpayers take their trip.

A good man can't do nothing in office because the system is against him, and a bad one can't do anything for the same reason.

I'm up in the old gold mining district in California, where, in the old days, if you wanted any money, you got yourself a pick and went out and got it. Not out of the government, like you do now; nowadays, why, the government just gives it away.

Ah for the good old days, when the boys used to dig the gold out of the hills, and the girls used to dig it out of the boys.

This is the age of miracles. I read where the Secretary of the Treasury informed all the Treasury Department people to keep out of politics.

There wouldn't be any such luck to have that spread to all departments?

I tell you, this finding out how to govern a country, or even a state, or county, or even town, has got the whole world licked.

There is not a type of government that can point with complete pride and say: There, this is the best that can be had!

Things in our country run in spite of government, not by the aid of it.

Our government is not a business, it's a charity organization. Half the people in the United States would rather get one dollar from the government in some way, than make 10 dollars honestly.

Those in charge of government planning are fine men, honest and mean well, and if it was water they were distributing, it would help people. For water trickles downhill and moistens everything on its way. But gold, or money, goes uphill.

The Reconstruction Finance Corporation lent money to medium and small banks, and all they did was to pay off what they owed to New York banks. See, the money went uphill, instead of down.

You can drop a bag of gold in Death Valley, which is below sea level, and before Saturday it will be home to Papa J. P. Morgan's bank.

The more men that have anything to do with trying to right a thing, why, the worse off it is. The government has not only hundreds, but literally thousands in Washington to see that no man can personally tend to his own business.

I doubt that this new method of "Government by Telegraph" which we are developing is quite as effective as it's advertised to be.

There is a good deal of difference between a vote and sending a telegram. In our system of voting they generally stop you after about once, or maybe twice, but any one person can send as many telegrams as they have money and can think up names to sign 'em.

We used to have a rule that our government wouldn't recognize any new government that had come into power by force and revolution. Then somebody, that had accidentally read our history, happened to ask: "Well, how did our government come into power?"

So now we recognize 'em no matter who they shot to get in. All they have to promise is that they will buy something from us, even if it's only guns for the next revolution. There is no such thing as a thief anymore, as long as he can pay his way.

THE CONSTITUTION

You see, the men that laid out our Constitution in the first place looked far enough ahead to see, in fact they must have had a premonition that at some time in the distant future there would be a bunch of men in there that didn't know any more about Government than I know about Einstein's theory.

Well, those old fellows in those days almost made it foolproof, so due to their farsightedness no one we put in can do us a whole lot of damage.

The old founders of the Constitution made it so it didn't matter who was in office, things would drag along about the same.

The fuss raised over Prohibition has done twice as much harm as the drinking has. The Drys wanted it in the Constitution, and they got it in there. The Wets wanted to drink, and they got it. So what is all this shooting about, anyhow?

There is no use getting excited over a little thing like an amendment to our Constitution nowadays. It's pitiful when you think how ignorant the founders of our Constitution must have been. Just think what a country we would have if men in those days had had the brains and foresight of our legislators today!

The law should in some way allow certain injustices to be remedied. Of course the other side says: We got where we are as a great nation by this set of laws that we're living under. So why change them? Let the Constitution alone! And that's mighty good logic, too.

But there is something that they forget. You, or I, can rightfully say we got where we are by these laws, but there is a lot of folks that ain't got anywhere under 'em. And the prospect ain't any too bright for 'em to get any further. So they might not be averse to some small change in the Constitution. They might say, Yes! Give us what you've got and we'll say it's a perfect Constitution, too.

So it all gets back to just how good has the Constitution been to you. That's all it is.

TAXES

Taxation is a serious subject with most Americans. There is something abhorrent about sharing one's earnings with a seemingly irresponsible structure of management. While governments and their employees come and then go, taxation, by contrast, goes on forever. There seems to be an irrefutable law which stipulates that governmental spending increases in direct proportion to the money collected. No matter how much money the government—whether federal, state, or local—collects, civil servants are most ingenious in finding ways to spend even more. Will Rogers discovered that axiom long ago. He carried it to its ultimate conclusion in a radio broadcast on April 28, 1935, in which he explained to the country the intricate points of a new inheritance tax:

> Well, there comes a plan from Secretary of the Treasury Henry Morgenthau, to put a bigger and better inheritance tax on these tremendous estates. On an estate of say $10 million, why, the government will take about 90 per cent of it and then give the offspring 10—after Mr. Morgenthau gets through with it.
>
> And then, on an estate of a 100 million, 200 million, a billion, like that, well, the government just takes all of that and notifies the heirs: "Your father died a pauper here today, and he's being buried by the MEBA, that is the Millionaires' Emergency Burial Association." It's a kind of branch of the RFC.
>
> Now mind you, I don't hold any great grief for a man who dies and leaves millions and billions. But I don't believe Mr. Morgenthau's plan will work, because he gives figures in there that show what his new inheritance tax would bring in every year—that is, as long as the Democrats stay in. He seems to know just who is going to die each year, and how much they're going to leave. Now brother, that's planning, ain't it?
>
> Now suppose, for instance, he's got scheduled to die J.P. Morgan in a certain year. And you can bet, if they can arrange it, they'll have him die while the Democrats are in and they can get the benefit of that estate. Now according to plans, J.P. Morgan he's got to die in order for Mr. Morgenthau to reach his quota for that year. Now while I think Mr. Morgan is a nice man, and I think his patriotism might compare with some of the rest of us, but whether he'd be patriotic enough to want to die on this year's schedule or not—just to make Mr. Morgenthau's budget balance—I mean that's asking a good deal of a man. He might be rather unreasonable and not want to die. I say, old men are contrary—and rich old men is awfully contrary; they've had their own way so long—so in order for Mr. Morgenthau's plan to work out a hundred percent, he's got to bump these wealthy guys off, or some-

thing. Well, the government's doing everything else, but there is a Humane Society.

While his radio audience appreciated Will's explanation, the government did not change a single comma in its new inheritance tax. Even Will Rogers could not make an impact on the tax system of the United States.

Taxpayers cheer, not from the heart but from the pocketbook.

Democrats have a sort of native shrewdness. They figured out that the only way to get the money away from the Republicans was to put on a bounty, or as the Romans called it—a tax on 'em.

You see, a tax is the thing you pay if you have anything, and if you don't have anything, you don't pay it, naturally. Well, the Democrats knowing the Republicans had money, and knowing that the Democrats didn't, why, they put it on.

Andrew Mellon, our Secretary of the Treasury, comes in with a mighty welcome suggestion. He says we can cut taxes by $160 million.

We deal in billions in expenditures, and millions in savings.

Every time the government suggests putting a tax on something, the manufacturers of that object rush to Washington, demanding that it's an injustice.

But no matter what the tax is put on, the man that makes it don't pay it; it's the bird that buys it who pays. But we have never yet heard of a "purchasers' lobby" rushing down to Washington.

Just announce that there is something to be divided up and you got the whole nation interested in national affairs. Announce there is something to pay, and you got one hundred and ten million anarchists on your hands.

They took the automobile tax off, they took the theater tax off on cheaper tickets, and they lowered the inheritance tax. So now you can buy an automobile, go to a cheap show and you can die. I don't know why the tax should be taken off any one of them. They are all luxuries.

The high Inheritance Tax, so the Secretary of the Treasury argues, discouraged dying; that with that tax on, a lot of men that would otherwise be dead, was still living.

Congress says: We'll frame a tax law that will get 'em alive or dead, living or deceased.

Now they got such a high inheritance tax on 'em that you won't catch those old rich boys dying promiscuously like they did. This bill makes patriots out of everybody. You sure die for your country if you die from now on.

The Senate slept on the tax bill over the weekend. But the birds that are going to have to pay it didn't sleep any.

The Capitol Comedy Company of Washington, D.C., put out something called "Non-Taxable-Bond" or "Let-the-little-Fellow-pay." The main character in this one is a working man on salary with no capital to invest, paying more on his income than the fellow who has capital and draws his money just from interest.

It ain't taxes that's hurting this country, it's interest.

No slick lawyer or income tax expert can get you out of a national sales tax.

People don't want their taxes lowered nearly as much as the politicians try to make you believe. People want JUST taxes more than they want LOWER taxes. They want to know that every man is paying his proportionate share, according to his wealth.

Spent the afternoon in Washington, D.C. (Don't Complain). Congress was in session and I was in the Speaker's office. I asked him why he wasn't in there and he said: "I am Speaker, not Listener."

"What are they talking about in there?" I asked him.

He said: "Taxes."

I said: "Why, that ought to be a good, live subject. I'm going in there and hear it."

He replied: "Go ahead; you do it at your own peril."

I went in. I was all alone in that gallery. Somebody was talking, but there was only four members present in their seats. Oh, it was lonesome in that place. It reminded me of the night I played Madison, Wisconsin.

Monaco has the right idea. Fix a game where you are going to get the dough but the fellow don't know you are getting it. People don't mind spending their money if they know it's not going for taxes.

This being an election year for a lot of these "statesmen" they will go home and run on "I cut your taxes."

Then they will come back next year, find a huge deficit and will have to dig up something else to raise the money on.

Say you started a political party and had this as its slogan: "No Taxes are to be paid at all! We will borrow on our National Resources for all current Expenses! No Taxes as long as we can borrow!"

Well, I bet you, you would have the biggest political party in America.

Noah must have taken into the Ark two taxes, one male and one female, and did they multiply bountifully! But with all their multiplying proclivities, the politicians out-multiplied them.

The gasoline tax, which is nothing but a national sales tax, has proven productive and punitive.

Now if a tax on gasoline keeps up the roads, why wouldn't a tax on light wines and beer keep up the House of Representatives, one on Coca-Cola and Jamaica Ginger and Camembert cheese keep up the Senate, White Rock and cracked ice the state legislatures, and so forth?

And let each stay within the budget. For instance, if people wasn't drinking much beer, we wouldn't have many Congressmen; if toothpaste and facial creams had a slump, cut the President's salary in proportion.

It looks like a good scheme.

I been looking since yesterday into this new income tax plan. Now I can't find a single group to shoulder that tax either. There just doesn't seem to be any volunteer taxpayers.

I see now what makes a Congressman so unpopular. He just will not fix a tax that falls on nobody.

Course everybody knows that one of our great ills today is the unequal distribution of wealth. You are either at a banquet in this country, or you are at a hot dog stand.

There is no doubt that the ones with money are the ones that could pay more taxes. But if the government takes all their money in taxes, it don't leave any and after all, it's those durn rich ones the rest of us got to live off of.

A movie star getting 300 thousand dollars a year would be taxed over half of it. While a financier receiving 300 thousand dollars a year in interest from tax-exempt bonds wouldn't pay a cent to the upkeep of his government from which he received not only protection for himself and his family, but also his government guarantees him his original investment!

Those tax-exempt bonds were put in so that a town or a state or a government could sell more bonds than it ought to.

Write to your Congressman and tell him to do away with tax-exempt bonds.
Even if he can't read, write to him.

Say, did you read in the papers about a bunch of women up in British Columbia, as a protest against high taxes, sit out in the open naked, and they wouldn't put their clothes on?
How far is it to British Columbia?

How is the government going to get the extra taxes? Out of the rich —or just out of the poor, as usual?

This money the government is throwing away, where is it coming from?
Well, I don't know, but off-hand I'd say it was coming from those that got it.

NATIONAL DEBT

I never thought we would live to see a Democrat that would put down that many figures and get 'em right. President Roosevelt says that by the end of next year, 1936, our per capita debt will be $270 each. Course, if you think that's too high, you got a perfect right to die and beat it.

Of course Mr. Mellon, our Secretary of the Treasury, might feel bad about his books not balancing. Think of how you'd feel if you counted up at night and found you was nine hundred million short.

Mr. Roosevelt is trying to get rid of Congress and the poor man can't get rid of 'em. They have appropriated more money than any Congress ever did, but I guess that is all right—we are not paying our national debt, anyhow, we just keep on adding to it, so it don't matter how much it is, anyway.

All I know is just what I read in the papers. In fact, all I know is what I read about criminals and Congress.

Congress has been getting more money out of us lately than the criminals. The criminals don't take it till after you get it, but Congress is making us all sign I.O.U.s for all we will ever get during our lifetime.

There should be a tax on every man that wanted to get a government appointment, or be elected to office. In two years that tax alone would pay our national debt.

The Secretary of the Treasury, Andrew W. Mellon, has skimped and pinched here and there and saved some money because he foolishly thought that was his business and duty. Well, the news got out that Mellon had a surplus.

Now get this, we owe billions. Now if you owed a sum of money and you suddenly happened in some way to make some—what would you do with this extra money? Why, you would apply it on what you owed and cut down the principal, wouldn't you? Certainly you would!

Well, what a fine chance you would have of ever becoming a politician! You got to split that up with the loyal boys back in the home wigwam! There is an election coming on and the best way to split this is so it will do the most good at the polls.

We owe more money in our national debt, and we are lowering taxes! Statistics say that 70 percent of every dollar paid in taxes goes to payment of interest.

Well, if two thirds of what you pay goes to just interest, why don't we do our best to try and cut down the principal, so it will lower that tremendous interest?

We howl and holler about why don't European countries pay us. Why don't we pay ourselves?

We are so far in the hole now that we will never get out anyway. We are behind now billions of dollars in our national debt so let's go ahead and make it a good one.

We are not only the richest nation in the world, but we are the poorest. We got more than any of them, but we owe more.

One of my broad-minded papers wired me: Didn't use your article today because you attacked credit and loans!

Well, credit means interest, and I will attack interest, because interest attacks me and you. There is not a man that's in the hole today, that can't look back and wish the first guy had never loaned him anything.

We have become kinder reconciled to the fact about this great National Debt. Course, there is lots of folks that think we are just so far in debt that there will never be any head above water again and they are worrying what our grandchildren are going to have to pay. Well, most folks say, "Well, our children seem to think they are smarter than we are, so if they are that smart, why, maybe they can think of some substitute for money to pay off the National Debt with, and they'll wonder why we didn't have a bigger one." Imagine you wanted to start a society on the following platform: "Everybody try to borrow all you can personally, and save nothing. Leave your children plenty of debts!"

Say, you wouldn't get ten to join that. You would be arrested for being crazy. But we will let the coming generations pay 70 percent of each tax dollar they pay in, just for interest on what we borrowed during our generation. Our children shouldn't pay for the billions of dollars we spent. That was not the coming generation's fault. They will have their own problems to look after, without paying for ours.

BUDGET

The politicians have overdrawn our bank balance so that it has set a record for an overdraft.

We got to stop Alexander Hamilton, who thought he had established a sound financial system, from laughing in his grave.

Japan has been kicking up a mess lately because they had a budget that wouldn't balance. So they changed Cabinets.

Our Secretary of the Treasury has never thought of that idea.

We are billions in the hole and will be billions more next year, and not a Congressman has got the nerve to ask voters to pay part of it in taxes.

The biggest handicap for a balanced budget is that there is an election in the Fall.

WELFARE

We got a powerful government, brainy men, great organizations, many commissions, but I don't want to discourage Mr. Mellon, our Secretary of the Treasury, and his carefully balanced budget, but you let folks in this country go hungry and they are going to eat, no matter what happens to budgets, income taxes or Wall Street values!

Washington mustn't forget who rules when it comes to a showdown.

The only thing I see for the fellow that don't believe in the government spending all this money on welfare, is not to participate in receiving any of it.

For instance, the government pays out for the relief to a starving child, or for people to eat, and here they go to pay the bank loan with it! Now the bank don't believe in the government spending all this money, but when the man comes to pay his loan with government money, the bank don't say: "I don't believe in the government spending all this money. No, I can't take it! I'll just carry you myself." Boy, what a laugh that would be.

So don't be too critical as long as you are living on some of the loot.

Tax relief, farm relief, flood relief—none of these have been settled by Congress, but they say they are getting them in shape for consideration at the next session of Congress with the hope that those needing relief will perhaps have conveniently died in the meantime.

We shouldn't be giving people money and them not do anything for it. No matter what you had to hand out for necessities, the receiver should be given some kind of work in return, say four hours a day, instead of money being doled out as charity—you work for it at some state or national public work. It wouldn't cheapen labor; it would cheapen public works, the thing that belongs to all the people, and the thing we would like to have cheapened.

It may not be a great plan, but it sure beats the one we got now.

They say that this thing can't go on, that the government is spending all the money, that it's not a good state of affairs to exist.

Course, one remedy would be for people to refuse to take some of it when it comes our way; but you haven't heard that, have you?

This plan that broke out yesterday, where you help out these young folks, that sounds awful good. Course I look for a bountiful editorial condemnation for it's going to cost money. But if you help out the young folks up to twenty, and the old ones over 60, that only gives a fellow a little stretch of about 40 years where he has to do any worrying for himself (or herself, as the sex may be).

If we can keep the young happy, and the old satisfied, why, all the middle aged have to look out for is women automobile drivers.

DIPLOMACY

England, France and Germany have diplomats that have had the honor of starting every war they ever had in their lifetime. Ours are not so good—they are amateurs—they have only talked us into one.

Of course we have ambassadors over there, but they are more of a social than a diplomatic aid to us.

Lending money to other nations never made friends with anybody. If a few million dollars is going to part our friendship, why, the friendship was never very deep.

If we keep our nose clean and don't start yapping about somebody else's honor, or what our moral obligations are, we might escape being dragged into some war. But it's going to take better statesmanship than we have been favored with heretofore.

The steamship lines must be giving tourist rates to foreign diplomats. There is no other way of accounting for 'em all coming over. Poor Washington, D.C., can't hardly tell what flag to hang out.

You talk about actors being jealous. You haven't seen any jealousy till you watch diplomats work.

Diplomats have a thing they call a Diplomatic Language. It's just a lot of words and when they are all added up, they don't mean a thing.

We got the most thorough training in every line of business in this country, except statesmanship. In that you just decide overnight yourself: I am a statesman!

That thing "Diplomacy" that these other nations dote so much on, why, we don't go in so much for that. We train men for everything else. We just wait until we hear of a conference somewhere and send a man, or a bunch of 'em, whose only bargaining up to then had been with their grocer.

When it comes to Diplomacy, why, we generally pick a man socially equipped so that he won't cut himself while eating. When we have done that, we feel we have succeeded.

When it comes to gathering to negotiate around the old mahogany table, where there is not a dish on the table, where other nations train 'em for years to say one thing and mean another, why, about all America ever comes out with is the check.

ECONOMY

I represent a new class of people in this country, the newly poor.

The value of the English Pound dropping 30 percent caused our newspapers twice the worry that the American dollar dropping 75 percent has.

Did you read this in the papers this morning: The American Dollar is down to 75 cents abroad?
   Be a good time to go over and buy some, for they are still worth a dollar over here.

Our problem is not what is the dollar worth in London, Rome, or Paris, or what even it is worth at home. It's how to get hold of it, whatever it is worth.

When money is going down in value, you want to have it in something besides a bank.

Everybody is talking and preaching economy, but the only ones that are practicing it are the ones that ain't got anything.

October 10, 1932. On a South and Central American trip, Will stops to chat with American troops stationed in Nicaragua. (Courtesy National Archives)

September 25, 1934. Completing a round-the-world trip, Will and Betty arrive in New York City aboard the French liner Ile de France.

With future member of baseball's Hall of Fame, centerfielder Tris Speaker, in Detroit during 1934 World Series. St. Louis won the Series 4 games to 3.

On one of Will's frequent trips to Washington, D.C., the "National Joke Factory," with Senators Joseph Taylor Robinson, (Arkansas), Democratic majority leader, and Royal Samuel Copeland, (New York).

England and America and France are trying to find out what the dollar is worth, and what the Pound Sterling is worth and what gold is worth.

Nations and their currency sure are like mothers with their babies —each thinks theirs is the best.

The main thing that's agitating everybody is the financial situation. I've heard of a nation being frightened of war; people worried over the health of a loved one; but we'll go on record as being the first nation that is literally scared about what's going to happen to its dollar.

This is the only time when the fellow with money is more worried than the one without it.

No nation in the history of the world was ever sitting as pretty. If we want anything, all we have to do is go and· buy it on credit.

So that leaves us without any economic problem whatever, except perhaps someday to have to pay for them. But we are certainly not thinking about that this early.

This country is not prosperous. It's just got good credit. We live better and owe more than anybody in the world.

Lowering the value of money from a dollar to 59 cents didn't have quite the effect that the economists thought it would. That's one of the drawbacks to a professor, his work is entirely with a pencil. But the moment the dealings are with somebody else, why it's entirely different.

I can sit in a grand stand with a race program and a good, sharp pencil—well, I have even done it with a dull one—and I can write down the winning horse. But the minute I walk under the stands and reach for a five dollar bill, instead of a pencil, that horse just seems to know it and runs differently.

It's like driving a car. If you are the only one on the streets, you are like the professor with the pencil—you can have things pretty much your own way. But when they commence to coming from every way, all making for the same corner, no man living can tell you exactly what will happen.

And it's the same way with money.

They showed that the Department of the Treasury had saved money, but that it cost $50 million more this year to save it than it did that same department last year, showing that even the cost of saving money has gone up.

All the financial papers are talking about how cheap money is now, with the Federal Reserve Bank charging around 3 and 3½ percent. I don't see why they don't say it's half of one percent, for there is no way of getting any of it, anyway.

The last economy Congress voted was more salary for themselves and then they adjourned to go home on their regular business. You know that Government is just a sideline with them.

If ever there was a time to save, it's now. When a dog gets a bone he don't go out and make the first payment on a bigger bone. He buries the one he's got.

Don't make the first payment on anything. First payments is what made us think we were prosperous, and the other nineteen payments is what showed us we were broke.

We say our government is nutty. That seems to be the general opinion that the way the government is run is all nutty, and that it's throwing away money. But anytime any is thrown our way, why, we've never dodged it.

DEPRESSION

We used to call depression a "state of mind," but it's just about reached a state of health. It moved from the mind to the stomach.

We got one thing to be thankful for, anyhow. The country is not in as bad a shape as the rumors have it. If ever a land was rumored to death, it's us.
  If we did pass out as a great nation, our epitaph should read "America died from fright." [September 3, 1931]

It wasn't what we needed that was hurting us, it was what we was paying for that we had already used up.

The bountiful harvest is the very thing that's the matter with us. Too much wheat, too much corn, too much cotton, too much beef, too much production of everything.
  So we are going through a unique experience. We are the first nation to starve to death in a storehouse that's over-filled with everything we want.

This Depression must have finally hit the Senate. They are investigating it.

Things are in a poor state right now. I know a hitch hiker out here that is having such poor luck getting a ride that now he is standing in the middle of the road, offering to go either way.

This New Year's Day there's nothing much in the papers but optimistic predictions by all prominent men who are doing well.

No news in the papers on the Depression, and no more news than truth in optimistic predictions.

We not only cured our "big men" from predicting, but we about cured 'em from thinking they was "big."

Old Hollywood has reconciled itself to conditions of the Depression better than anywhere. They have just charged off 50 percent of their husbands as a total loss, voluntarily cut alimony, reorganized with less overhead and some are even going back to pre-war mates and conditions.

The world ain't going to be saved by nobody's scheme. It's fellows with schemes that got us into this mess. Plans can get you into things, but you got to work your way out.

Douglas Fairbanks [Sr.] got back a couple of weeks ago from the Fiji Islands, or some outlandish place that he had been. He said that down there you could live on 90 cents a week. That is about 10 cents more than what some have to live on here.

Congress hasn't done anything in so long that even the lobbyists that work on commissions are starving and hollering for personal aid.

Honest, as we look back on it now, somebody ought to have taken each one of us and soaked our fat heads. We bought everything under the sun, but where was our payments going to be if we lost our jobs? Why, that had never entered our heads. Why should we lose our jobs? Wasn't all our big men telling us things was even going to get better? Was our prominent men warning us?

If we had had a "prominent" man he would have, but we just didn't have any.

Everybody has some scheme or plan to save the country. Everybody has some scheme to set the world right again. But come to think of it, I can't remember when it was ever right. There has been times when it has been right for you and you and you, but never all at the same time. The whole thing is a teeter board, even when it's supposed to be going good. You are going up, and somebody is coming down.

But all this kind of "NUT" thinking is not my business. It's for some economist, that stuff is his racket. We all got a racket and I'm not going to try and muscle in on some thinker's racket.

The other day at the movie studio they claimed that all stories had to be made modern and up to date, that the old idea of the mortgage on the old farm was all out of date, that the villain robbing the train and hiding the money was all the hooey.

Say, listen, there never was a time in our lives when the foreclosing of a mortgage was as timely as it is today. It almost comes under the heading of standard equipment with most homes and farms, and as for villains being out of date, why, villains are getting as thick as college degrees—and sometimes on the same fellow.

If there is a man in this country that hasn't had a pamphlet printed giving his views on "How to solve the Current Situation," it's because there is no more paper to print 'em on.

Our principal worriment in this country is our unemployed, and it's the only problem that I see we have in this country. But if it's any consolation to the unemployed, I've been in countries where our unemployed would be arrested for being Capitalists!

INFLATION

Two friends were going into a cafe, and not knowing what to order, they finally decided to split an egg.

That's one advantage of the cafeteria. You get to see the food, even if you can't afford to buy it.

Most places are using girl waitresses now—well, they can do it, even a child could carry all you can afford nowadays.

Inflation ain't nothing but old man interest gnawing away at us.

This society woman says she don't know how she is going to educate her little Sturdie on an $85 thousand apartment house and $50,000 worth of diamonds.

Why, $85 thousand, where I was born in the old Indian Territory, there wasn't that much money in the whole Cherokee Nation. For a hundred thousand you could have bought the whole state of Oklahoma. And if you happened to have $14 over, you could have bought Kansas.

Course I guess it has advanced now; chances are the price of Kansas has doubled since then.

I have been accused of being worried over this "Inflation." I wasn't worried. I was just confused. There is quite a difference. When you are worried, you know what you are worried about, but when you are confused, you don't know enough about a thing to be worried.

You see, medical science has developed two ways of actually determining insanity. One is if the patient cuts out paper dolls, and the other is if the patient says: I will tell you what this economic business really means.

The House of Representatives is going to limit debate on inflation to five hours tomorrow. I wish to goodness there was a way to limit individuals that try to explain it to you to five hours.

There is one thing about inflation. It's made every man's intelligence equal.

CENSUS

Say, have you had your census taken yet? That's the last thing we've got left to take from us.

If at times you feel your government is not interested in you, you are all wrong. Why, every ten years they send around to see if you are still living, and why. They take your name and address and if anything shows up during the next ten years, they will notify you.

Knowing how many of us there is don't mean a thing. Censuses are just for Chamber of Commerce's oratorical purposes. The new census will give California six new Congressmen. Now if you call that adding to human welfare, you are an optimist.

California is sure excited over this census. They have instructed every one of us on just what assumed names to give to the different census takers. The more voters we show we have, the more Congressmen we will be allowed in the next Congress.

Well of all the silly arguments. Who wants more Congressmen? There ain't much quality in numbers.

We spend millions of dollars every ten years trying to collect the census of this inglorious commonwealth of America, when all we would have to do is to wait until a presidential year, and then count the candidates.

Now is a good time for Congress to pass something on its merit, for all the lobbyists will be home, having their census taken.

Read the census? Talk about putting a quota on immigration. Why the Yankees are swarming into the South like locusts.

Only one drawback—these rascals bring their Republican politics with 'em. They ought to be met at the Mason-Dixon line and deloused.

DISARMAMENT AND OTHER CONFERENCES

Well, the disarmament conference is off to a flying start. There is nothing to prevent their succeeding now but human nature.

Conferences are just like the poor and the Democrats, they will always be with us.

The only time we ever attract any attention at a conference is when we don't go.

America, that's a funny thing about us, we never was very good in conferences; we are great talkers, but we are mighty poor conferrers. Individually we are not bad, but as a delegation we are terrible. I don't know why that is.

I bet you right now, that they could have an egg-laying conference in Czechoslovakia, and if America could find out where it was, we would send more delegates and lay more eggs than any nation in the whole hen house.

There is one line of bunk that this country falls for, and always has: "We are looking to America for leadership at this conference; she has a great moral responsibility!" And we, like a big simp, just eat it up and really believe that the world is just hanging by a thread and the American delegates control that thread.

Why, they didn't discover us till 1492 and by that time the world had had 1492 wars, 1492 peace and economic conferences, all before we was ever heard of. England controlled all the oceans, half the land, over half the world's commerce; France is no Babe in Arms, Japan and Russia are of age; yet it's America they kid into thinking she is the whole cheese.

These conferences started after the war. When these nations quit fighting, they had nothing to do, so they started in to confer and it's always been a matter of doubt as to whether the fighting wasn't better than the conferring is, you know, because we had more friends when we was fighting than we have now since we started into conferring.

Well, the London conference closed today. That is, it just disbanded today, but it ended the day it started. Now every delegation goes home and tells tales on the others. Of course we leave as the principal villain. We were supposed to bring the pie they were to cut. When we didn't bring it, the banquet was a total loss.

Mr. Cordell Hull, our Secretary of State, a mighty able man, arrived and told Roosevelt what the London conference had done. That took five minutes.

Then he told Roosevelt what could have been done if the nations had really wanted to do something. That took hours.

Every day you meet a delegation going to some convention to try and change the way of somebody else's life.

The President has done all in his power to try and further peace and at the same time leave us a musket loaded in the corner.

It's all right to go to these conferences. But it's always well to come home and reload your gun after each one is over.

Well, today Austria says they want a gun. Yesterday it was Germany. England's got a gun. All God's children wants guns, going to put on the guns, going to buckle on the guns and smear up all of God's heaven.

All these come from treaties which say: "I shall have two guns, and you have one." It just don't make sense to say that one nation shall have more than another in anything.

It's like I always preached, why hold these conferences? There is always more hatred formed at any meeting than there is friendship; no matter what they agree to, they know they should have done better. The nations in the world that get along and never have any trouble are the ones that never meet in conference at all.

The poor disarmament conference, it's just dropped plum out of the papers. It just shows you how we can get all excited about something and think that life and death depend on it, and in six weeks nobody can remember it.

Those poor delegates, they were fairly well known a month ago, now their own folks don't know where to send the mail. I am going to ask for contributions for funds to build a home for delegates who have been sent off to conferences and forgotten.

Suppose some delegate to this disarmament conference says: "Airplanes are an unfair method of warfare, for they can drop things on defenseless people, what do you say we abolish them?" They would send that delegate home to have his head examined. And if some fellow gets up and says: "What do you say about prohibiting the use of chemical gases during the next war?" Say, they will throw that guy in the river.

Now we gather to disarm, when a gun has put every nation in the world where it is today. It all depended on which end of it you were —on the sending or receiving end.

Well, the conference met today and appointed a commission to meet tomorrow and appoint a delegation which will eventually appoint a subcommittee to draw up ways and means of finding out what to start with first.

A lot of people feel discouraged that there was no more accomplished at this Pan-American conference, but I tell you, the United States did mighty well. They didn't give up anything, and any time we can attend a conference and come out as good as we went in, why, we are ahead.

Of all the fool things that we go into (and we don't miss many), why, these disarmament conference will go down as the prize.

No nation can tell another nation how little it shall protect itself.

At these conferences they always bring a pack of experts and technical men along to advise. I have always noticed that any time a man can't come and settle with you without bringing his lawyer, why, look out for him.

WAR AND PEACE

America has a very unique record. We never lost a war or won a conference in our lives. It's cheaper for us to fight a nation than to confer with them.

Ammunition beats persuasion when you are looking for freedom.

You know, you can be killed just as dead in an unjustified war as you can in one protecting your own home.

Did you notice all those war films coming out of Hollywood? Now if we are so crazy about all this war stuff now, why, maybe we might be interested in the boys that made all these wonderful pictures possible—you know, our soldiers and sailors and marines and airmen. Why, those are the boys who put on the original war. These days everybody seems to be making some money out of wars, but them.

I've been reading all day in the papers about all these bright young college boys and girls marching—marching to keep from going to war. It's a good joke on them! We ain't got no war.
   These students learning to march in the Peace Parade, that would give them just about the training we give our soldiers in a regular war. They'll be just about ready for it then.

I am a peace man. I haven't got any use for wars and there is no more humor in 'em than there is reason for 'em.

Nobody's ever found any particular good use for salt water. We've never found out what salt water was fit for, but I'll tell you it's awful handy when they've got three or four thousand miles of it between you and an enemy.
   You just let somebody sneak up some night and take all the water out of the Atlantic and Pacific oceans, and brother, by noon the next day we'll be beating our Fords into muskets.

I would rather have a nation declare war than peace against me. In war at least you know who your enemies are. But in peace you don't know either friend or foe.

They are talking of having another war, just as soon as they get it straightened out just who won the last one.

One sure certainty about our Memorial Days is that as fast as the ranks from one war thin out, the ranks from another take their place. Prominent men may run out of Decoration Day speeches, but the world never runs out of wars.

People talk peace but men give their life's work to war. It won't stop till there is as much brain and scientific study put to aid peace as there is to promote war.

Do you think we are prepared to go to war with an enemy? I think we could, if we used good judgement in picking our enemy. I think we could defeat Switzerland, and we would have a chance with Monaco.

Then you mean to insinuate that we couldn't whip a major country?

Not unless it was fixed and we bought them off.

If you think there ain't going to be no next war, you better see some of these nations preparing; they are not people that will go to work and learn a trade that they are not going to work at.

Course these are only tips. I am like the old rooster when he brought out the ostrich egg and showed it to all the hens and said: I am not criticizing but I just want you to know what others are doing!

Women love to say that they don't want war, and that they have to bear the brunt of it, which of course, they really do.

For all the wars in the world, even if you won 'em, can't repay one mother for the loss of one son. But even at that, when she says to you "That's my oldest boy's picture, he was lost in the war," there is behind that mist in her eye a shine of pride.

A nation is just like an individual. If a man's neighbors all hate him and he is continually in trouble, and all his fights and troubles are always over in the other fellow's yard, he must be wrong.

If he won't stay at home what he needs is a good licking, or a muzzle.

Peace and good-will with your neighbor is a nation's greatest recommendation. You show me a man that gets on fine with his neighbors, and he must be a man with some good in him—even if it's just good judgement.

A war either makes or breaks a nation, so you always got a fifty-fifty break.

Wars are not fought for Democracy's sake—they are fought for land's sake. And we are the only country that ever went to war and come home with nothing.

We haven't got any business in these Far East wars. Seven thousand miles is a long way to go to shoot somebody, especially if you are not right sure they need shooting.

It's their war and they have a right to fight it as they see fit, without any advice from us.

If we pulled together as much to put over a siege of peace as we do a spell of war, we would be sitting pretty. But we can hardly wait for a war to end to start taking it out on each other.

Peace is kinder like prosperity. There is mighty few nations that can stand it.

Lots of news today about that war. Now how can they fight that long without getting all their war material from some other nations?

That's why there will always be wars. Everybody makes money out of a war except the nations fighting.

Wars are just like depressions, they come when you least expect 'em.

Everywhere an American went to invest some money in the hope of making 100 percent, why, there would be a gunboat to see that he had all the comforts to which he had been accustomed.

Ever since I can remember telling jokes on stage, and years before I started writing for any papers, I have used kidding stuff about us going into somebody's country, and it's always been tremendously popular stuff, for not a soul wanted us to be sending Marines out over the world. Like a big city would send policemen to places where they heard there was trouble. It had just become almost impossible for a country to have a nice home talent revolution among themselves without us butting into it.

I have a plan that will stop all wars. When you can't agree with your neighbor, you move away; or with your wife, she either shoots you or moves away from you. Now that's my plan, move nations away from each other. Take France and Germany, they can't agree. Now take

France and trade places with Japan. Let Japan live there by Germany and if those two want to fight, well, let 'em fight.

We don't always agree with Mexico; well, trade Mexico off for Turkey—harems and all. Then that would solve the Irish problem. Take England and move 'em away from Ireland. Take 'em over to Canada, let 'em live on their son-in-law. But when you move England away from Ireland, don't you let Ireland know where you're taking 'em, or they'll follow 'em and get 'em.

SUPREME COURT

In his career, Will Rogers starred in seventy motion picture films. One he particularly enjoyed making was *Judge Priest*. It was based on the chief character of a number of short stories written by Will's friend Irvin S. Cobb. The locale of the Judge Priest stories was in the South in the immediate post–Civil War era. The film was, of course, in period costume.

Premiered in 1934, *Judge Priest* was an instant success. John Ford, its director, considered it his favorite motion picture. Critics and audiences alike raved about the film. Almost everybody seemed to like it—except one lady from the South. She wrote Will a letter, complaining:

> You played the part excellently, but you did not understand
> the South and only southern men and southern women
> should play the parts portraying life in the "Old South" as
> they only understand the South.

Will answered the lady's letter as part of a weekly column* and gently pointed out that his native Oklahoma was definitely south of the Mason-Dixon line. He further assured the letter-writing lady that both his parents had been born in the South, and that he, Will Rogers, had taken to wife a lady from that noble part of the country. With tongue in cheek he allowed that if the story were ever written again, perhaps it should be written by someone born even farther south than Mr. Cobb—whose birthplace was Paducah, Kentucky.

---

*November 11, 1934.

There was, however, at least one other fan who wrote a letter. It was dated October 8, 1934, and was written on White House stationery:

DEAR WILL:

We saw "Judge Priest" last night. It is a thoroughly good job, and the Civil War pictures are very true to life as I remember the battles of that period.

Also, I am very glad to see that you took my advice in regard to your leading lady—this time you have one who is good to look at and can act.

I suppose the next thing you will be doing is making application for an appointment on the Federal Bench. I might take you up on that!

ALWAYS SINCERELY,
(*signed*) FRANKLIN D. ROOSEVELT

The Supreme Court said today that New York City subway riders could ride for a nickel but it didn't say they could get a seat.

Charles Evans Hughes is a fine fellow, and smarter, too, than you would think. He will make us a good man on the Supreme bench, and he can't possibly do us any harm, for Supreme Court decisions will always remain the same, five against four.

When it's six to three, that's called unanimous.

You give us long enough to argue over something and we will bring you in proofs to show you that the Ten Commandments should never have been ratified.

The Supreme Court of the United States yesterday prohibited the sale of anything in which liquor might be held or transported—bottles, jugs, barrels, buckets, gourds, flasks, corks, labels, boxes, mails and burlap sacks. You can't sell any of these, but you can sell the wheat and corn that it's supposed to be made with. In other words, according to the decision, you are allowed to make it but not allowed to have anything to hold it in.

You see, it's on account of decisions like this why they got to be careful the type of men they put on the Supreme Court bench.

The Supreme Court decided that it was not illegal to be the buyer of booze. In other words, they said that your freedom was not in jeopardy, but your life was. They say you can buy it, but it's illegal to transport it. You got to gulp it right where you made the deal for it.

Now how are you going to get liquor to your mouth without transporting it? To really be within strict keeping of the law, the bootlegger is going to have to pour it into you, and you are not allowed to lift a hand to assist.

I have told a lot of alleged little jokes about the Supreme Court splitting 5 to 4 on everything, including the weather. But regardless of that, I think they are a mighty trusty pillar for our country to lean on.

In our Decoration Day speech-making, President Taft spoke at some unveiling of a monument in Cincinnati. He made an alibi for the Supreme Court. I don't know what prompted him to tell the dead what the court was doing, unless it was some man who had died of old age waiting for a decision from that august body.

La Follette* has got it in for the Supreme Court and wants to abolish some of their power. Well, that's not an issue, that's just a grudge. Besides, if he would only think for a minute he would know that when Congress passes a bill to abolish the power of the Supreme Court, why, all the Supreme Court has to do is say the bill is unconstitutional. I might say I am going to fire my boss, but I can't fire him as long as he is my boss.

The Supreme Court, they've been the talk of the town this week. You know, they hadn't agreed on anything unanimously in over eight years. Even I've kidded them so much that I think they all got together and said: "Boys, we got to agree on something."

They knew that folks were kidding about them always disagreeing five to four. And they said: "Ain't there something in the world that we could possibly agree on?" Well, they met and they sat and they talked, and then they pondered. You see, a young man he just thinks, but an old man when he's sitting and thinking, why, he's supposed to be pondering.

Well, those nine, very fine old gentlemen—old lawyers, you know—they pondered and they finally thought of something. They

---

*Robert M. La Follette, Sr., Republican; Wisconsin; governor (1900–1906), U.S. senator (1906–1925).

came to the conclusion that the National Recovery Administration, the NRA, was 100 percent in disfavor with them, so they all agreed.

Poor old NRA, it did one thing for history. It brought the Supreme Court to a unanimous decision; it's the only thing in our time that's ever done that.

You don't have to listen to some fellow telling you how bad things are going for the President or what's to become of the Constitution. They all seem to forget that those nine justices in kimonos will look after the Constitution, and the President will just have to look after himself. He has to do our worrying, but we don't have to do his.

Hurray for the old Constitution! Nobody wants to see the old lady led astray. But wouldn't this amendment to her be helpful? When Congress passes a law, or a President exceeds his authority, have some person notify the Supreme Court and get them to examine the medicine and see if it's poison, before it's given to the patient, and not at the funeral.

This amendment would make the Supreme Court a preventative and not an autopsy jury.

The Supreme Court is divided almost in half on the decisions. Talk about an international court. How would we ever agree with a lot of foreigners when we can't even agree among our own judges?

Well, the big news of the last week was the Supreme Court decision handed down in the "Prohibition on Boats" case. It was kinder unique in decisions. It said: "You can sell booze on American boats, but you are not allowed to have it on there."

There is one for the book for you. I bet you nobody in the world but a Supreme Court could have ever thought of a decision like that. It would be like saying, you can shoot a man, but not with a gun.

The biggest news that has hit the financial section of this country was yesterday when the Supreme Court of the United States ruled that a bootlegger had to pay income tax.

We ought to have our national debt paid in a couple of years.

We don't any more get a law halter broke and get people kinder used to it, when some judge comes along and says it ain't so. Last week Judge Knox comes out and decides that a doctor in prescribing for the modern American illness—suffering from the effects of Prohibition— can prescribe any amount he thinks necessary. Now according to the

Volstead Law* as passed by Congress, no patient is allowed to get sick over a pint's worth every ten days. So along comes this Judge and says "Congress is no doctor (they all are patients). How do they know how sick a man can get? Why, for a pint every ten days, a man would really not be sick at all; he would just be indisposed."

So now when a fellow comes to see the doctor, the doctor will say: "What's the matter with you?" The patient will say "Why, about a gallon, doctor."

Or the doctor, after looking over one of his perpetual patients, will say "Why, you are looking great today; your case has improved from two quarts to one. If you don't look out you will get well."

Instead of doctors studying at medical school as they used to, now he takes a course in rapid penmanship. It looks like a great year for fountain pens!

Heretofore druggists used to make their deliveries by a boy sent from the store. Now every drug store will have to deliver in a truck. They will fill your prescription now in a two-gallon milk bucket.

Of course, all this is right now, but you wait till that Supreme Court of the United States gets a hold of that Judge's opinion! They are liable to diagnose the case different. They are liable to cut out the patient's illness entirely.

---

*Volstead Act, federal prohibition act providing for enforcement of Eighteenth Amendment.

Chapter VI

PRESIDENTS

*W*ill Rogers' career as a performer spans roughly three decades, from the early 1900s to 1935. His act was initially silent and centered on his artistry with the lariat. His fame as a political humorist did not spread appreciably until his appearance in Ziegfeld's *Midnight Frolic* in 1915.

During Will Rogers' show business career, the United States elected seven different presidents: Theodore Roosevelt, William Howard Taft, Woodrow Wilson, Warren Harding, Calvin Coolidge, Herbert Hoover, and Franklin Roosevelt. Of these, Will Rogers admired Theodore Roosevelt the most. He was on the best of terms with the occupants of the White House, with the exception of Warren Harding. As did any president, Warren G. Harding provided ample material for the jesters. His preference for golf over serious attention to state business, his political clubhouse style of entertaining, his card parties—all provided grist for the mills of those reporting on government.

Will Rogers wrote a humorous sketch for the *Ziegfeld Follies* showing an uproariously chaotic cabinet session under the leadership of President Harding. Harding's addiction to golf was another favorite target for Rogers' humor. President Harding, so it was reported from the White House, did not appreciate this type of humor. Will Rogers was greatly disturbed by the president's rejection, especially since he bore no ill feelings toward the chief executive. He continued his humorous observations and praised Harding repeatedly when it was deserved. After Harding's death, Will wrote a touching eulogy.

His friendship and counsel were sought by Calvin Coolidge and Franklin Roosevelt and his daily and weekly columns were required reading in the White House.

But the president who first advanced Rogers' career was Woodrow Wilson. Will maintained that it was . . . but why not let Will Rogers tell his own story, written after the president's death on February 3, 1924:

Some of the most glowing and deserving tributes ever paid to the memory of an American have been paid in the last few days to our past President Woodrow Wilson. They have been paid by learned men of this and all nations, who knew what to say and how to express their feelings. They spoke of their close association and personal contact with him. Now I want to add my little mite even though it be of no importance.

I want to speak and tell of him as I knew him, for he was my friend. We of the stage know that our audiences are our best friends, and he was the greatest audience of any public man we ever had. I want to tell of him as I knew him across the footlights. A great many actors and professional people have appeared before him, on various occasions in wonderful high class endeavors, but I don't think that any person met him across the footlights in exactly the personal way that I did on five different occasions.

Every other performer or actor did before him exactly what they had done before other audiences on the night previous. But I gave a great deal of time and thought to an act for him, most of which would never be used again, and had never been used before. Owing to the style of act I used, my stuff depended a great deal on what had happened that particular day or week. It just seemed by an odd chance for me every time I played before President Wilson that on that particular day there had been something of great importance that he had just been dealing with, for you must remember that each day was a day of great stress with him. He had no easy days. So when I could go into a theater and get laughs out of our president, by poking fun at some turn in our national affairs, I don't mind telling you it was the happiest moment of my entire career on the stage.

The first time I shall never forget, for it was the most impressive and for me the most nervous one of them all. The Friars Club of New York, one of the biggest theatrical social clubs in New York, had decided to make a whirlwind tour of the principal cities of the East all in one week. We played a different city every night. We made a one night stand out of Chicago and New York. We were billed for Baltimore but not for Washington. President Wilson came over from Washington to see the performance. It was the first time in theatrical history that the president of the United States would be coming over to Baltimore just to see a comedy show.

It was at that time that we were having our little set-to with Mexico, and when we were at the height of our note exchanging career with Germany and Austria. The house was packed with the elite of Baltimore.

The show was going great. It was a collection of clever skits, written mostly by our stage's greatest man, George M. Cohan, and even down to the minor bits was played by stars with big reputations. I was the least known member of the entire aggregation, doing my little specialty with a rope, and telling jokes on national affairs, just a very ordinary little vaudeville act by chance sandwiched in among this great array.

I was on late and as the show went along I would walk out of the stage door and out on the street and try to kill time and nervousness until it was time to dress and go on. I had never told jokes to a president, much less about one, especially to his face. Well, I am not kidding you when I tell you that I was scared to death. I am always nervous. I never saw an audience that I ever faced with any confidence, for no man can ever tell how a given audience will ever take anything.

But here I was, nothing but an ordinary Oklahoma cowpuncher who had learned to spin a rope a little and who had learned to read the daily papers a little, going out before the aristocracy of Baltimore, and the president of the United States, and kid about some of the policies with which he was shaping the destinies of nations.

How was I to know but what the audience would rise up in mass and resent it. I had never heard, and I don't think anyone else had ever heard of a president being joked personally in a public theater about the policies of his administration.

The nearer the time came the worse scared I got. George M. Cohan and others, knowing how I felt, would pat me on the back and tell me, "Why, he is just a human being; go on out and do your stuff." Well, if somebody had come through the dressing room and hollered "Train for Claremore, Oklahoma, leaving at once" I would have been on it. This all may sound strange but any who have had the experience know that a presidential appearance in a theater, especially outside Washington, D.C., is a very rare and unique feeling even to the audience. They are keyed up almost as much as the actors.

At the time of his entrance into the house, everybody stood up and there were plain clothes men all over the place, back stage and behind his box. How was I to know but what one of them might not take a shot at me if I said anything about him personally?

Finally a warden knocked at my dressing room door and said, "You die in 5 more minutes for kidding your country." They just literally shoved me out on the stage.

Now, by a stroke of what I call good fortune, (for I will keep them always), I have a copy of the entire acts that I did for President Wilson on the five times I worked for him. My first remark in Baltimore was, "I am kinder nervous here tonight." Now that is not an especially bright remark, and I don't hope to go down in history on the strength of it, but it was so apparent to the audience that I was speaking the truth that they laughed heartily at it. After all, we all love honesty.

Then I said, "I shouldn't be nervous, for this is really my second presidential appearance. The first time was when William Jennings Bryan spoke in our town once, and I was to follow his speech and do my little roping act." Well, I heard them laughing, so I took a sly glance at the president's box and sure enough he was laughing just as big as anyone. So I went on. "As I say, I was to follow him, but he spoke so long that it was so dark when he finished they couldn't see my roping." That went over great, so I said, "I wonder what ever become of him?" That was all right, it got over, but still I had made no direct reference to the president.

Now General Pershing was in Mexico at the time, and there was a lot in the papers for and against the invasion. I said, "I see where they have captured Pancho Villa. Yes, they got him in the morning editions and then the afternoon ones let him get away." Now everybody in the house before they would laugh looked at the president, to see how he was going to take it. Well, he started laughing and they all followed suit.

"Villa raided Columbus, New Mexico. We had a man on guard that night at the post. But to show you how crooked this Villa is, he sneaked up on the opposite side." "We chased him over the line 5 miles, but run into a lot of government red tape and had to come back." "There is some talk of getting a machine gun if we can borrow one. . . . The one we have now they are using to train our army with in Plattsburgh. . . . if we go to war we will just about have to go to the trouble of getting another gun."

Now mind you, he was being rode on all sides for our lack of preparedness, yet he sat there and led that entire audience in laughing at the ones on himself. At that time there was talk of forming an army of 2 hundred thousand men. So I said, "We are going to have an army of 2 hundred thousand men. Mr. Henry Ford makes 3 hundred thousand cars a year. I think, Mr. President, we ought to at least have a man to every car. . . . See where they got Villa hemmed in between the Atlantic and Pacific. Now all we got to do is to stop up both ends." "Pershing located him at a town called Los Quas Ka Jasbo. Now all we have to do is locate Los Quas Ka Jasbo."

"I see by a headline that Villa escapes net and flees. We will never catch him then. Any Mexican that can escape fleas is beyond catching. . . . But we are doing better toward preparedness now, as one of my senators from Oklahoma has sent home a double portion of garden seed."

After various other ones on Mexico I started in on European affairs which at that time was long before we entered the war. "We are facing another crisis tonight, but our president here has had so many of them lately that he can just lay right down and sleep beside one of those things."

Then I first pulled the one which I am proud to say he

afterwards repeated to various friends as the best one told on him during the war. I said, "President Wilson is getting along fine now to what he was a few months ago. Do you realize, people, that at one time in our negotiating with Germany that he was 5 notes behind?"

How he did laugh at that! Well, due to him being a good fellow and setting a real example, I had the proudest and most successful night I ever had on the stage. I had lots of gags on other subjects but the ones on him were the heartiest laughs with him, and so it was on all the other occasions I played for him. He come backstage at intermission and chatted and shook hands with all.

Some time I would like to tell of the things he laughed at during the most serious stages of the great war. What he stood for and died for will be strived after for years. But it will take time, for with all our advancement and boasted civilization, it's hard to stamp out selfishness and greed. For after all, nations are nothing but individuals, and you can't stop even brothers from fighting sometimes.

But he helped it along a lot. And what a wonderful cause to have laid down your life for. The world lost a friend. The theater lost its greatest supporter. And I lost the most distinguished person who ever laughed at my little non-sensical jokes, I looked forward to it every year. Now I have only to look back on it as my greatest memory."*

PRESIDENTS

Presidents become great, but they have to be made Presidents first.

You can get your name easier on a button than you can get it on the letter box in front of the White House.

We don't any more get a President in the White House and he learns where the ice box is than we want to move him.

I don't know who started the idea that a President must be a politician, instead of a businessman. A politician can't run any other kind of

---

*Weekly article, published February 17, 1924.

business, so there is no reason why he can run the U.S. That's the biggest single business in the world.

I would rather tell 'em what I think and retire with satisfaction than be President and be hampered.

I have always maintained that the office of the President should be for six years, with no re-election. It's not fair to him. He is naturally human and going to use every legitimate means of staying in office, so that takes up too much of his valuable time. He owes the nation that time. He don't owe it to his political henchmen that want to stay in with him.

Everybody figures politics according to what they have accumulated during the last year. Maybe they haven't earned as much as they did a few years ago; all they look at is the old balance sheet and if it's in the red, why, his honor the President is in the alley, as far as they are concerned.

But it takes about 20 or 30 years to really tell whether any President had anything with him besides sunshine and showers. We have to look over his achievements in view of what they have to do with the future.

Being great as President is sorter like a World Series—you got to have the breaks.

You give me a few showers just when I need them most, and let me have the privilege of awarding them around the doubtful states as I see best; let a certain demand for steel crop up which I didn't even know was going to crop; let the Argentine and Russia have wheat failure; let the foot and mouth disease hit every country except out west of the Mississippi; let, as I say, all these things happen over which I have no control and have even me in there as President, and I will give Lincoln a run for his laurels, even if I can't spell "cat," eat with my knife, and don't know a tariff bill from a T-bone steak.

After an election, here is how this two-headed President thing works out. We have a President that's in, but has no authority; a President that's out, but has no authority; a Senate that's in, but has no leader; a House that's in, but has been voted out.

We've got a budget that both sides are afraid to balance, debts which we keep adding to; we are sore at the world because they won't disarm and in the midst of it all, we tell the Philippines what constitutes "Liberty."

You know, when a President wants to make a speech, he just touches a button and says to some research assistant, "Get me a speech on Norsemen! Say they are blondes and they live in Minnesota. Put in something about them being a hardy race. And also put in about the Norsemen being the backbone on which our country was founded. And be careful about calling them common people. Nobody wants to be called common, especially common people."

GEORGE WASHINGTON TO FRANKLIN D. ROOSEVELT

On two separate occasions Will Rogers spent a night in the White House. To indicate impartiality, the two events were equally divided between the two major parties: one occurred during the presidency of Republican Calvin Coolidge, the other when Democrat Franklin Roosevelt was its occupant. Of his stay with Calvin and Grace Coolidge, Will Rogers described a closely guarded White House secret:

> We are sitting there at the table, just the three of us, chatting away about a little of everything . . . The Coolidges have a couple of flea hounds and they was handing out things to them all the time . . . Well they was feeding the dogs so much that at one time it looked to me like the dogs was getting more than I was.
>
> We had fish that night for dinner. Well, I never paid much attention to the fish. I paid enough attention to it to eat it, but I never gave it any more thought. But the next day at lunch—get this! The next day at lunch—I was still there the next day at lunch!—when the lunch bell rang I was the first one in to the table. I had been there so long by then that I knew my place, I knew just what chair to pull back.
>
> Well, during the lunch the butler come to Mr. Coolidge with a platter of something that resembled some kind of hash. The president looked at it and asked, "Same old fish?"
>
> I had eaten turkey hash for generally about two weeks after holidays and weddings. Chicken hash generally runs two days. I had partaken of Beef hash, and I have eaten hash that nobody knows what the contents were. But when you get down to eating fish hash, you are flirting with

economy. This old thing of saying he preaches economy but he don't practice any of it is the bunk."*

George Washington was the most versatile President we ever had. He was a farmer, civil engineer and gentleman. He made enough with civil engineering to indulge in both the other luxuries.

I bet after seeing us, George Washington would sue us for calling him "father."

You know, America celebrating for Washington—a man who was so truthful—seems kinder sacrilegious. A lot of lying Americans get together and celebrate. Americans celebrating a truthful man's birthday always reminds me of a snake charmer celebrating St. Patrick's Day.

Did you read what this writer dug up in George Washington's diary? I was so ashamed I sat up all night reading it.

This should be a lesson to Presidents to either behave themselves or not to keep a diary. Can you imagine, 100 years hence, some future writer pouncing on Calvin Coolidge's diary? What would that generation think of us?

Calvin, burn them papers! Yours for the suppression of scandal.

Washington crossed the Delaware, with everybody rowing but him. I don't remember whether he crossed it to get to or away from Philadelphia.

Jefferson seemed to be the only Democrat in history with any kind of business ability.

I hope the Democrats win this election, just for one thing. I have heard 5,000 hours of speeches on a "Return to Jeffersonian principles" and I want to see what "Jeffersonian principles" are.

Is it just an oratorical topic, or is it an economic condition? I know that Jefferson was for the poor, but in his days that was good politics, for practically everybody was poor.

Jefferson, sitting up there on his hill, believed in equality for all. But he didn't divide up the hill with any poor, deserving Democrats.

---

*Saturday Evening Post article, January 8, 1927.

Our children are delivered to the schools in automobiles. But whether that adds to their grades, is doubtful. There hasn't been a Thomas Jefferson produced in this country since we formed the first trust. Rail splitting produced an immortal President in Abraham Lincoln; but golf, with 20 thousand courses, hasn't produced even a good, A number-1 Congressman.

Andrew Jackson was the one who said: "If you don't get out and work for the Party, you don't get in on the gravy after election!"

This writer, Hughes, wrote a book exposing Washington. Why don't he hop on Andy Jackson? There's a lad that never missed a shot or a drink while in the White House.

Did I ever tell you about the time I broke bread with the Democrats in Washington? I passed myself off as a Democrat one night, just to get a free meal.
    They call it a Jackson Day Dinner. I made the mistake of my life. I went there with a speech prepared about Jackson, telling how "he stood like a stone wall," and here it wasn't that Jackson that they were using as an alibi to give this dinner to. It was old "Andy" Jackson.
    Well, to tell the truth, I am not so sweet on old Andy. He is the one that run us Cherokees out of Georgia and North Carolina. I ate the dinner on him, but I didn't enjoy it.

Another Decoration Day passed and Mr. Abraham Lincoln's 300-word Gettysburg address was not dethroned. I would try to imitate its brevity if nothing else. Of course, Lincoln had the advantage. He had no foreign policy. That's why he is still Lincoln.

Lincoln is the one that said "You can fool all the Democrats part of the time, and part of the Democrats all the time, but a Republican is the only one you can fool all of the time." You know it takes nerve to be a Democrat; but it takes money to be a Republican.

Just imagine if Lincoln had had golf to add to his other accomplishments—there is a boy you would have been proud of.

The papers today say: "What would Lincoln do today?" Well, in the first place, he wouldn't chop wood. He would trade his axe in on a Ford; being a Republican he would vote the Democratic ticket. Being in sympathy with the underdog, he would be called a Radical Progressive. Having a sense of humor, he would be called an eccentric.

If Abe Lincoln from Illinois was resurrected and was to fill an unexpired term, and he still insisted he was a Republican, there would be a party vote against him.

Teddy Roosevelt was a man who wouldn't even waste hatred on nothing.

Any President with political knowledge always fights shy of the Tariff coming up during his administration. They tried their best to drag Teddy Roosevelt into it, and he just took a wellworn elm club and wrapped it over any friend or foe's head who suggested that his administration get tangled up with that yellow fever. That's where he got the reputation of the "Man with the Big Stick." It was for hammering on guys who wanted some Tariff gravy.

An old, long-whiskered man once said to Teddy Roosevelt: "I am a Democrat, my father was a Democrat, my grandfather was a Democrat." Roosevelt then said: "Then if your father had been a horse thief and your grandfather had been a horse thief, you would be a horse thief?"

"No," the man said, "I would be a Republican."

The story is not true. All Republicans are not horse thieves. At the biggest estimate, not over 90 percent are horse thieves. Every once in a while you meet a pretty nice one.

President Wilson lays all the world's troubles on the Peace Treaty not being signed.

I suppose when it is signed you can even find a place to park your car.

President Wilson would turn over in his grave if he knew what has happened to his idea of "Self-Determination for Small Nations."

People had never heard of Harding, but after his nomination as the Republican candidate, you would have thought he was dead, the nice things the papers said about him.

It seems almost impossible a man could be so competent and his party never think of him before. Only two detrimental things have come out in Harding's whole record. One is his middle name is Gamaliel, and the other was he used to play a B flat cornet in a band. So it seems like a smooth scheme of the Republicans to capture the B flat cornet vote in this country.

President Harding gave a luncheon for visiting governors where they discussed but didn't try Prohibition.

It's been stated President Harding won't run next time. The Republicans want him to because he is the only man they got that is known.

I think the Democrats are the wisest. They are trying to find somebody to run who ain't known.

Harding was the most human of our late Presidents. There was more of the real "every-day man" in him. If he had a weakness, it was in trusting his friends, and the man that don't do that, why, there is something the matter with him, sho nuff.

Betrayed by friendship is not a bad memorial to leave.

Coolidge knows that he come into the Presidency from the Vice-Presidency, where nothing is expected; he knows that he didn't look like much when he arrived; he knows that even the atheists, after looking him over, prayed for the salvation of the country.

So he knows that anything he did was a surprise and he knows that he come into our public life when we had just about all the government laws and advice that we needed. He saw that the less he did, the more satisfied we would be with him.

Both sides are busy watching what Cal will do. When he first become President, there seemed to be quite a sentiment to nominate him again for Vice-President.

Lots of people can't understand the popularity that Mr. Coolidge is deservedly enjoying all over the country at the present time. I can tell you. It started the minute he opposed Congress. The people said: "If he is against Congress, he must be right!"

That was one great thing about Coolidge. Coolidge never thought half the things that were wrong needed fixing. He knew that over half the things just needed leaving alone. It's like writing a letter to everybody you hear from. He knew that if you leave nine-tenth of 'em alone, it didn't need answering.

Mr. Coolidge is the only one that ever seemed to relish official dinners. They never worried him. He had the same expression and the same conversation for Queen Marie of Rumania as he had for Senator Moses. "Hello" when they came in and "Good bye" when they passed out. He just went about his eating, and they went about theirs, and nothing didn't mean nothing to him.

My Dear Mr. President: The American Club in London, on Piccadilly, wanted to give me a dinner, and you know what I think of these dinners. You remember the one you and I attended at the Gridiron Club in Washington? The speeches, outside of yours and mine, was terrible.

If I remember right, even yours wasn't so good.

Mr. Coolidge, why, you never caught him appointing a commission to find things out. If the salmon wasn't biting in the Columbia River, or the League of Nations wouldn't enforce birth control in Abyssinia, you wouldn't catch Mr. Coolidge to send someone to bring back data. No sir! If Wall Street sold Short, or Long, or Crooked, you never caught him even reading about it. He just said: What is, is, and I am not going to un-is it!

Mr. Coolidge kept his mouth shut. It was such a novelty among politicians that it just swept the country. You see, originality will be rewarded in any line.

Mr. Coolidge's vetoing days will soon be over. I bet you the first two weeks he's out of there, in a hotel, when the head waiter hands him a menu, he will mark it VETO and hand it back.

Mrs. Coolidge could run things; Calvin couldn't, but Grace could.

I always did want to see Hoover elected. I wanted to see how far a competent man could get in politics. It has never been tried before.

Mr. Hoover said Prohibition was a noble experiment, and he believed in noble things, even if they were only experiments.

Hoover gets rid of something useless every day. Wait till he sees Congress.

Two news items in the papers today: I see where Mr. Hoover invited Mr. Roosevelt to the White House—and then I see where Mr. Roosevelt had his life insured for a half million dollars.

One thing we have always heard of President Hoover, that while he may not be a political spellbinder, and able to sway vast audiences, that he could take a small bunch of men, talk to 'em and he could have them coming out of the conference, promising to cut off a leg, quit smoking, or give up golf.

Mr. Hoover, there was nothing personal in the vote against you. We all know that you was handed a balloon that was blowed up to the utmost. You held it as carefully as anyone could, but the thing busted right in your hands.

This fellow Franklin D. Roosevelt never gets through surprising us. We just find out now that he speaks French fluently.

That's the second linguistic surprise he has handed us. We knew he could speak English, but he's the only guy who can talk "Turkey" to the Senate.

Now we will take this fellow Franklin Roosevelt. He was born an outcast. The doctor said: "We can save him, but he will be a Democrat." His father, being a Republican, was for drowning him then, but his mother, a very charitable woman, even to the extent of saving a Democrat, said: "Let's keep him, it would be cute to have one around the house."

America hasn't been as happy in three years as they are today with a new President. No money, no banks, no work, no nothing, but they know they got a man in there who is wise to Congress, wise to our big bankers and wise to our so-called "big" men.

The whole country is with him. Even if what he does is wrong, they are with him. Just so he does something. If he burned down the Capitol we would cheer and say: "Well, we at least got a fire started, anyhow!" We have had years of "Don't rock the boat," so, Mr. President, go on and sink it if you want to. We just as well be swimming, as like the way we are.

Guess you all heard Mr. Roosevelt on the radio Wednesday night. These so-called big boys can all get up before their little audiences and yell for stabilization, amortization, gold standard, or platinum finish.

Then the President can come to the microphone with that convincing manner of his and the rest of 'em just as well wash up their little speeches and go home.

Just suppose Congress kind of crosses Mr. Roosevelt in something, he can go on the radio Monday night, and if his cause is just, he can make a plea, and he will have so many telegrams going into Congressmen and Senators the next morning that you will think Roosevelt went on the air just as a benefit for Western Union.

Say, this Roosevelt is a fast worker. Even on Sunday, when all a President is supposed to do is to put on a silk hat and have his picture taken coming out of church, why, this President closed all the banks and called Congress in extra session.

And that is not all he is going to call 'em either, if they don't get something done.

They are accusing Mr. Roosevelt of being a dictator. Well, a dictator is just like a parachute, they are made for a crisis, you can use one if you like, or you can jump without it.

PRESIDENTIAL ADVISORS

I have always maintained that no President can be as bad as the men that advise him. We don't need a different man as bad as we need different advisors for the same man.

A lot of people are kidding the President, they say the men that advise him are former inmates of Columbia University.

That's all right. We have had Presidents that acted like they were advised by the inmates of Matteawan, the Institute for the Criminally Insane.

STATE OF THE UNION MESSAGE

Kareful Kal Koolidge read his message to Congress. At a great telegraphic expense I have gathered together the opinions of some of the best paid politicians:

Senator Lodge, Republican: It is a message that could not possibly be improved upon.

Senator Robinson, Democrat: I have been reading messages ever since I can remember and if that is a message, then I am Babe Ruth.

Senator McKinley, Republican: The President's message is what I call a real message. It is short, concise and to the point.

Senator Dill, Democrat: It was the longest, most garbled message and got nowhere at all.

Senator Green, Republican: It makes me proud that I am a Republican.

Senator Wheeler, Democrat: It makes me proud that I am a Democrat.

Speaker Gillett, Republican: It will please the country immensely.

Senator Harrison, Democrat: He didn't guess a single problem right.

Mrs. Coolidge: It was simply wonderful.

Congressman Carter, Democrat: It was the best message I ever slept through. *

CABINETS

Say, some on that list of new Cabinet members sent everybody scurrying to Who's Who, World Almanac and the United States fingerprint department, trying to find out who they were.

The rogue's gallery photographs show us that three of 'em escaped from the Senate. That's like going to the old men's home to get an athlete.

This thing of getting rid of a man in the Cabinet is all right, but there is one bad feature to it that few of the people realize. That is, that unfortunately every one of them is replaced by someone else.

If it just wasn't for that, this resignation business would be great.

Every editorial writer has been expressing his views on our new Attorney General. Now I like to sorter deliberate before passing judgement.

Well, he stands 6 foot 6 inches going into the Cabinet. No one knows what his height will be coming out. That Attorney General's office has lowered the stature of so many of its occupants that some of them have come out of there hid under a rubber heel.

Hoover appointed this William D. Mitchell, who is a Democrat, as Attorney General. If they are going to transfer Prohibition enforcement over to his department, that's a pretty slick trick of appointing a Democrat to enforce it.

If you got something that can't be done, appoint your political enemy to do it.

*Henry Cabot Lodge, Massachusetts; Joseph T. 'Joe' Robinson, Arkansas; William B. McKinley, Illinois; Clarence C. Dill, Washington; Frank L. Green, Vermont; Burton K. Wheeler, Montana; Frederick H. Gillett, Massachusetts; Byron Patton 'Pat' Harrison, Mississippi; Grace Anna Goodhue (Mrs. Calvin) Coolidge; Charles D. Carter, Oklahoma.

Catching up on the news before writing tomorrow's syndicated column between takes on the set of Life

Will listens attentively in a scene from David Harum, *1934.*

You know what a Cabinet is? It's a band of about nine men that go to the White House every Tuesday to see if the President has lived through the past week. If he had passed out, they, being the Cabinet, would be the last to hear it. News travels slow in the Cabinet.

They take up subjects—that is they take 'em up to the White House, then take 'em back home again. Then bring 'em back again the next Tuesday.

At those meetings they take care of crises. You know when we sometimes read about a crisis and afterward wonder what become of it? Well, they took it up. It takes a good crisis to last a Cabinet discussion.

PRESIDENTIAL COMMISSIONS

Appointing a commission is not a crime; it's been considered a very fine way of handling anything, but it just seems like a Presidential Commission don't get nothing done, you know. They don't really earn the breakfast that they give 'em at the White House the day they appoint 'em.

The more I see of public affairs and public offices, the more I realize that a comedian has a wonderful opportunity if appointed to one of the high Presidential appointments.

Comedians always held these positions and there is no reason why I can't go in there and do as bad as some of the rest.

Of course nothing is ever done about a commission report, except, they say, one man at the state prison for the criminally insane actually read one once clear through. Then he did something about it. He made a bonfire that lasted a week.

Commissions have contributed more to humor than they have to achievement in America.

VICE-PRESIDENTS

A Vice-President answers about the same purpose as a rear cinch on a saddle. If you break the front one, you are worse off than if you had no other.

I had lunch with the Vice-President. I only did it on condition that we ate alone. The reason that I did it was I dident want it to get out that I ate with a Vice-President.

I asked the Vice-President how he had everything running and he said: "Oh, things are going along pretty good here now if the President just don't butt in and spoil it."

I would not nominate a Vice-President. That is generally done through malice, and I hold no Vice-Presidential malice toward no one.

Will somebody please tell me what they do with all the Vice-Presidents a bank has?

Why, the United States is the biggest business institution in the world, and they only got one Vice-President and nobody has ever found anything for him to do.

After being sworn in, Vice-President Charley Dawes was supposed to get up and thank the Senate for the high position and the privilege to be allowed to rule over such an august body.

But boy, he cut loose and told those bobbed-haired longhorns that it was bad enough to be Vice-President, but that to have to sit all day and listen to them yap was absolutely the limit.

In his speech he lost the friendship of the Senate and gained the respect of the other 109 million Americans.

Congress kinder got the Vice-President going now. He sits up there with a hammer, but none of them are close enough that he can really do much good with it. It's a terrible job, and why they ever wished it on as important a person as the Vice-President, Lord only knows.

The following is one of the bravest statements made in a political decade. I just got off and held a caucus with myself, and said, somebody has got to be sacrificed for the sake of party harmony. I hereby and here-on put myself in nomination, and to save some other man being humiliated by having to put me in nomination, why, I will just nominate myself.

Here is a certificate to show that this is bona fide: "I, Dr. Isadore Moskowitz, of 234 East Mott Street, have examined the enclosed patient, Mr. Will Rogers, and find him to be of sound mind and body. (In fact, sounder in body than mind.) This certifies that if he wants to run for Vice-President, I see no way of preventing it. (Signed) Isadore Moskowitz, Horse doctor's commission expires June 1, 1925."

So I, Will Rogers, of Claremore, Oklahoma, Hollywood, California, and Forty-Second Street and Broadway, New York, do hereby step right out and declare myself not only as a receptive, but anxious candidate for the second position on the forthcoming ticket.

Now on first hearing this, it might sound like a joke, but when I relate to you some of the qualifications which I possess, why, I think any fair-minded man will give me serious consideration. But the trouble is there are no fair-minded men in politics.

In the first place, they have got to nominate a farmer who understands the farmer's condition. Well, I got two farms in Oklahoma, both mortgaged, so no man knows their condition better than I do. He also has to be a man from the West. Well, if a man came from 25 feet further west than I lived last year, he would have to be a fish in the Pacific Ocean.

Another big reason why I should be nominated is that I am not a Democrat. Another, still bigger reason why I should be nominated is that I am not a Republican. I am just progressive enough to suit the dissatisfied, and lazy enough to be a standpatter.

Oil has never touched me. The reason I know it never has, I drilled a well on my farm in Oklahoma and never even touched oil, much less oil touching me. I never worked for a big corporation.

When the President can't go anywhere, why, the Vice-President has got to go speak or eat for him. Now I could take in all the dinners, for I am a fair eater. I could say, "I am sorry the President can't come but he has pressing business." Of course, I wouldn't tell the real reason why he didn't come. So, you see, I am just a good enough liar to be a good Vice-President.

I am not much of an after-dinner speaker but I could learn two stories; one for dinners where ladies were present, and one for where they were not. Of course, I have no dress suit. The government would have to furnish me a dress suit. If I went to a dinner in a rented one, they would mistake me for a Congressman.

It won't take much to launch my campaign. We will wait and when some dark, or light, horse is eliminated, we will take their headquarters and buy their buttons and badges cheap.

I can hear a lot of you all say, "Yes, Will, you would make a good Vice-President, but suppose something happened to the President?"

Well, I would do just like Mr. Coolidge. I would go in there and keep still and do nothing.

P.S. I was born in a log cabin.*

---

*Syndicated article, June 26, 1924.

MISCELLANEOUS

Say, who writes these long-winded, uninteresting speeches that our public men deliver? It must be just one man in Washington that turns 'em all out, for regardless who is President, they are the same speeches.

I guess it's some guy down there that has the speech contract.

No matter what man is in office, the one that you put in his place is worse. I advocate electing our officials for life. If we had kept our original cast, we would have been better off. We had no business letting Washington go. We ought to have kept him till we got a hold of Lincoln, then have been more careful of the protection of his life and preserved him to a ripe old age down to where Teddy Roosevelt was, say, 15 years old.

Then we could have turned it over to him. He would have run it as good at that age as most men could at 50.

If I was a President and wanted something, I would claim I didn't want it. For Congress has not given any President anything that he wanted in the last 10 years.

Be against it, and then he is sure to get it.

A President's personal habits, his looks, his dress, whether he is a good fellow with the boys, why, that don't mean a thing. He can shut up for the entire four years, or he can go out and talk everybody deaf, dumb and blind; he can be a teetotaler or he can have a drink whenever he likes, in all these things he can be either on one side or the other and it won't make a bit of difference. If the country has enjoyed prosperity over ninety percent of which he had no personal control, he will be renominated.

I am going out to the movies and I may pick up just the type for President. I understand just the type you want. We want a man in there who can handle men; a man, who, when his hired help gets to acting up down at the other end of Pennsylvania Avenue, can hop in his car, go down there and tell 'em who is boss, and where to head in. Don't confer with them—just soak 'em.

The head of our Foreign Relations Committee come nearer to a Prime Minister than anyone. You see, France has a President, too, but we never know who he is, and neither do most of them. And they think that our President is like him, sorter decorative.

They don't know that we think so much of ours that we hold him responsible for everything that happens, whether it be in the sky, on the earth or in a Senate Committee room.

The Presidential market fluctuates. You see, conditions in this country change so rapidly that a man that would be a good President today might tomorrow be entirely unsuitable for the job. Take the case of William Jennings Bryan; he would make an ideal Sunday President, but would be an absolute liability on weekdays.

We used to be worried about one of our public men when we hadn't heard anything of him in a long time. Now we don't worry any more. We know he is writing a book.

Chapter VII

POLITICS

W ill Rogers enjoyed politics. He read every available newspaper, covered political conventions, listened to campaign speeches, made innumerable trips to Washington, D.C., and broadcast and wrote on politics during all his reporting years. Politicians—whether local, state, or federal, whether Democrats or Republicans—were his friends. Yet he took little of it seriously.

Several times, however, Will Rogers found himself actively, though involuntarily, involved in politics. The first time, in 1922, it was at the request of one of Teddy Roosevelt's sons—*The New York Times* claimed it was Kermit, while Mrs. Will Rogers recalled that it was Theodore, Jr. Republican Congressman Ogden Livingston Mills, representing New York's exclusive "silk-stocking" district, was running for reelection; would Will please speak on his behalf? Will Rogers felt he could not turn down such an invitation from a son of the late president he admired.

At the appointed hour Will appeared and made a speech as only he could. "The poor fellow don't know it yet whether I am for him or against him," Rogers declared afterward. Even the prestigious *New York Times*, while reporting the speech, was somewhat mystified. The audience seemed to enjoy it and either because of Will's speech, or

143

in spite of it, Mr. Mills was reelected; in fact, he later served as secretary of the treasury.

The next step in Will Rogers' involuntary political career came in 1926. Returning to his home in Beverly Hills, California, during the Christmas break in his nationwide lecture tour, he learned that he had been named honorary mayor. His "reign" was riddled with beneficial acts, paid for by His Honor out of his own pocket; among other things Rogers built a gymnasium for the local police department and a hand-ball court. The Right Honorable Will Rogers, Mayor of Beverly Hills, stayed in office less than a year, as the California state legislature decreed that a town of the "sixth class" was to have no mayor; in such a town the president of the board of trustees automatically took the position. Will Rogers was "shocked":

> A few months ago I read in the papers that the legislature had passed a bill applicable to cities of the sixth class. Well, I never paid any attention when I read it, knowing it was one of those things they do during the session to try and make it look like they are doing something. It was just among the list of jokes that they had passed. Like in Minnesota one time, when they introduced a bill to demand more roosters. They claimed the pro rata share of hens versus roosters was too one-sided, so some good humanitarian friend of old Cock Robin was coming to his rescue by an act of the legislature. When you look over a barn yard it does look like he was asked to carry on a little too much. It's all right for a man or animal or fowl to do what they can to perpetuate his race but there is no use asking him to do the unusual.
>
> Well, the first thing I knew people got to calling me up and saying: "I see where you are going to lose your job as mayor." I never paid much attention to that, for about two-thirds of the talk in Hollywood or Beverly Hills can't be depended on. Then I commenced to hear that this joke of the legislature was to take effect the first of August.
>
> It looks like a direct dig from the legislature; you see, a few months ago I played on my tour of enlightenment in the city of Sacramento and the legislature was in session and I was asked to speak before them in joint session. That is, men from every joint in the legislature was allowed to

come in, including the governor, which he did. I had the joint packed, it was free; none of them come that night where it was three dollars.

Well, I didn't want to appear critical but I told them a few things about how their joke foundry was operating. The men that come in '49 and stole each other's grub stake would have been Aimee McPhersons* in comparison to this elected and selected bunch of Robin Hoods. Well, the truth hurts, I don't care how thick the hide is, even a rhinoceros can't shed off true facts, so I just figured that after I had left town they cooked up this bill to knock me out of a position that I had filled with honor and high-mindedness.

There is only one thing that makes me sore about the whole thing and that is this. This law applies to cities of the sixth class only. My Lord, if I had known that I was ruling in a city of the SIXTH class I would never have taken the thing in the first place. I should sue them for lowering my standing—why, I will be years living that down.**

Another milestone in Rogers' political "career" was reached late in August 1927 when the National Press Club "conferred" upon him the commission of "Congressman-at-Large." Will Rogers' most distinguished "entry" into the political arena came in 1928, when he ran a mock presidential campaign as the candidate of the "Bunkless Party." The battle was waged strictly in the pages of *Life*, which then was a humor magazine. Will made but a single campaign promise to his readers: "If elected, I will resign."

The Republicans that year nominated Herbert Hoover, while the Democrats selected Al Smith. The campaign was fierce and dirty, pitting the secretary of commerce against the Catholic governor of New York. Not only was much made of the religious difference but the opposing views on Prohibition furnished millions of forgettable words in newspapers and over the radio.

In his daily column of November 4, 1928—Will's birthday and just two days before the presidential election—he summed up the entire campaign:

---

*Aimee Semple McPherson, American evangelist, founder of the International Church of the Foursquare Gospel.
**Syndicated weekly article, August 28, 1927.

In this campaign season, I have promised nothing and am the only one of the three that can make good, so I am openly out for myself.

I am not the "Greatest Administrator of all time" neither am I "The Greatest Executive a state ever had." I have never spent "twenty years abroad" and if I was born of poor parents, either city or farm, I have kept it a personal affair. I have neither lived off tax payers or corporations. But those other fellows would like to live in the White House, and in order to get in there, they will promise the voters anything from perpetual motion to eternal salvation.

In the issue following the November 1928 election, *Life* announced that Will Rogers had been elected president of the United States by the "silent majority," the dissatisfied voters. Will kept his promise and immediately resigned:

I do want to thank the Silent vote for not voting and getting mixed up in any way with this dog fight we have just had. They talk about a man not being a good citizen if he don't vote. If everybody didn't vote then none of them could get elected and that would be the end of politics, and we would just go and hire some good man to run the country, the same as we should now.

Apart from his name being placed in nominations at the Democratic national conventions of 1928 and 1932, Will Rogers' "career in politics" had peaked. He discouraged any and all attempts to draw him into active participation:

There was a piece in the paper this morning where somebody back home was seriously proposing me for President. Now when that is done as a joke, it was all right, but when it's done seriously, it's just pathetic. We are used to having everything named as Presidential candidates, but the country hasn't quite got to the professional comedian stage.

There is no inducement that would make me foolish enough to ever run for any political office. I want to be on the outside where I can be friends and joke about all of

them, even the President. As long as it's all right with him,
why, my conscience is clear.

Should the Democrats, however, become successful, I
would accept the post office in Beverly Hills and Claremore,
Oklahoma. I can take care of both letters.*

To make his position clearer still, he put his determination into
plain words:

If you see or hear of anybody proposing my name humor-
ously or semi-seriously for any political office, will you
maim said party and send me the bill?

I not only "don't choose to run," I will say "I won't run,"
no matter how bad the country will need a comedian by
that time.**

Will Rogers summed up his stand: "I certainly know that a comedian
can only last till he either takes himself serious, or his audience takes
him serious, and I don't want either of those to happen to me till I
am dead (if then)."

Will Rogers had no further personal brushes with the body politic,
even though he remained America's foremost political analyst and
most listened-to commentator.

POLITICS

I tell you folks, all politics is apple sauce!

With politicians horning in, our comedian business is overcrowded.

Politicians are just a bunch of local bandits, sent by their local voters
to raid the public treasury.

You can't, in politics, go against your constituency.

---

*Syndicated daily column, February 2, 1928.
**Syndicated daily column, June 28, 1931.

The more I see of politics, the more I wonder what in the world any man would ever want to take it up for.

Then some people wonder why the best men of a community are not the office holders.

Any one of our big men could take this country and run it fine, if he just didn't have to mess with any political machine, or a lot of red tape.

These politicians, when they can't make politics pay, can always fall back on—the honorable practice of law.

You are a politician just in proportion to the loot you have pilfered while in Washington for the old home state. If you can come back with a couple of Boulder Dams, a few government hospitals and jails, and an appropriation to build roads somewhere where nobody lives, or wants to, why, if you do all these things, you will be putting yourself in line with becoming a statesman.

But that's all as it should be, I reckon. It's there where the money is, and they won't pay off the National Debt with it, that's the last thing that was ever suggested. So as long as we are going to spend it anyhow, why, there is no reason why the old home town, or home state, don't grab off what we think is more than our Pro Rata!

Politicians are like the rich—they're always with us.

Politics is not the high class, marvelous thing that lots of you picture. Our whole government workings are crammed with "baloney."

But with all the hooey, it's the best system there is in the world and the honesty of our men in big jobs is very high—there is many dumb ones get in there, but no downright dishonest ones.

Los Angeles is what is called an average American city; that is, the politicians are arguing over where to put their municipal airfield. Each politician is trying to sell the ground that belongs to his friend. Who ever thought politics would get into aviation?

Say, politics will get into a prairie dog hole, if it can sell the ground the hole is on!

You can't stop a politician, even by defeating him.

American history records no return of anything once it got into politics.

Politics is a business where most of the men are looking for glory and personal gratification more than they do for money. It's one of the easiest ways of horning into some publicity.

Just quit listening to the politicians. They have to make a noise the nearer it comes to election. The President ain't going to ruin the country. The Constitution will remain with us. The Russians are not going to take us. Let folks quit arguing over who did or didn't do what.

Making good in office is kinder like gambling. You can go in with plenty of money and the best intentions, but the old system is against you.

That law of percentage against a man becoming great in politics is working night and day.

Each nation can produce something better and cheaper than the rest. Maybe it's by nature, climate, talent, or thrift. So why is it if I raise something and you make something that we can't make a trade? Why do I have to attempt making what you make, while you try to raise what I raise—maybe on land that's not suitable?

Among the commodities which we excel in is office holders and politicians. For instance, we could trade Russia some Senators for some vodka, and little Nicaragua some Congressmen for some bananas.

I tell you, this fool scheme is worth trying if just for the sake of this last part. If we can furnish the world with our politicians, we can compete with 'em.

Our public men are speaking every day on something, but they ain't saying anything.

Politicians will never announce anything until everybody else knows all about it. Then they do it as though it was a great mystery.

If more men in politics would raise children instead of issues, we would have a bigger and better country.

No other business in the world could afford to carry such deadwood. But we got 'em and they are going to live off us someway, so we just as well put long-tail coats on 'em and call 'em statesmen.

There is no more independence in politics than there is in jail. I really don't see how anyone can take the whole thing serious, backtracking, all the changing of opinions, all the waiting to see what the majority will be liable to do, all the trading back and forth with each other for support. They are always japing about "public service." It's public jobs they are looking for.

All the politicians are trying to stir up some excitement in their line of work. But I can't find much interest in their graft, outside the ones that are in it. The outside people have just about come to the conclusion that there ain't a worry's worth of difference in any of 'em, and they just try and forget it and live it down if they ever did take any interest.

It sure is a bad time for a man to get ambitious and want to get into politics. There has never been a time when public office was at such a low ebb, and maybe not on account of the man in there. Sometimes it's just a case of a good man in at the bad time.

Politics is the best show in America. I love animals and I love politicians, and I like to watch both of 'em play, either back home in their native state or after they've been captured and sent to a zoo—or Washington.

I am reading about a Texan who has invented a serum called Scopolamine, a thing that when injected into you will make you tell the truth, at least for a while, anyway.

If it could be brought into general use it would, no doubt, be a big aid to humanity. But it will never be, for already the politicians are up in arms against it. It would ruin the very foundation on which our political government is run. If you ever injected truth into politics, you would have no politics.

I knock 'em all, and occasionally boost 'em when they do something meritorious, which is rare.

Did you ever know a politician that was not "facing the most critical time in the world's affairs" every time he spoke in public?

If there is one thing that a politician hates worse than a recount, it's somebody that is not in their business.

Politics is the only sporting event in the world where they don't pay off for second place. For a man to run second in any other event, why, it's an honor. But any time he runs second for President it's not an honor; it's a pity.

Politics sure is a great character builder. You have to take a referendum to see what your convictions are for that day.

Children, what was the first thing you learned about politics in school? It was that Politics was Business, wasn't it? That it is advertised under the heading of idealism, but it was carried out under the heading of business, and the bigger the business, the bigger the politician.

I have written on nothing but politics for years. It was always about national or international affairs. I have been in almost every country in the last few years. I have talked with prominent men in those countries, our ambassadors or ministers, and I would have to be pretty dumb to not soak up some information.

Now I read politics, talk politics, know personally almost every prominent politician, like 'em, and they are my friends, but I can't help it if I have seen enough of it to know that there is *some* baloney in it. I am going to keep on the same as I have in the past. I am going to call 'em like I see 'em. If I don't see things your way, well, why should I? I hope I never get so old that I can't peek behind the scenes and see the amount of politics that's mixed in this medicine before it's dished out to the people as "pure statesmanship."

DEMOCRATS AND REPUBLICANS

The trouble with the Democrats is that they all want to run for President.

A Democrat never adjourns. He is born, becomes of voting age and starts right in arguing over something.

There is always plenty of things to denounce as long as there is a Republican administration.

Don't blame all the things that have happened to us lately on the Republicans—they're not smart enough to have thought 'em up.

Democrats are the only known race of people that give a dinner and then won't decide who will be the toastmaster till they all get to the dinner and fight over it. No job is ever too small for them to split over.

Democrats have spilled more oratory and convinced less voters than any party I know of, outside the Socialists.

I am anxious to see these newly elected. Some are Republicans but Liberals; some are Democrats but not Liberals; some are Democrats and just use the label; some are Republicans just to try and keep an old custom alive.
This next Congress is sure going to be a pack of mongrels.

You take a Democrat and a Republican and you keep them both out of office, and I bet you they will turn out to be good friends and maybe make useful citizens, and devote their time to some work instead of 'lectioneering all the time.

There is no difference between Republicans and Democrats; they are both good if things are going good, and both terrible if things are bad; so just throw up a coin and go to the polls.

History says that the Republicans was a rather kindly people and were good to their young. And they was a thrifty race, too. They had a certain foresight, you know, and they'd take over the reins of government about the time things were going good. Then, when they saw that pestilence and famine was about to overtake the land, why, they'd slip it back to the Democrats.

The Democrats are better denouncers than the Republicans, for there has been so much more time that they had practice at it. Denouncing is not an art with the Democrats, but it's a profession.

In a Sunday article I stated that the Donner Party was our only case of cannibalism. I was wrong, as usual, for I just learned of this case.
Crossing the divide from Utah to Colorado in 1872, a man named Packard evidently practiced it. He was convicted in Del Norte, Colorado, and the judge passed sentence as follows: "Packard, you have committed the world's most fiendish crime. You not only murdered your companions, but you ate up every Democrat in Hillsdale County. You are to be hung by the neck till you are dead, and may God have mercy on your Republican soul!"
We knew the Republicans live off the Democrats, but this was the only one they ever convicted.

Say, did you read what Jim Reed, the Democratic Senator from Missouri, called the Republicans? Why, you would think if they had any pride at all they would come out and deny it.

I guess they would if they could.

The Democratic candidate says the country is not prosperous. He means, of course, by that, that the Democratic end of the country is not doing as well as it would if they were in office.

There are a great many Democrats who are now forced to earn a living by the sweat of their brow, when all they should be doing is endorsing a government check.

Democrats don't care, they will forgive you if you will just argue with them. But when you won't say anything, that's what makes 'em sure enough sore.

There is a few peculiarities that apply to the Democrats that don't apply to any other sex. One is, they will always leave a clambake as soon as they are through listening to themselves, and the other is that they won't come unless they can speak.

Did you read this Senator's appeal this morning to the Republicans "to please clean up before election"?

He intimated that they could get back to normal after election but to kinder lay off till some of this had blown over. Now that's not an unreasonable demand to make of a party—to remain decent one year out of four.

I like to talk to Democrats. They have a better sense of humor than Republicans. Republicans are serious, for they never know at what moment they will be caught, investigated and thrown out.

I hate to admit it, but those birds, the Republicans, are just shrewder. The Democrats stay in power in city government, the Republicans know the dough is on the Potomac; the Democrats worry their heads off over who is going to be Justice of the Peace, and Republicans' minds are on: What two highbinders will we send to the Senate?

Democrats have their principles, their ideals. That's why the Republicans always get somewhere. They have no ideals; it's just cold business with those babies. You don't hear those guys shouting about "Get us back to Lincolnian Principles or the Taftonian Methods!" No, sir. They know that the people don't want to "GO BACK" to anything;

they want to go forward, or what they think is forward; it may be backward, but if they think it's forward, let 'em have their own way about it.

Lots of people never know the difference between a Republican and a Democrat. Well, I will tell you the difference. The Democrats are the ones who split. That's the only way you can tell them from the Republicans.

If the Democrats never split in their lives, there would be no such things as a Republican.

The old Democrat, he is still so old-fashioned that he thinks being a politician is one of the honored professions. Just let him head a few committees, and make a few speeches every once in a while, and he is in his glory.

He will miss his supper to explain to you what Jeffersonian principles are. He don't know what they are, but he has heard 'em spoken of so often in speeches that he knows no speech is complete without wishing that we would return to those principles—and the only thing that keeps us from returning to them is that very reason that we don't know what they were.

A Republican, he would naturally rather make some money under a Republican Congress, but rather than not make any at all, he'll get out and make some under the Democrats.

That's one peculiar thing about a Democrat; he would rather have applause than salary; he would rather be told that he is right, even if he knows the guy is a liar, than he would to know he is wrong, but belongs to the Republican party.

It's not training or education that makes a Democrat. The more education he gets, the less likely he is to be a Democrat; and if he is highly educated, he will see the applesauce in both parties. And as for training—you can't train a man to be a Democrat. He acts like he is trained, but he ain't; most of that devilment he just comes by naturally.

The Democrats met in Washington to try and dig up ways and means to get enough dough to carry on another campaign. Somebody proposed they raise six million dollars. Why, that flabbergasted all of 'em. Six million dollars for the Democrats? Why, they were becoming Republicanized overnight.

On the set with good friend and fellow polo player, motion-picture star Spencer Tracy, who is made up for his role in Dante's Inferno, *1935.*

Will's closest friend, Broadway star Fred Stone (seated far right) visits cast of Fox production Doubting Thomas; *seated Billie Burke, Alison Skipworth; standing with Will, Andrew Tombes, 1935.*

Using his nonprescription reading glasses to keep abreast of the latest news, while co-star Billie Burke, Florenz Ziegfeld's widow, tries to read over his shoulder. During filming of Doubting Thomas, 1935.

Fox Film Corporation's and Hollywood's top box-office attractions of 1935, Shirley Temple and Will Rogers.

Will Rogers and Wiley Post (center) attend the premiere of David Copperfield, starring Will's one-time Ziegfeld Follies co-star, W. C. Fields, 1935.

You see, a Republican moves slowly. They are what we call conservatives. A Conservative is a man who has plenty of money and doesn't see any reason why he shouldn't always have plenty of money. A Democrat is a fellow who never had any, but doesn't see any reason why he shouldn't have some.

So the idea of closing a bank of your own free will and accord is as foreign to a Republican as selling stock which you don't own is foreign to a Democrat. It's not that the Democrat's conscience would hurt him, it's just that he never thought of the thing.

Now you take, for instance, a Republican. There is lots of people that won't speak or associate with one. They think they would catch some grafting disease, but I have met several of them and you take one when he is out of office, and he is as nice a fellow as you would want to meet.

Now take the Democrats. Every time they got in office and started to get ahead and accumulate something, why, the Republicans would rise up and crush them. So it has got the Democrats so hardened against them that when he does get in power, all he thinks of is to so completely put the Republicans out of commission that they can't possibly recover and attack them again—at least not in his lifetime.

You keep a Republican getting interest on his money and he doesn't care if it's Stalin of Russia who is doing it.

It's dissatisfaction what makes a Democrat; it's not environment. Why, a Democrat can run with a bunch of Republicans for a year and come out as honest as he went in; and he can run with a bunch of Democrats for a year and come out knowing just as little as he did when he went in. But dissatisfaction is his stock in trade.

CORRUPTION

Corruption and golf is two things we might just as well make up our minds to take up, for they are both going to be with us.

Democrats have talked more corruption and got less of it than any known denomination.

Jimmy Cox of Ohio, the Democrat running for the Presidency in 1920, run on "Corruption in the Republican Party!" He lost.

There were seven million more people in favor of it than there was of abolishing it.

It's awful hard to get people interested in corruption, unless they can get some of it. You take a fellow that hasn't received any corruption, and it's kinder like the fellow that has never drank sauerkraut juice; he ain't much interested in whether it's good or bad.

Corruption is really not new. It has been in existence for years, but mostly in a small way. In fact, the Democrats were supposed to have started it.

Democratic graft was mostly confined to sorter rounding the saloon keepers into line with a campaign collection every year. They thought that was just about the height of "big business." They never gave any other business a tumble. I guess it was because they didn't know there was any other business.

So the Republicans just was wise enough to see that the same principle applied to one business as to the other. If it was good for the saloons to stand in with the government, why, it was good for all other business. So they commenced working out the idea in a big way.

While the Democrat was still fooling his time away with the "jitney" fellow, the Republican said: "There is only one way to be in politics and that's to be in in a big way!" They just kept working and building their business right up, till, look what it is today.

There is two types of Larceny, Petty and Grand. They are supposed to be the same in the eyes of the law, but the judges always put a little extra on you for Petty, which is a kind of a fine for stupidness. "If that's all you got, you ought to be in jail longer!"

The Republicans have always been the party of big business, and the Democrats of small business, so you just take your pick. The Democrats have their eye on a dime, and the Republicans on a dollar.

PROHIBITION

In his book *The Cowboy Philosopher on Prohibition*, Will Rogers stated:

> I don't knock Prohibition through any personal grudge as I
> do not drink myself, but I do love to play to an audience

who have had a few nips, just enough so they can see the joke and still sober enough to applaud it.

Will Rogers very rarely had a drink. He did not smoke, and he could nurse a single drink for an entire evening and when it was time to go home, he would still have half a glass left. During the years of his lecture tours, he was known to have a rare small glass of wine, on occasions when he felt that he had eaten something that did not agree with him.

There is, however, his own description of his first encounter with vodka. It was in a "Russian Restaurant that used to be a coal cellar" in Paris; the year was 1926:

> They asked me if I had ever had a taste of Vodka, and they poured out a little small glass of what I thought was water. It was the most innocent looking thing I ever saw.
> Then all said just drink it all down at one swig; nobody can sip Vodka. Well, I had no idea what the stuff was, and for a second I thought somebody had loaded me up with molten lead, and I hollered for water.
> Now over in Europe the water is in quart bottles, and here was this Vodka in another quart bottle, and it looks exactly like water; and they immediately grabbed the Vodka and loaded up the glass again, and me thinking it was the water, and my throat a-burning, why, I gulped it down quick, and here I was just twice as bad off as I had been. If I could have seen which one to hit I would have swung on him, but they already were blurred. Lord, what quick results that stuff delivers!
> I asked, "Where do they get this white iodine?" They informed me then that that was Russia's national dissipation. Why, that old white corn down South would be branch water compared to this stuff. Jack Brandy and White Mule would be used as a chaser where this stuff comes from. How they can concentrate so much insensibility into one pre-scription is almost a chemical wonder."*

There is no record that Will ever again gulped, or even carefully sipped, vodka. Even though Will claimed to have the secret recipe for

*There's Not a Bathing Suit in Russia & Other Bare Facts; c. 1927.

the manufacture of the libation, he certainly never assembled it. Will, however, was more than generous in sharing his find with the rest of America, parched by Prohibition:

> One half bushel of old potato peelings; fourteen ears of Russian corn, or maize—cob and stalk included; four top and soles of worn Russian boots; five grains of Giant Powder; three bombs chopped up fine; mix all this in a washtub of Volga River water, add two revolutions and serve.

The South is "Dry" and will vote "dry." That is, everybody that is sober enough to stagger to the polls, will.

Prohibition was never an issue in the South. Their habits and their votes have nothing in common. They feel they are the originators of the still, and large corporation breweries would be unfair competition and would perhaps destroy the entire revenue of hundreds of thousands of small still owners who would have no other means of support.

We would be a fine liberty loving country if we allowed a few Yankees to dictate to us what we could make and what we could drink. Prohibition isn't an issue down here, it's a privilege.

Is there too much drinking going on over home? I am for anything that will cut drinking down and get it over with as soon as possible. If we must sin, let's sin quick and don't let it be a long, lingering sinning.

So get Vodka; it will cut the drinking down one-half and maybe three-fourths and it will do the same amount of damage to mind and body that an American strives for for hours.

Prohibition originally started out with us as a moral issue. It was either good or bad for you to drink. Then it drifted to economics: did people save money when not drinking? Then into racketeering; and then it drifted into the worst angle of any, that is politics.

I flew down here to Claremore, Oklahoma, my home town.

There's nobody here in Oklahoma. They are driving to Missouri to get their beer. In that way the state retains its morals . . . and its appetite, too.

Do you people know anything about moonshining? Oklahoma has always been "Dry"—certainly I am laughing, what did you think I was doing—and on account of our years of experience we do build better stills than anybody. I can show you stills there 100 years old. It's a tradition with us; it's not a get-rich-quick industry. We take pride in the quality, not the price.

When you speak of Oklahoma corn, you are talking right up our alley. We gather our corn in airplanes. Why, our corn last year in Oklahoma ran over 200 gallons to the acre!

Our corn keeps the world merry. Most of our hogs are fattened from the mash from the still, so that's why Oklahoma pork brings more on the market than any other. It's from satisfied and liberty-loving hogs. One Oklahoma ham fattened from still mash runs 3.75 percent intoxicant.

POLITICAL PARTIES, GENERAL

It would drive a person near crazy to dope out really what does divide the two parties. Prosperity don't divide the two parties, for under either administration the poor get poorer and the rich get richer.

Our politics is just a revolving wheel. One party gets in and through a full stomach and a swelled head it oversteps itself, and out they go. And then the other one gets in and that's all there is to it.

Well, that's the way it should be, I guess, for there'd be no living with one of 'em if they didn't know there was another one in existence. So I guess that's why we got to have two of 'em, to keep the other one kind of scared.

So that about concludes the bedside story of the two great political parties which we work night and day to support.

Now which is the narrowest: religious intolerance or political intolerance?

Why, say, politicians think an umpire's decision is based on "what will my decision do for the party?"

It may be more profitable and more satisfying to belong to the party that's in, but it's certainly more amusing to belong to the party that's out.

If political parties are supposed to have to vote together on everything, let each party only send one man from the entire United States. Party politics is the most narrow-minded occupation in the world. A guy raised in a straightjacket is a corkscrew compared to a thick-headed party politician.

All you would have to do to make some men atheists is just tell them the Lord belongs to the opposition political party. After that they could never see any good in Him.

Some fellow named Watson says he will put up one hundred thousand dollars to back a third party.

At the present price, that would buy just eight votes.

Everybody is asking, "What's the matter with the Democratic Party?"

There ain't nothing wrong with it; it's a dandy old party. The only thing wrong with it this time is that the law killed it. It won't let a man vote but once, and there just wasn't enough voters at one vote each to get anywhere.

This country runs in spite of parties, in fact, parties are the biggest handicaps we have to contend with.

I thought at the time of the Jackson Day Dinner that the Democrats were going mighty far back to find some hero that they could worship. But I happened to be in Cuba when President Coolidge delivered his speech to the Latins, and the Republicans had to go even further back then the Democrats did for Jackson. He went back to Columbus.

I had never known or even heard Columbus's political faith discussed before. But he must have been a Republican, the way Cal was boosting him.

I generally give the party in power, whether Republican or Democrat, the more digs because they are generally doing the country more damage and besides, the party in power is drawing a salary to be knocked.

Chapter VIII

BUSINESS

*A*part from his real estate investments, Will Rogers' various forays into the business world can hardly be termed auspicious. He admits freely that as a budding rancher in the Indian Territory he was less interested in the finer points of animal husbandry than in a variety of what could best be described as more personal diversions; while he loved the ranch life of a cowboy, the adolescent Will appreciated many of the exhilarating pastimes a nineteenth-century Indian Territory had to offer. Those amusements ranged from socials and dances, fast racing horses and rigs, all the way to active participation in rodeos. He was not yet twenty years old when one such event made quite an impression on his life:

> It was at a little Fourth of July celebration at Claremore, Indian Territory, on July 4th, 1899, they had a steer roping and I went to it. It was the first one I ever was in, the very first thing I ever did in the way of appearing before an audience. I know it had quite an influence on my little career, for I kinder got to running around to 'em and the first thing I knew, I was just plum "honery" and fit for nothing but show business. You see, once you are a showman, you are plum ruined for manual labor again.

161

After some experience as a performer in rodeos, Wild West shows, the circus, and even a short stint in vaudeville, Will confidently entered show business wearing the hat of a producer. It became an expensive learning process. Whenever he tried to switch from being strictly the performer, he acquired additional knowledge of what not to do and little else. He experimented with producing Wild West shows and failed to make money. In his own vaudeville act, an Oklahoma cowboy, Buck McKee, rode Will's horse, Teddy, across the stage for Will to rope. The act at times barely earned enough to pay for the upkeep of both men, their wives, and the horse. Will reminisced once that on occasions their combined funds were so low that Buck had to ride Teddy to the next engagement, while he, the two ladies, and all their ropes and gear went by day coach.

Will Rogers tried to enlarge his own vaudeville act by adding horses, cowboys, and cowgirls. He went on the assumption that more is better and learned that more merely meant more paychecks. His venture to produce his own motion picture films ended in financial ruin.

Having inherited the family ranch upon his father's death, Will Rogers continued to ranch and farm it. As Will was only rarely able to visit his holdings, his first cousin Herb McSpadden managed the spread. Even though Herb was an outstanding rancher and familiar with every phase of farming, this operation rarely broke even, and needed Will's additional financial support. The Depression years allowed few endeavors to be profitable.

Will Rogers did not invest in the stock market, despite the general mania of the time. His moral sense did not feel at ease with the concept of making money without earning it. Similarly Rogers abhorred the idea of collecting interest on money lent. While he saw the need for mortgages, and borrowing in general, he wanted no part of any interest thus made. But for a single stock market venture at the insistence of Eddie Cantor, Will Rogers bought no stocks, either outright or on margin. Thus when the crash of 1929 wiped out many "rich" performers, including Eddie Cantor, Will Rogers was not among them. He had his investments in land. As an ex-rancher and a rancher's son, he knew land values. He had invested wisely.

I guess we will all just give thanks we had invested in land, instead of Wall Street; even if we can't sell the land and have to pay taxes on it, we can at least walk out on it.

Still, I got some land in Florida where you can't, unless you have divine power.

Will Rogers may not have been successful in business, but he knew his own worth and anyone who dealt with him prospered. Sam Goldwyn may not have become rich on the thirteen films Will made for his studio, but there was a profit. Hal Roach, too, had other stars who made more money for him, but he never had cause to regret signing Rogers to a dozen silent films. Florenz Ziegfeld took a chance, and it was Rogers who assured him of hit shows. For onstage Will could use his most valuable asset, his verbal humor. And in 1929, Fox Film Corporation, which took the biggest financial gamble on Will, was shrewd enough to know that in a medium which now had sound, Will Rogers' personality was a certain winner.

Without succeeding in the world of commerce by the standards business sets, Will Rogers amassed a fortune and gave away a large part of it. Without fanfare, or publicity, he revealed that there were few to equal his success in the "business of daily living," which is, after all, being of comfort and service to one's fellow man.

BUSINESS

Nothing is going to be stopped anywhere that there is any money in.

In the old days there was mighty few things bought on credit. Your taste had to be in harmony with your income, for it had never been any other way.

I think buying on credit has driven more folks to seek the revolver as a regular means of livelihood than any other one contributing cause.

Every manufacturer is forever bragging about our "high standard of living."

Why, we could always have lived this high if we had wanted to live on the installment plan.

At the price this government sells things to other nations we may be able to go bankrupt without having another war.

A "Holding Company" is a thing where you hand an accomplice the goods while the policeman searches you.

Everybody likes to make a dollar his way, but if he finds he is not allowed to make it his way, why, he is not going to overlook the chance of making it your way.

Some people will bet on anything. Take Life Insurance companies. You like a fool will bet them that you will die, when they have every available information from doctors and everybody that you will live.
    Why, if it looks like you will die, they won't bet you.

You know how these head nurses are. There's nothing outside of a motor cycle cop with more authority than a head nurse.

WALL STREET

Will wanted to have as little as possible to do with Wall Street. Unlike other Americans, he was puzzled by the antics of the stock market. On November 4, 1924, Will's forty-fifth birthday, Calvin Coolidge was elected to a full term. Will liked President Coolidge; what he could not accept was the impact of that election on the stock market:

> We are able to report much jubilation on the part of the disgracefully rich, or Republican, element of the entire country. They are celebrating the country's return to Wall Street.
> And stocks, why, anything that looked like a stock would sell. People would wire in, "Buy me some stocks." The broker would answer, "What kind?" The buyer would wire back, "Any kind; the Republicans are in, ain't they all supposed to go up?"
> Men bought stocks who had never even bought a toothbrush before. People bought wheat and sent a truck to the Exchange to get it. Even moving picture companies' stock went up, figuring I guess that pictures would be funnier with Charley Dawes as Vice-President than they would have been with Charley Bryan. And my old friends Bill Hart and

Tom Mix—why, the way stocks are going, buyers evidently feel that they can whip twice as many men in a fight as they could under any previous administration. What is worrying me is what they will do with movies that were made under the late divided administration. They will perhaps just destroy them and make new ones.

Personal fortunes have been made. I read of one who cleaned up 10 million in cast iron pipe. Here cast iron pipe has been laying around for years and we never thought much of it. It was all right to hit someone over the head with, or to stumble over, and here all it needed was a president from Vermont to put it on its feet. You know it is really remarkable how near cast iron pipe is linked up with New York's 45 electoral votes.

Coca-Cola took a jump right out of the glass. That seems kinder strange that a summer drink stock should wait until November to show its value. I thought we elected Mr. Coolidge to lower our taxes and keep us at peace with the world. I didn't know that we had to drink Coca-Cola.

International Harvester was another. Now harvesters are all in the sheds and will be until next June; still, people are just crazy about them, even idle. What makes these things worth so much more on November 5th than they were on November the 3rd? I was old-fashioned enough to think that supply and demand regulated the price of everything. Now I find November the 4th regulates it. Who is going to pay all these extra profits these things are supposed to earn?

You mean to tell me that in a country that was really run on the level, 200 of their national commodities could jump their value millions of dollars in two days? Where is this sudden demand coming from all at once?

Will Rogers' question was published across America on the weekend of November 23, 1924. Few Americans asked the same question until October 29, 1929, when the counterfeit prosperity ended with a crash; but by that time the answer to Will's question had become academic.

Let Wall Street have a nightmare and the whole country has to help get them back in bed again.

The stock market not only operates on O.P.M. (Other People's Money) but O.P.R. (Other People's Rumors).

Let a rumor get out that Ford was building a 6 door sedan and wheat would jump 10 points.

There is a lot of folks that not only lost confidence in Wall Street, but they lost money.

But I am telling them that this country is bigger than Wall Street, and if they don't believe me, I'll show 'em a map.

We are living in an age of mergers and combines. When your business is not doing good, you combine with something and sell more stock.

It's one of the mental weaknesses of the American people that if two things go together, they think it must be great.

I bought some stock in a Chinese bandit corporation yesterday. I studied whether to buy that or New York hotel stock.

Their ideas are similar; they both work on the ransom plan.

To people away out on farms and ranches, where people make a living off what you are supposed to make it off of, why, it don't make much difference what happens. The stock market could have closed "strong," or closed forever, and it wouldn't matter to a big bunch of Americans.

You can't sell a pair of shoes in New York, without it being done through the stock exchange. I got an order in with a broker for ten subway tickets.

Everybody said that if people didn't trade in stock, why, Wall Street couldent exist. So I says: What can we do for them so they will keep on existing?

Why, restore confidence! they said.

So that's what I have been doing for weeks. 'Course I haven't been buying any stocks myself, I wanted to give all the other folks a chance to have confidence first.

The past few weeks Wall Street has gone into one tailspin after another. You would pick up the morning paper and read the stock report and you wouldn't think there was that many minus signs in the world.

Mr. Roosevelt has cut the stock market down to three hours a day. He just told them: Now you be good boys! I will give you three hours a day to work on these suckers, and the other twenty-one hours they are under the protection of the fish and game laws.

One-third of the people in the United States promote, while the other two-thirds provide. There are more commissions paid out to stock salesman than there are profits ever collected by stock buyers.

How about that tear gas attack on Wall Street? Say, that old boy, with one shot of tear gas on the New York Exchange, did more than Roosevelt. He closed it.

It must have been quite a novelty to see the broker crying, instead of the customers.

BANKS AND BANKERS

In Russia the government owns everything. Well, that ain't so different than it's over here. The banks own it over here.

The good old U.S.A. still holds one international record. Our international bankers have loaned more of other people's money to foreign countries on less security than was ever loaned before, even with security.

Now there is a record we want to see beat, but no other bankers are dumb enough to beat it.

I think we just about been cured of foreign loans. The big boys have come in for such a rawhiding from all over that it's made them realize it.

I guess there is no race of people that it is so universally agreed that they pulled a boner as the international banker. Now our home bankers, both large and small, are in bad through an over-expansion in good times, but the international one is in bad through malice aforethought. His devilment was premeditated. He knew he was loaning on no security, cause there is no security over there. He got his commission for peddling it out, so what does he care?

I suggested that Congress pass a bill that no person could borrow a cent because you can't break a man that don't borrow.

Well, you will say what will the bankers do? I don't care what they do. Let 'em go to work, if there is any job any of them could earn a living at. Banking and after-speaking are two of the most non-essential industries we have in this country. I am ready to reform if they are.

The day I was in Washington, one fellow testified that Andy Mellon's bank backed the bootleggers and loaned money on warehouse certificates. Well, I know a lot of bankers out in the farming and cattle country that have been loaning on farms and live stock that would like to have as good collateral as a few hundred barrels of Old Crow.

Everybody that I hear kicking about the Federal Reserve Bank is someone trying to make money by speculation.
    So I about come to the conclusion that the Federal Reserve might accidentally be working in the interest of the millions of us who don't know a stock from a stockyard.

A good deal of debts have gone under the auctioneer's hammer since I last communed with you—both private, national and international. Some of those countries around the world got a moratorium, the big international bankers got theirs guaranteed, taxpayers got another tax assessment, and the farmers got exactly what everybody had been predicting they would get—two bits for their wheat.

J. P. Morgan has nothing but a secured mortgage on the world at 7 percent.

LABOR

Tomorrow is Labor Day, I suppose set by Act of Congress. Everything we do nowadays is either by, or against, Acts of Congress.
    How Congress knew anything about Labor is beyond us.

Say, did you read about this fellow in Washington saying that our standard of living had advanced so far in this country that we could lay off two million men from work and the rest of the people would live just as good as they did ten years ago.
    He didn't say what would become of the two million he laid off. But you take a busy man like that, he can't stop to worry about trifles like a couple of million men.

Never did things look brighter for the working man, but none of us want to work. If we got to work for the money, we are just as bad off as if there were no prosperity.

Machinery is just doing fine. If it can't kill you, it will put you out of work.

Unemployment is confined practically to college graduates and Harvard men. There's no prospect of relief for this type of unemployment until the education system is changed to teach them to work, instead of teaching them that with an education they won't have to.

The greatest and most urgent need in our land is the settlement of strikes. Can't the government make arbitration compulsory? Everybody knows there is wrongs, everybody knows there are strikes with just causes, and some that are not. But let each side negotiate—the Labor Union send one man, the employer one man, and the Government one man.

It looks like the side that wouldn't agree to that, there is something wrong with it. Let everybody stay on the job during arbitration. Then if they get the raise of wages, it starts back from the day the complaint was made.

All strikes that deal in a commodity are hurting nobody but the people that use and want that commodity.

No nation will buy anything to eat or anything to wear from you, but if you got a gun they will buy it and more than likely shoot it back at you.

Looks to me like if every nation made their own ammunition, it would relieve their unemployment.

TARIFF

Tariff is an instrument invented for the benefit of those who manufacture, to be used against those who buy. As there is more buyers than there is makers, it is a document of the minority.

But what a minority.

Twenty men can enter a room as friends and someone can bring up the topic of Tariff, and you will find nineteen bodies on the floor with only one living that escapes.

The Argentine wants lower tariff on beef. So we told them, why, we can't settle any tariff question. Our Congress has been trying to agree on that for 150 years, so the best way for you to get your beef in cheap is to smuggle it in. The people bringing in bootlegged liquor seem to be doing all right.

Some of the smartest men in our national life have been divided on the tariff question. It's not all politics, a lot of it is a matter of real opinion based on a long study.

It's a smart man's business, it's not just for mere politicians to mess with.

You see, a lot of manufacturing establishments try to cover up their own business ability by having the government protect them against somebody that handles their business better than they do.

Every little industry that can't make a big profit hollers for protection.

LAWYERS AND LAW

The American Bar Association—that's a gang of lawyers who think that if you are not one of them you are in rompers intellectually, and they take that Association as serious as a Chamber of Commerce does a cold-potato lunch.

Two lawyers can make a scandal out of anything they have anything to do with. One hundred will bring a revolution.

You almost have to be a lawyer in Washington, just to hold your own.

We have got more toothpaste on the market and more misery in our courts than at any time in our existence.

Everybody says for you to leave a will. By all means leave a will. Yes, leave a will so the lawyers can misinterpret what you meant when you knew enough to know what you wanted to do with your money.

Modern history has proven that there has never been a will left that was carried out exactly as the maker of the money intended. So, if you are thinking of dying and have any money, I would advise you to leave the following will: Count the lawyers in the state and divide it among them!

If it wasn't for wills, lawyers would have to go to work at an essential employment. There is only one way you can beat a lawyer in a death case—that is to die with nothing; then you can't get a lawyer within 10 miles of your house.

OIL INDUSTRY

I'm here in San Angelo, the real heart of the cow business, but it's so poor that these old cattlemen are eating their own beef, and the bread lines in these towns are composed of independent oil men. They are worse off than the cotton farmers.

I read where they say that ranches are all gone. Yea? Well, I am on one right now of 600,000 acres belonging to W. T. Waggoner here in Vernon, Texas, with 25,000 cattle and some of the best horses in any state. He is one cowman that was smart enough to solve the low profit on cattle and he makes ranches pay.

Here, every cow has got her own oil well.

One of the very next things Mr. Roosevelt is going to do, so I was told in Washington on the best authority, is to appoint an oil "czar."

No industry needs a warden worse.

Frank Phillips [Oklahoma oilman and banker] was out to our home the other day. He said he was going to Washington where the oil men were going to draw up a code of ethics.

Everybody present had to laugh. If he had said the gangsters of America were drawing up a code of ethics, it wouldn't have sounded near as impossible.

SHOW BUSINESS

As Hollywood's number one box-office attraction, Will Rogers was in constant demand as a public speaker, as master of ceremonies, and as a general drawing card for benefits. He accommodated as many such requests as he could. One such occasion raised quite a furor at the time but was soon forgotten; another episode is one where Will Rogers' involvement was soon overlooked, though his innovation is still being followed to this day.

Event number one took place in April 1932. It was the premiere of the film *Grand Hotel*, starring Greta Garbo, Lionel and John Barrymore, Wallace Beery, Joan Crawford, Lewis Stone, and Jean Hersholt. The gala was to be presented at Sid Grauman's Chinese Theatre, and a lengthy live show preceded the film. Will Rogers, as master of ceremonies, introduced the various stars of the film, with the exception of Greta Garbo and John Barrymore. While the latter had a good excuse by being out of the city, the seclusive Greta Garbo had no intention of putting in an appearance. After each star had taken a bow, Will Rogers announced that because of the importance of this film Metro-Goldwyn-Mayer, the producer of *Grand Hotel*, had persuaded Miss Garbo to be present on the stage after the film. There was a gasp in the audience. It would be the first time that most had seen the beautiful star in person.

After the film, as the houselights came on, a murmur of expectation ran through the crowd. Will Rogers stepped onstage to make the formal introduction. As he tells it:

> Well, I had framed up a gag with Wally Beery, who I knew would be a big hit in the picture that they had just seen, and he got some "dame" clothes. And he was my Greta Garbo. Sounds kinder funny, don't it? Well, it wasn't to them. Wally did it fine. He even looked like her—but not enough to satisfy that crowd.

Will thought that the audience "got their waiting's worth by seeing Wally Beery in skirts," but vowed in print never again to play a practical joke on an audience.

The other event was the Academy Awards ceremony of 1934. In the few years since the founding of the Academy of Motion Picture Arts and Sciences, the awards ceremony had been a staid event. On March 18, 1934, Will Rogers was master of ceremonies, and the character of the ceremony was changed forever. He injected humor where there had been tedium. He set the tone with his opening statement:

> I was always a little leery of this organization. The name Arts and Sciences—I think that name has bluffed more people than it attracted. This is the highest sounding named organization I ever attended. If I didn't know so many of the people who belonged to it personally, I would have taken that name serious. Call them "Arts and Sciences,"

but do so with your tongue in your cheek. Everything that makes money and gives pleasure is not "art." If it was, bootlegging would have been the highest form of artistic endeavor.

Wrote *Photoplay Magazine*, in its issue of June 1934, of the event: "Will's wit changed the big affair from the customary ceremony of long-winded speeches into a joyous riot." And ever since, the annual ceremony has attempted to live up to the "joyous riot" Will Rogers left as his legacy.

One night, a few years ago, I was asked to introduce Charlie Chaplin at the Lambs Club in New York, that's the most exclusive actors organization. I told them that in all my little years on the stage and screen, that I had only met one person that I could honestly call an "artist." Every other person I ever saw, someone else could do what he was doing just as good, that it was all a trick. But that Chaplin was all that these real so-called artists was supposed to be.

Whether you like him, or not (and how you couldn't I don't know), but he is one of the few geniuses developed in our time in any line.

A movie actor is no better than his double.

Shakespeare is the only author that can play to losing business for a hundred years and still be known as an author.

I have looked politics and movies both over, and while they have much in common, I believe politics is the most common. So I will stay with the movies.

At the studio they was talking about changing a story. But there are no new situations. Wives are leaving husbands, husbands are leaving wives, robberies, where they used to take your horse and if they was caught they got hung for it, now they take your car and if they get caught, it's a miracle.

Your movies won't be changed much more than your morals, or your taxes, or any other of the things that you think should be re-modeled.

The other night at a benefit, back stage, I introduced a dozen friends to each other, and then had them say: Why, Will, we used to be married to each other!

I just got discouraged and quit trying to be sociable and introduce anybody.

If the public judges the movie people by some of the interviews that appear in print, they must wonder how they ever kept out of the asylum.

This is the big day for the Academy of Motion Picture Arts and Sciences Awards. You'll see great acting tonight, greater than any you will ever see on the screen.

We'll all cheer when somebody gets a prize that every one of us in the house knows should be ours.

Yet we'll smile and bear it. Boy, that's acting.

AVIATION

First thing we have to do is get to the aviation field. It took us just an hour and a half to drive through the traffic to the field. Ain't autos grand? What would we do without them?

If we had had a dirt road, with no expense to the taxpayers, we would have got there with a horse and buggy in about forty minutes.

Airlines have flown millions of miles and no injuries to anyone. By comparison get the record of automobiles that may run 50 miles a day and you will find that they got more accidents than they have cars.

But you don't have to stop to figure out which is safe. All you have to do is to compare the intelligence of the men that pilot planes with the intelligence of everybody that drives a car.

This is what I am trying to get you to understand, Calvin: Nobody is walking but us; everybody else is flying. So in a few years, when somebody starts dropping something on us, don't say I dident tell you.

Five people killed in a plane yesterday and it is headlined today in every paper. Saturday in Los Angeles at one grade crossing seven were killed and six wounded and the papers didn't even publish their names.

It looks like the only way to get any publicity on your death is to be killed in a plane; it's no novelty to be killed in an auto anymore.

AGRICULTURE

Farmers, get out your sense of humor! Congress meets to relieve you again next week.

August 12, 1935. Arriving on relatively narrow, tree-lined Chena Slough in Fairbanks, Alaska. Having that day left the mighty McKenzie River in northern Canada, Will convulsed the reception committee with: "Is that all the river you got?"

August 14, 1935, Fairbanks, Alaska. Because of dismal weather reports from Barrow, nationally famous Alaskan pilot Joe Crosson (left), tried unsuccessfully to dissuade his two friends from flying there. Two days later, with Communications Superintendent Bob Gleason as radio operator, he flew through the same dangerous conditions to pick up the bodies at Barrow.

The sprawling ranch house nestled in the Santa Monica hills of Pacific Palisades, California. The family moved here in 1928.

Cattle are so cheap that even cowboys are eating beef for the first time in years.

If the farmer could harvest the promises made him, he would be sitting pretty.

I just found out what a soft shell pecan is. It's one you can crack with just a small hammer.

Congress says they are helping the farmer. But they are in Washington, drawing a salary. The farmer is home, trying to pay that salary. Farmers have had more advice and less relief than a wayward son.

People can raise things faster in this country than anybody can buy it—even the government.

There is just one thing that will help the farmer. That is eliminate the middlemen and let the two ends meet.

When a steer starts from the feed pen to the table, there is about 10 to take a bite out of him before he reaches the family that pays for him.

Rain in Iowa, or an epidemic of appendicitis among the boll weevil, play just as big a part in the national career of a man as his executive ability.

It looks to me like the candidates are trying to relieve the farmer of his vote, instead of his debts.

Ah, to be out in the wide open spaces, where men are men and farms are mortgaged! Where the government has showed them every way in the world where they can borrow money and never introduced an idea of how to pay any of it back. Where women are women, and only get to town when they have to go to endorse a note with their husbands.

There is lots of politics in Missouri. Wherever you find poor soil you will find politics. When you see you ain't going to raise anything, you just sit down at the end of the row and cuss the party in power.

When will they quit taxing farmers' land, regardless of whether it made anything? Or selling people's homes for taxes?

Walking Monday afternoon through one of the most famous of the historical California Missions, San Juan Capistrano, and who should I find in meditation before a wonderful old picture depicting the joy of the harvest, and the merrymaking at the sale of the crops? It was the Secretary of Agriculture Wallace.

Tears were in his eyes and he kept murmuring: "Oh, what have I done Father, that I couldn't have been Secretary of Agriculture in days like those?"

These old boys with a pair of specs and a tablet and pencil can sit and figure out how much wheat, corn and oats can be raised each year in order to sell each bushel of it at a profit. Then along comes a guy called "elements." This bird "elements" never went to college, he has never even been called an "expert."

But when this guy "elements" breaks out, he can make a sucker out of more experts than anybody.

Somebody had a plan to teach hogs birth control, and now it's a habit with them. Somebody had a plan to plow under every third acre of wheat, and then the wind come along and blew out the other two acres. Now we find there is more people eating than there is raising, and if you get a thing too high, the guy that eats is going to commence hollering.

So plans don't work; if they are milk and honey to you, they are poison ivy to somebody else.

Glad to see that re-forestation bill pass. We got to have a lot more forests and trees, otherwise these cigarette smokers won't have anything to burn up.

We sure are living in a peculiar time. You get more for not working than you will for working, and more for not raising a hog than for raising it.

Coolidge said: "There is lots of people worse off than the farmers."

I don't know who it could be unless it is the fellow who holds the mortgages on the farms.

Coolidge closed his speech by saying: "The future of agriculture looks to be exceedingly secure!"

Agriculture is secure. In fact it's secured by at least two mortgages.

Steak on the plate went up, steak on the hoof went down.

Prosperity remained with them that had.

AUTOMOBILES

Politics ain't worrying this country one-tenth as much as trying to find a parking spot.

It seems strange that we Americans don't hold the automobile speed record, for we have millions trying to break it every day.

Henry Ford says: "America is on wheels today!" He means America is on credit today.

If an automobile manufacturer could make a car so good that he could advertise it as follows: "This car will last 'til it's paid for," why, he could put all car manufacturers out of business.

Everything is sold on credit nowadays. Even the most experienced can't tell by looking at a fancy car how many payments are yet to be made on it.

The Automobile men, as an association, arrived in Washington. They claimed that . . . if Congress would just do away with that tax, why, they would have a chance to make a living.

They never thought that it might be the quality of their cars that might be holding back sales. Lord, grant that I never take it serious.

It's getting so a man that has a car now walks further than he ever did in his life, walking back from where he parked it at.

This is liable to bring walking back among grown people.

Suggestions to solve traffic problems: Everybody traveling west, go Monday; east, Tuesday, north Wednesday, south Thursday.

Sundays reserved for weekend drivers alone, Sunday night—caring for the injured.

Those darned motorcycles! No motorist has ever been able to discover a good word for a motorcycle.

There is something that we all read in the papers every morning of our lives, no matter what paper it is we pick up. "Four Killed and

Three Wounded Yesterday by Automobile!" Maybe it's more, maybe it's less, but it's there every day.

I have the Chicago Tribune in front of me, and here is yesterday's toll: "12 killed, 13 hurt by Autos in City Sunday. Cook County death toll goes to 169 in 1926, an increase over this time last year of 44 deaths, or 34 percent." And right over in the adjoining column of the same edition of the paper is the following: "Annual Auto bill of U.S. is 14 Billion of dollars per year."

In another part of the paper it tells that 22 thousand met their death last year by auto and that we are well on our way to beat that record. We paid 14 billion dollars to kill 22 thousand—about $635,000 a piece, with no charge at all for the wounded. They will run at least two or three times as many as the killed, and FOR WHAT? Why, just to get somewhere a little quicker, that is, if you get there at all.

Now they call all these accidents PROGRESS. Well, maybe it is progress. But I tell you it certainly comes high-priced. Suppose . . . when automobiles were first invented, that a man, we will say it was Thomas A. Edison, had gone to our government and he had put this proposition up to them: "I can in 25 years' time have every person in America riding quickly from here to there. You will save all this slow travel of horse and buggy. Shall I go ahead with it?"

"Why sure, Mr. Edison, if you can accomplish that wonderful thing, why, we, the government, are heartily in accord and sympathy with you."

"But," says Mr. Edison, "I want you to understand it fully . . . when it is in operation, it will kill 15 to 20 thousand a year of your women and children and men."

"What! You want us to endorse some fiendish invention that will be the means of taking life! Why, you insult us by asking us to listen to such a plan. Why, if it wasn't for our previous regard for you, we would have you thrown into an asylum. How dare you talk of manufacturing something that will kill more people than a war? Why, we would rather walk from one place to another the rest of our lives, than be the means of taking one single child's life."

Now that is what would have happened, if we had known it. But now it don't mean a thing. It's just a matter of fact.

Too bad.

How to pass one car without meeting another one gives people in this country more thought than all the messages to Congress since Washington wore golf breeches.

I went to Henry Ford's home and it was the time when the *Star* car was supposed to cut quite a dash in the Ford sales, so I asked him: "Mr. Ford, I know it is rather inquisitive, but in case the opposition gets to cutting the price, just how cheap could you sell your car?"

He said: "Well, Will, that is kind of personal but if the worst comes to the worst, I could give it away, as long as we retain the selling of the replacement parts. You know, Will, one of these things will shake off enough nuts in one year to pay for itself."

Chapter IX

THE WORLD

*B*efore he was twenty-five years old, Will Rogers had made his first round-the-world trip. While circling the globe may not be quite so noteworthy nowadays, at the beginning of the twentieth century it was a feat, especially the way Will did it.

Actually, that trip started out as a fulfillment of Will's long-harbored interest to see the gauchos of the pampas. In his early geography lessons, Will had come across pictures of those Argentineans who were so much like, yet different from, the cowboys he knew. In 1902, Will decided to sell the small herd he owned and use the money to travel to South America. For company on this adventure, Will asked Dick Parris, a boyhood friend, to come along.

The plan was perfectly simple and logical though, as it turned out, infeasible. Since Argentina was in South America, Will reasoned, all one had to do was to go south to New Orleans and catch a boat for Buenos Aires. Early in March, Will and Dick packed their bags, took their saddles, and set out for Louisiana. On March 15, Will, now at Hot Springs, Arkansas, received a letter from his father, Clem V. Rogers, stating that a draft for $1,300 had been sent to New Orleans. Probably that money came from the sale of Will's cattle. By the time Will collected the money, the two young men had learned that no boats were scheduled to leave New Orleans for the Argentine. To get to Buenos Aires, so they were told, they would have to start from New York City.

Three days later, on March 18, Will wrote to his sisters in Chelsea, "Leave in the morning for New York to get a boat to South America." On Wednesday, March 19, 1902, Will and Dick were aboard the steamship *Comus* en route to New York City, where they were expected to arrive on Monday, March 24.

New York was far less intimidating to the two young men from the Indian Territory than might be expected. They checked into a hotel, then walked around town and took in some of the sights. What turned out to be disturbing was the news that no ships were scheduled to leave for the Argentine in the foreseeable future. The advice was to go to England, which maintained regular, scheduled traffic with South America. The two men, now practically seasoned travelers, booked passage for England aboard the USS. *Philadelphia*.

Among the souvenirs from this trip is a draft (number 55418) dated March 24, 1902, made out to W. P. Rogers. Drawn on the London and River Plate Bank Ltd., Buenos Aires, it calls for "100 Pounds Sterling." Since the date coincides with Will Rogers' arrival in New York City, it is safe to assume that Will converted some of the money rather than carry so much cash on his person.

The Times of London reported the arrival of the USS. *Philadelphia* on April 3. Since Will and Dick were to leave England aboard the *Danube* on April 10, the two young men had a week to explore London. They visited the Houses of Parliament and Westminster Abbey, stood outside Buckingham Palace, and went through the Tower of London. It was all part of their great adventure.

"Steaming along the west coast of Africa . . . 9th day out," Will wrote to his father in a letter, mailed when the ship stopped briefly at St. Vincent, Cape Verde Islands.

By April 24—two weeks after leaving England—Will and Dick were in the province of Pernambuco, Brazil. Reporting faithfully to his family back home, Will wrote that the ship was scheduled to "get to Rio de Janeiro in 4 days."

On May 5, Will and Dick landed in Buenos Aires and checked into the Phoenix Hotel. In less than three weeks Will would be faced with a hard decision; it would affect his entire future while clearly showing the character of the man.

The two friends had been away from home for two months. They had seen New Orleans and New York City; they had been to London; they had crossed the equator and traveled by ship for thousands of miles; they had experienced more adventures, seen more sights, and met more people than their homefolk could imagine. There would be much to tell when they returned to the Indian Territory.

Walking around Buenos Aires, hearing only a foreign tongue, home seemed far away and Dick Parris was homesick. He suggested that they return to Claremore, that they had seen enough for two lifetimes. Will tried to persuade his buddy to stay, to think of all they had yet to see and experience, but Dick was adamant. Feeling responsible for his friend, Will paid for Dick's passage home. He also asked him to take along some presents for "Papa" and his sisters.

On May 24, Dick Parris left for home. Will, now almost without money, remained alone in the Argentine.

It would have been easy for Will to give in. He could have claimed that he was practically broke; he could have used his friend's return as an excuse to go back with him; he could have argued that he did not wish to continue alone. A restless curiosity, a passion for finding out what lay beyond the horizon, would not allow him to quit.

Will stayed behind, saw the gauchos, and admired their exceptional skills. He ran out of money and sold his saddle—the last item any cowboy will sell. He looked for work, did odd jobs, and went hungry. "Years and years and years ago I spent six months in the Argentine republic and inhaled enough Spanish to ask for something to eat and to cuss," he recalled some twenty years later. *

But the decision not to go back with Dick Parris led Will to South Africa and his entry into show business. He continued his trek eastward. When he finally completed his first trip around the world and came back to the Indian Territory, he had learned many valuable lessons. "I left home first class," he wrote less than five months before his death, "and it took me two years and nine months to get back third class. That's what a clever lad I was, and had to go all the way around

---

* Syndicated weekly article, May 2, 1926.

the world to do it."* But Will Rogers had accomplished what he had set out to do, and he had done it all by himself. He had seen how other people lived, for he had lived among them. He had learned to understand that "it was their country, and they had a right to run it as they saw fit." He never remonstrated or complained. Will Rogers would continue to travel extensively throughout his life, and he would retain his understanding of others. He saw more of the world than almost any observer of his day, and when he wrote or spoke of other lands, it was based on his personal knowledge. And when Americans returning from abroad would complain or protest a real or imagined violation of their "rights," Will would tend to side with the other country:

> I left home as a kid and traveled and worked my way all through Argentine, South Africa, Australia and New Zealand. . . . But I never found it necessary to have my AMER-ICAN rights protected. Nobody invited me into those countries and I always acted as their guest, not their advisor.**

TRAVEL, TOURISTS

We Americans unfortunately don't make a good impression collectively. You see a bunch of Americans at anything and they generally make more noise and have more to say than anybody, and generally create a worse impression than if they had stayed at home.

They are throwing rocks at us, but sometimes you think it is deserved. There should be a law prohibiting over three Americans going anywhere abroad together.

There ought to be a law against anybody going to Europe till they had seen the things we have in this country.

If the President had the authority and he kept Americans at home one summer, and made them see their own country, it would be the greatest

---

*Syndicated weekly article, March 24, 1935.
**Syndicated weekly article, published June 28, 1925.

thing that ever happened in the world to this country, and incidentally give Europeans a chance to laugh at something else, besides us.

I tell you, a tourist is one of the worst, if not the worst investment there is. He knocks everything and buys nothing. He don't know where he is going, only that he wants to get away from his own home. He is sore at his wife and family that are in the car, and he takes it out on your part of the country.

A tourist contributes nothing but empty tin cans and profanity to the up-building of your state.

I am on my way to China. Boy, there ought to be a law against making an ocean this wide.

When you reach the 180th meridian sailing west, you lose a whole day. Don't ask me why. If you come back this way, you get it back. If you don't, you just lose it.

The way days are now, it don't look like it's worth coming back for.

Crossing the Pacific aboard the SS *Empress of Russia* we lost a whole day yesterday. Everything is cockeyed to us, anyhow, for here we are traveling straight west to get to the Far East; and Japan, the land of the Rising Sun, is where it sets.

We had some terrible rough weather. One whole 24 hours we only made 50 miles—and most of that was up and down.

The Aleutian Islands, there is nothing on 'em, they are barren. Being in that state, of course we own 'em. If they had anything on 'em, why, some other nation would have taken 'em over or at least hold the mandate over 'em.

You know what a mandate is? It's a thing you take over a country when you haven't quite got the gall to take over the country. It's a kind of a fashionable way of grabbing it, and still have a speck of pride left.

My dear President Coolidge: Will you kindly find out for me through your intelligence department who the fellow is that said a big boat didn't rock!

Hold him till I return. Yours, feebly . . .

THE AMERICAS

Since I crossed into Canada, I don't know a thing that happened at home. Here they don't pay any attention to their little, innocent sister to the South.

Speaking of enforcing Prohibition, we sent a delegation to Canada to ask them if they wouldn't prohibit liquor from being sent out of their country; but our committee is coming back empty handed—with the exception of just what little they can carry.

Canada told them: "If it's against your law to bring it in and then you can't stop it from coming in, how are we going to keep it from going out when it's not even against our law?"

We will have to get the League of Nations to get other nations to help us take care of our business.

Canada has a great system of dealing with their native population away up in the far North. You look on a map and all the country that is north of the real mainland of Canada, all those tremendous islands and gulfs up there, a white man is not allowed to fish, hunt or trap in. It's entirely for the support of the Indians that live up there. We never had thought of that.

I come up to Canada to see for the Boss if this country was worth taking over. Now I have no idea but what we could take them over and make a paying proposition out of them, for Canada now is supplying about everything we use in the way of raw material. But I hate to interrupt a friendship that has been going on now pretty steady since the battle of Lake Erie. You see, they don't owe us and they still think we are pretty good neighbors, so if we can just keep from annexing them, and keep from loaning them anything in the way of a government loan, why, we ought to be friends for years to come.

I was told to not drink the water in these tropical countries. I had never tried their beer with ham and eggs in the morning, but I am managing to gulp it down.

However, I have heard of worse hardship.

Been reading President Hoover's speech yesterday to the Puerto Ricans. The keynote of the speech was "the rapid increase in population of the islanders."

He was in a tough spot. He didn't know whether to compliment 'em on being a virile race, or to condemn 'em for making the usual American mistake of over-production. You see, there is not enough jobs there to take care of the increase, so what he tactfully wanted to impart to them was to control themselves till industry was on a par with affection.

He finally departed for the Virgin Islands where he hoped conditions would be better regulated.

The President didn't think much of the Virgin Islands. He thought we were bunkered on that deal. I think myself, we was perhaps influenced by the title.

Mr. Hoover hadent been sworn in over three-quarters of an hour till the desire to be President on the part of half of Mexico broke out. It looks like his being inaugurated kinder put the same idea into 34 generals' heads in Mexico. All you had to do to be President was to shoot the one that was, and that brought on some pretty fancy marksmanship. It was the old way of electing Presidents by the bullet, instead of the ballot.

Now in Mexico boys are taught "If my ammunition holds out, and I can get them before they get me, I not only can be President, but will." There was a fellow named Porfirio Diaz, a dictator, and he had a rule "The best way to keep a good man down is with bullets." Then Madero got in and he and his Vice-President come to an accidental death by murder. Then Huerta takes out a revolutionary permit. About this time Carranza died what is a natural death in Mexico, he was shot, practically totally. So Huerta was supposed to be provisional President—that is President until he was shot. Then Obregón comes in by election, something unheard of until then.

In Mexico it's just a question of whether he will be shot before he becomes President or after.

I was in Mexico City the other day when they had just thrown a bomb at General Obregón's* car. He will be Mexico's next President. He told us it cost him over a thousand dollars to send messages thanking people who had wired him, congratulating him on his successful escape.

He said: "It would have been cheaper if they had hit me. I couldn't afford to be missed again."

---

*Alvaro Obregón, president of Mexico [1920–1924]; reelected 1928, but assassinated before taking office.

Here in Mexico City, I was up and paid a call on our friend, Mr. Estrada, their Secretary of State today, and he got out a wonderful bottle and gave me a swig of what he called Mexican Hospitality.

It was Tequila. Then he asked me how I liked Mexico. Why, with one more swig of that, a person would even be fond of Siberia.

I brag on Mexico. I'm always blowin' about Mexico. I like Mexico. I like the Mexicans. Folks say: "Why, Will, you know that Mexico is run all wrong!"

Well, that don't make any difference to me. It's their country. Let 'em run it like they want to.

Just been reading about this fellow Augusto Sandino* down in Nicaragua. As to whether he was a George Washington, or a Jesse James, that's for his own people to judge.

But there is one thing that he and I agree on, and that was that American armed forces had no right down there.

The government says that the Marines were sent to Nicaragua to supervise an election and have to stay until it's held, which is next October.

In the meantime the Marines are doing all they can to see that there are fewer votes to supervise, and Sandino is doing all he can to see that there are fewer Marines to supervise.

It looks like Washington is so busy trying to make Nicaraguan elections pure like ours.

Say, what right have our Marines got settling an election in Nicaragua? I thought even at home, our Army and Navy was supposed to never enter politics.

Evidently our Army and Navy have to go to Central America to get into politics.

Nicaragua voted the other day not to have us supervise their election, but that's not official as we didn't supervise that vote.

Nicaragua and some Caribbean islands want to put a tariff on imported Marines.

---

*Augusto C. Sandino, Nicaraguan revolutionary who waged guerrilla warfare against occupying U.S Marines; assassinated 1934.

We mean well; we don't go anywhere to put it over on anybody, and we don't go into wars to get anything out of 'em; we go with the best intentions in the world. But we get into more things for less reasons than any nation in the world.

Not long ago Nicaragua was having trouble; they just wanted to have a good time among themselves and put on a little civil war and just use home talent. They just wanted to have a little shooting and use each other as targets. Do you think they could have a little war? No sir! Before they could fire the opening overture, we was right there.

Tomorrow is Pan-American Day. We are celebrating by rushing two cruisers to Nicaragua.

Everybody is excited over who will win the election. Why, the side with the most machine guns will win it.

There's no doubt that Cuba's run cockeyed, but what country ain't?

Cuba, it's their country. It's their sugar. Take the sugar out of Cuba and we would no more be interested in their troubles than we would in a revolution among the Zulus.

This President of Cuba has been in now two weeks. One more week and he will be retired by the Cuban Constitution for "Long Service to his Country."

This fellow in Cuba, he hasn't got many votes with him, but he has some of the best marksmen in Cuba.

The minute there is any trouble in any Latin American country, that should be the tip right there for us to crawl in a hole and not even be allowed to poke our head out till it was all over, for as sure as we could see it, we would either be in it or offering advice. We can't help it, it's just second nature with us. We mean well, but the better we mean, the worse we get in.

Another thing about all this trouble in Cuba, Bolivia, Paraguay, and all those is that folks forget that a Latin American country must have so much revolution and war anyhow. They don't look on a revolution as being such a terrible thing like we do. They are a people that don't get much excitement and a good revolution is a sort of relaxation for 'em.

We stood while twenty-one nations played their national anthems. The conference is already a standing and musical success.

I have one suggestion to offer for international good-will, that is have an international anthem that goes for everybody when it is played. Make it short and it will please every nation. Some of these anthems are longer than their countries' records. I propose Irving Berlin as its composer.

When you have stood in the tropical sun for twenty-one airs, you are about ready to vote for your nation to annex the other twenty.

Yours, groggy from martial music.

Somebody at the Havana conference Saturday brought up the question of revolutions, which, when and how to treat 'em. The delegates want to vote to make revolutions unlawful. That is, while they are in power, but when they are out, they want to have them declared legal again.

It's rather embarrassing, for all the delegates are there by grace of a revolution at some time.

You give Ecuador England's navy and right away Ecuador's ambassador would be seated next to the President at official functions.

You know, us up home, we just can't understand Latin politics. Do you know that the only time they ever get to cheer in some of those countries is when one side overthrows the other—and then they got to cheer mighty fast.

I am down here in the Argentine, in Buenos Aires, to be exact.

Like all countries, the President is just in from day to day. He may be on the same plane with me going out.

The Argentine, why, the Englishmen have got this country tied up tighter than Senator Borah has his home state of Idaho.

USSR, COMMUNISM

To get any kind of idea of Russia, everything in the world we do, every viewpoint we have, is entirely different in Russia.

I was surprised they didn't walk on their hands instead of their feet, just to be different from Capitalistic nations.

You heard of equality of sex in Russia? That's not so. The women are doing the work. They are digging the subway.

You know, you have to work in Russia, or you don't eat.

That's one thing about America. We don't give everybody a job, but everybody's certainly got a car.

The main question everybody asks me about Russia is—are they happy? It's awful hard to look at a person and tell just how happy they are. We looked at 'em at hundreds of stations crossing on the Trans-Siberian Railway. They just be kind of standing at the stations with a dull, blank expression on their faces—no joy, no smile.

But I've sat in the gallery of the Senate in Washington, and I've seen the same dull, blank expression on their faces.

I bet you, if I had met Trotsky, and had had a chat with him, I would have found him a very interesting and human fellow, for I have never yet met a man that I didn't like.

When you meet people, no matter what opinion you might have formed about them beforehand, why, after you meet them and see their angle and their personality, why, you can see a lot of good in them.

Russia is a country that looks like it was invented for arguments' sake. Four years sitting at Cabinet meetings wouldn't muddle up your mind as much as one trip to Russia.

We Americans do something for every fool thing in the world. One time, in New York, I played a benefit to get a Statue of Liberty for Russia.

Now can you imagine Russia with a Statue of Liberty?

Vodka is the only drink where you drink and try to grit your teeth at the same time. It gives the most immediate results of any libation ever concocted. By the time it reaches your Adam's apple, it has acted.

The Trans-Siberian Railway is the longest railroad in the world. Somebody said to me—of course you didn't get to see if it was double tracked, or not.

I said, no! I didn't get to see if there was a double track or not, but we kept passing trains at full speed going in the opposite direction and if there wasn't two tracks, there sure was some awful good railroading done there.

You know, those Russian rascals, along with all their cuckoo stuff, have got some mighty good ideas. If just part of 'em work out they are going to be mighty hard to get along. Just look at the millions of us here that haven't done a thing today to help the country, or that helps anybody.

Russia's liable, if it does just even half way work out, to have us winging on our foreign trade.

They start at the cradle with kids in Russia. Political propaganda starts with their ABC's.

The funny part about these American visitors you meet in Russia, they are all so nice and friendly and enthusiastic about Communism, and believe in it away over our form of government—BUT they all go back home.

It just looks to me that if Communism is such a happy family affair, why is it that no American Communist wants to stay where it is practiced?

A lot of friends had said to me: "Oh, you will get many a laugh out of Russia. I would like to be with you up there."

Funny? Say, I was just about the saddest looking thing you ever saw. I had seen pictures of long trains wending their way along the Trans-Siberian Railway, hauling heavy loads of human freight, when nobody had a return ticket but the conductor. So if I thought of an alleged wisecrack, it was immediately stifled before reaching even the thorax.

Talk about some of our states guarding what their schoolbooks contain—why, these children in Russia never get a chance to read anything only about how terrible everything is but Communism.

They say Russia is supposed, by their law, to be run by everybody.
    Well, it looks it.

Communism will never get anywhere till they get that basic idea of propaganda out of their head and replace it with some work. If they plowed as much as they propagandered, why, they would be richer than the Principality of Monaco.

The Bolsheviks have made everybody in Russia serious, but it's taken a gun to keep 'em from laughing.

The trouble is the Communists got their theories out of a book by that guy Marx. He was like one of those efficiency experts; he could explain to you how you could save a million dollars, and he couldn't save enough himself to eat on.

It seems the whole idea of Communism, or whatever they want to call it, is based on propaganda and blood. Their whole life and thought is to convince somebody else.

It looks to me like if a thing is so good, and is working fine for you, you would kind of want to keep it to yourself. I would be afraid to let anybody in on it.

In Moscow I attended a writers' convention.

You talk about everybody being equal. There is a guy over there named Maxim Gorki, that has sold 19 million copies of his books in the last five years. His income last year, they said, was seven million rubles. That guy has made all of that just writing about how terrible the rich are.

Here I was, sitting in this Russian airplane. What was a bonehead like me breezing off into Russia for?

I could understand a man flying out of Russia, but not in there.

GERMANY, HITLER

On his tour of 1906, Will Rogers appeared at Berlin's Wintergarten Theater. "W. Rogers (with assistant and horse)" was booked from April 1 to April 30. As can be imagined, his unusual routine with the lariat delighted the Germans. It was like no other act they had ever seen. This man on the stage could perform miracles with his rope. How did he do it?

Will was pleased with the reception he received. At one performance the audience just would not let him leave the stage. They applauded again and again. Will looked around for some special effect for an appropriate closing. There, in the wings, was a fine target for his seemingly unerring rope. It was the mandatory fireman, his sole duty to stand by in case of fire. He was dressed in a most impressive, shiny uniform, each button sparkling. Will swung the rope over his head and the loop sailed through the air, halfway across the stage and into the wings. The audience could not see what it was this American cowboy, Rogers, had caught. Then a laughing Will pulled the startled

fireman on stage. There he stood, his arms pinned to his sides, embarrassed. But instead of the laughter and applause Will had expected,
there was a gasp in the now-silent theater. Will had committed the
heinous crime of *lèse majesté*.

Will found himself arrested for "insulting" Kaiser Wilhelm by holding his civil servant up to public ridicule. After lengthy negotiations,
there were profound and profuse apologies all around and Will promised never again to rope a civil servant—at least not in Germany.

In January 1932, Will was on a solo trip around the world. In
London he began making arrangements to interview Germany's budding despot, Adolf Hitler, who was not yet chancellor:

> Say, this guy Hitler has grabbed off the spotlight from all
> the dictators. He is a Dictator to end all Dictators. When
> I was in Europe a year ago this last January, I made ar-
> rangements from London to go to Munich to see this Hitler
> for an interview, then some newspaper guys talked me out
> of it, saying, "Why, he is only a flash in the pan. Before
> you get your interview published he will be through."
>
> Doggone it, I wish now I had gone. I would like to see
> what kind of a bird he is. I don't know but what I will prance
> over yet and take a look at him. But he is so big now I guess
> I couldn't get an interview. If I did I would sure make it a
> nice one (all in his favor) till I got out of Germany, anyhow.
> For that old boy runs that country like a warden.

Been reading a lot lately about that guy Hitler, in Germany, that's
getting quite a following. He advocates forgetting everything connected
with the peace treaty and starting all over new.

And that is about what will happen in a few years. *

Germany, this morning in the papers, wants everybody to disarm,
saying that they disarmed.

Yes, but look what it cost to disarm 'em!

Germany has banned that splendid film *All Quiet on the Western
Front*, on account of it showing Germany losing the war.

---

*Syndicated daily column, September 29, 1930.

I guess they are going to take it back and make it with a different finish.

Do you know what inflation is? Well, these days it takes two and a half tons of German Marks to buy a stein of beer in Berlin. Before the war you could have bought two and a half tons of beer for a mark.

France says they are "willing to disarm," but they didn't say so till Germany went home from the disarmament conference and announced they were starting to build some more of those vest pocket battleships.

The papers say that farm prices have advanced 17 percent in the last month.
    Now that's better news than a speech on "good relations" by Mussolini and Hitler combined.

Of course we know our government is costing us more than it's worth, but do you know of any cheaper government that's running around? If you do, they sell you a ticket there anytime.
    Now you can try Russia. There's no income tax in Russia, but there's no income. Now Hitler, he ain't got no sales tax—but he ain't selling anything. Mussolini, you don't have to pay a poll tax to vote in Italy, but nobody votes.

Papers all state Hitler is trying to copy Mussolini. Looks to me it's the Ku Klux Klan that he is copying. He don't want to be emperor—he wants to be Kleagle.

Champion fliers from all over the world are gathering in here. This is the one official meet of the year! There is a German flier coming, his name is Ernst Udet, and he can do more crazy things in the air than Hitler can do on the ground.

ITALY, MUSSOLINI

Mussoliniland sure looks like pie and cake after coming out of India and China and Mesopotamia. They call this old boy a dictator, but he has done more with less to work on than any man in the world.

Now you take Mussolini. Lots of 'em knock him and say that's a terrible form of government. But you wait till he passes out and see what happens to that country.

Talk about Russia with her Five-Year Plan. Mussolini just saw their five years and raised 'em fifty-five. Italy is now with a Sixty-Year Plan.

Smart guy, that Mussolini. He laid out a plan where if it proved at the end that it wouldn't work, they couldn't find him.

That Mussolini is a card. Yesterday he interviewed ninety-two mothers with a gross total of 1,288 children, which divides out to about fourteen head per each. While our great slogan for the perpetuation of the civilization was "a car in every garage!" Mussolini's was "a baby in every arm, and more if you can carry 'em!" He knows no nation ever become great on garages.

These other dictators think they are doing some "dictating" when they announce a budget quota. But when you start laying out a maternity quota for the women, then you are really in the dictating business.

There is no war going on at the present time. But there is an awful lot of folks working on arranging wars. Mussolini sent his army down into Africa for a training trip hoping to annex some loose territory in route. That's your next war.

England was strongly remonstrating with Italy and told them the text in the Bible which reads: "Thou shalt not covet thy neighbor's territory, nor thy neighbor's prospective oil wells, nor thy neighbor's natural resources!"

Mussolini broke out laughing and asked England's representative, "Where was that verse and chapter when you boys was coveting India, South Africa, Hong Kong and all points east and west?"

The whole of Rome seems to have been built, painted and decorated by one man; that was Michelangelo.

If you took everything out of Rome that was supposed to have been done by Michelangelo, Rome would be as bare of art as Los Angeles.

The Colosseum is a great old building. That's where the Romans held their games. You see, these Romans loved blood. What money is to an American, blood was to a Roman. A Roman was never so happy as when he saw somebody bleed.

Some people over home say a dictator is no good; yet every successful line of business is run by a dictator. Just look at industry or your political parties; how many men run them?

So everything is really done by dictatorship, if you just sum it up.

Dictator form of government is the greatest form of government there is—provided you have the right dictator.

Remember there is always this difference between us and Italy. In Italy Mussolini runs the country. But here the country runs the President.

GREAT BRITAIN, PRINCE OF WALES

Will Rogers traveled to Great Britain a number of times. Early in his career he appeared on the London stage as a silent act, simply performing his rope tricks with fellow Oklahoman Buck McKee riding the horse. The press appreciated his talent:

> Another new turn is that of Will Rogers, who is a genuine cowboy and an expert lassoist. This is one of those strange exotic entertainments like the Pelicans at the Hippodrome, which occasionally appear, and are very welcome on the Music Hall stage. The skill with which this man can make a bit of rope do his bidding is incredible; he can throw two lassoes at once, catching a horse with one and the rider with the other, and that, though the most difficult, is not the most showy of his tricks. *

In 1926, Will was back in Europe with his family. Director Carl Stearns Clancy and cameraman John LaMond were also along to film enough footage to produce a dozen travelogues.

Alone, Will even visited the Soviet Union for two weeks. It was a most work-filled summer "vacation." Returning to England, Will made the motion picture *Tip Toes*. Co-starring America's Dorothy Gish and Britain's Nelson "Bunch" Keyes, the film was directed by Herbert Wilcox.

And still there was no rest. Charles Cochran, the "British Ziegfeld," had his annual *Revue* at the London Pavilion. It seemed to falter, lacking a centerpiece around which the various acts could be presented. Cochran and Rogers had known each other for a long time, and Cochran now suggested that Will join the show. Will was hesitant.

The Times, May 24, 1906.

Since he had last appeared in London he had completely changed his act. Instead of displaying his skill with a lariat, he now just commented on current events. After all, these were English audiences, and he wondered whether his type of act could be effectively transplanted. The two men did not settle on a salary, as this was to be simply an experiment. Still, on his first night, July 19, Will Rogers was quite concerned. Wrote *The Times* of London:

> Mr. Will Rogers, the American comedian and film actor, appeared on Monday night in Cochran's Revue at the London Pavilion. He is presenting each night for a season of at least six weeks, the "turn" that has earned him such popularity in America. He walks on to the stage in an ordinary, shabby suit—and just talks. At the first performance on Monday night, he talked a little too much, but that mistake can be rectified. At the beginning Mr. Rogers seemed a little timid. He need not have been. Humour of the kind in which he delights is international, and in a very few days he will be attracting all London to the Pavilion. *

And in the July 25, 1926, Sunday edition of *The Times*, James Agate, London's foremost critic, was moved to state:

> Mr. Rogers frankly and generously accepted our recognition of him as an exceptional person, belonging to an exceptional race . . . A superior power has seen fit to fling into the world, for once a truly fine specimen, fine in body, fine in soul, fine in intellect . . . America's Prime Minister of Mirth enchanted in both matter and manner.

Will Rogers was accepted in London; Charles Cochran's *Revue* was doing very well. When it was time for Will to return to America and the obligation of a fully booked lecture tour, Charles Cochran handed Will a blank, signed check, suggesting that he fill in the amount he though appropriate. Will Rogers tore up the check.

The Times, July 21, 1926.

Just between you and me, Calvin, this Prince of Wales [Edward] don't care any more about being King than you would going back to being Vice-President again.*

Nations have got a funny sense of humor, ain't they? English royalty waited till they had all married Germans, then they went to war with 'em. Germans all married Russians, then they fought.

Some nations go to war for gold, some nations for territory, some to make the whole world free for Democracy. But if you want to match a war with England, you just show them an oil well.

There is one thing about Englishmen, they won't fix anything till it's just about totally ruined. You couldn't get the English to fix anything at the start. No! They like to sit and watch it grow worse.
    Then, when it just looks like the whole thing has gone up Salt Creek, why, the English jump in and rescue it.

What is tradition? It's the thing we laugh at the English for having and we beat them practicing it.

You know we have always used the Court of St. James as a kind of springboard to dive from the ambassadorship into the Secretary of Stateship, and from there to oblivion.

In England, every time a problem comes up and is voted on in the House of Commons, why, if the side the Prime Minister is on loses, that means that the people have lost confidence in him, and losing confidence in a public official over there means he is not with you long.
    Imagine what would have happened if such a procedure had been in effect over here.

In the House of Lords, they have an outsider come in there every day and pray for them. One man couldn't do enough praying for them. But it can't just be an ordinary preacher. He must be an Archbishop.

---

*Weekly article, July 24, 1926.

You have to have had a lot of praying experience to know just what their wants and needs are.

The King is in Scotland, shooting at a grouse; Harry Lauder and some Scotchmen are helping to drive him up to the gun. The Duke of York is gone to Australia. Lady Astor has gone to America, and I have nowhere to eat now. Most everybody is out of London.

Oh, yes, the Prince of Wales is visiting England now.

Deer season opened in Scotland for all those who can't hit grouse.

Last summer I was in England and got stepped on in Hyde Park, when Mr. Oswald Mosley had his fascist Black Shirts there. It showed me that England, like America, can never have Communism, Fascism, or nudism, or any other "ism."

Here were those Black Shirts, and about a hundred yards away was the Communists, and in between was half of London laughing at both of them.

All went home satisfied. They all had had their say, and after all, nobody wants his cause near as bad as he just wants to talk about his cause.

I ain't going to tell you any jokes about this English Prince falling off his horse. I fall just as much; of course, my falls don't attract as much attention, but they hurt just as much.

The Prince of Wales, over in England, fell off his horse again today. That's got so it isn't news anymore. If he stayed on, that would be news.

England is all worked up over what to do as they are afraid he will be hurt. I should suggest they have men follow him along on foot with a net and catch him each time as he falls.

You know about the Prince of Wales falling off his horse. Never saw a picture of him falling unless the horse was falling too. Can't see any humor in that.

What are you going to do when your horse falls? Go down with him, or stay up in the air until he comes back up under you?

Buckingham Palace has the iron railings all wore off with the noses of Americans trying to peep through the cracks of the bars.

The night of the crash, August 15–16, 1935. Alaska's Walakpa Lagoon, eleven miles from Barrow; a mass of twisted metal and splintered wood in two feet of water is all that remains of the plane Wiley Post assembled from unrelated parts. (Courtesy The Alaskan Historical Aircraft Society, Anchorage)

August 18, 1935. In New York City's Pennsylvania Railroad Station, Will, Jr., Mrs. Betty Rogers, Jimmy, Mary, and Jesse Jones on their way to California for funeral services. (Courtesy National Archives)

IRELAND

Ireland is another pet of mine. If it's run cockeyed, that don't make any difference to me. I like it; and they run it.

If I was England, I would give Ireland "Home Rule," but reserve the motion picture rights.

These Irish, you got to watch 'em. Why, there was a few of 'em sneaked into Oklahoma and got mixed up with the Rogerses and the Cherokees, and I am a sort of an offshoot—an Irish Indian.

I have been in twenty countries and the only one where American tourists are welcome whole-heartedly by everyone is Ireland. And the funny part is, there is more to see there than in all others put together. They don't owe us and they don't hate us.

The lakes of Killarney is where Switzerland got their ideas of lakes. Americans, go where you are welcome! Ireland is a friend to everybody, even England.

FRANCE

What is the matter with the French? I will tell you what is the matter with them. They won't pay their taxes!

They have what they call an income tax, but it's practically voluntary.

France is having some excitement. Their changing Prime Ministers every few hours has been the prize governmental circus trick of Europe.

This guy Aristide Briand that's in this minute has been Prime Minister ten times.

I arrived in Paris late at night. The next day we had Briand as Premier for breakfast; Herriot was Premier for lunch; Poincaré for dinner; and I woke up the next morning and Briand was back in again. This is not a government; it's an old-fashioned movie, where they flash on the screen: "Two minutes please, while we change Premiers."

I have had a date to interview every one of them, but they were thrown out before the interview time come due.

Look at the Frenchmen! They look to us like they do everything cockeyed. Their House of Deputies looks like a Keystone Comedy Company, yet with all their excitement they have made the finest recovery from the war.

The staid old Britishers that we think does everything just about right, why, he is having his toughest sledding right now.

Americans are coming to France nowadays to look, and France can't find any way to keep 'em from looking without paying.

I suggest that they put in hot dog stands. Coney Island got rich on 'em out of the same kind of people.

American tourists are still coming by the thousands and bragging about where they come from. Sometimes I think France really has been too lenient with them.

Why don't we send Marines to Cherbourg, France? They was throwing rocks at us over there all last summer, and we never said a word.

We shouldn't have said a word. If anybody goes anywhere they ain't wanted, let 'em get hit.

At the Olympic Games, the man that is in laying out the cottages, or who will be next to who, says you learn a lot about what the League of Nations is up against.

For instance they found that they couldn't put France and Italy on the same hill. Then they asked France who they wanted to be near, and France said Germany. Well, that was fine. Then when the Germans got here they asked them, and the Germans said they didn't want to be near France.

The French couldn't hate us any more unless we helped 'em out in another war.

SWITZERLAND

I had always heard a lot about Switzerland. Every time we read a headline in the papers about universal peace, or "War is expected to break out in the Balkans tomorrow afternoon," why, the dateline is always Switzerland. It's the rumor factory of the world.

Switzerland knew something when they settled there, too. They said to themselves, "The best thing about a war is to keep out of it." But they also figured that there is a lot of jack in them, if you are placed right. So they commenced to figuring, "Where can a fellow go to be near enough to see a war but still not be in it?" So they picked out the spot they have now, and all they had to do was to get the hotels ready.

You would think it would be dull between wars, but that is where you are wrong. Switzerland has really what is an all the year round business. The minute a war was over, why, they would hold what they call a "Peace Conference" to prevent other wars.

You see, there really are more conferences than there is wars, because sometimes it takes two or three conferences before they can get a war started.

SPAIN

In Spain they have Primo de Rivera, the Amateur Dictator. He is a kind of second company of Mussolini. Kinging there is not what you would call a steady job.

I guess that the King of Spain will be buying a ranch in Canada or Mexico or some place. Spain just pulled off a bloodless revolution.

You know those bloodless revolutions are the ones that hurt the King business more than a fighting one does. A King can stand people's fighting, but he can't last long if people are thinking.

Spanish is the language. This old gag of having the children take up French, because it's fashionable, is the baloney! You don't see anybody in France but Americans, so you don't get a chance to try out your French anyway.

Spain is so far off to herself that she can't afford to pay transportation to any country she could lick.

PHILIPPINES

We will drag along with you folks in the Philippines on the pretext that we are protecting you, and someday we will get in a war over you. And if we ever do, we will lose you before lunch. Japan can be in there and have a crop planted before we could get a fleet across that ocean. Any nation that thinks they can go six thousand miles away from home and fight somebody is crazy.

Now if we will just give the Philippines their full freedom and get out of there!

Of course Japan might take it, but she would anyhow. A dog can protect only the bones that are right in front of him, he can't have one away off to itself in front of another hungry dog and expect to be able to hold it.

Pat Hurley, our Secretary of War in Mr. Hoover's cabinet, had been away over in the Philippines. The President said to him: "Pat, along with about 876 other difficulties I am having, why, the Philippines are perspiring to independence. Will you go over there and see if it's Communist propaganda, or just Democratic influence? You know, it's hard to tell nowadays which causes me the most devilment, the Russians or the Democrats."

I asked Pat if there is much Russian propaganda in the Far East. He said: "Much more than there is food."

President Coolidge refuses to give the Philippines their complete independence. I am with Mr. Coolidge. Why should the Philippines have more than we do?

I did want to meet Aguinaldo, that Filipino revolutionary leader. I have always been an admirer of that old hombre. We used to call him a bandit. Any man is a bandit if he is fighting opposite you and licking you most of the time; but if you are fighting against him, why, that's patriotism!

The difference between a bandit and a patriot is a good press agent.

CHINA, MANCHURIA, JAPAN

It never mattered to us who was President of China anyway, because we couldn't pronounce his name, whoever he was.

We will stop these Chinese from fighting among each other, if we have to kill them to do it.

China has been awful nice to us in the past; they have let us use their home grounds to send our Marines to when we didn't have any other war on at the time. Why, there has been times that if it hadn't been for China allowing us to go in and shoot at them, we wouldn't have had a soul in the world to shoot at.

Every nation in the world have their own land, and every other nation recognizes it—except China. Everybody looks on theirs as public domain.

England has been awful nice to China and helped 'em run their business even more than we have, if that is possible. There is one town called Shanghai that the Chinese were running so un-English that the English had to go right in and go to the trouble of taking over the whole thing, and now a Chinaman has to come in on a passport. English gunboats are so far up the Chinese rivers that it takes Chinese guides to bring 'em back down.

There is five hundred million Chinese and they are getting more civilized all the time. They are not only learning how to use opium from us, but they are learning how to sell it to us.

"The Chinese Problem!" We are always hearing about the Chinese Problem. To the Chinese it's no problem. We didn't find that they had a problem till we found that they had some money to buy something we had.
Then we found that they had some things to sell cheaper than the rest of the world, so that, naturally, made them a problem.

China learned us about two-thirds of all the useful things we do, and now they want to have a civil war. Now we had one and nobody butted in and told us we couldn't have one. They let us go ahead and fight. China didn't send gunboats up our Mississippi River to protect their laundries at Memphis or St. Louis.

Let me tell you about a Chinese dinner: Lots of folks have had Chinese dinners, but this orgy of bamboo shoots I was at started about 9:30 P.M. At 1:30 in the A.M. when we shoved away from the table, there was at least ten Chinese still bringing in arms loaded with more unnameable provender.
I wouldn't ask what all these dishes were, for I wanted to enjoy them, but I do know that we had Bird's-Nest soup. I was hoping that the old Blue Jay that had occupied the nest was part sanitary, anyhow.
Then, along in the middle of dinner, they had lunch.

There is one thing that handicaps the Chinese. Take one separate, and he is smart, alert, able, clever and can get things done. But let him be joined by another Chinese and their efficiency drops 50 percent.

Now there is China, called a Republic. Yet China is so big that nine-tenths of her people never found out that all these wonderful benefits that they are enjoying are called Liberty.

Well, there is quite a little in the papers about some Chinese bandits holding foreigners for ransom. Those heathen Chinese should not be allowed to have bandits in their country. If you let 'em keep on, the first thing you know they will have pickpockets and taxi robbers over there.

I bet you England wouldn't stand for them annoying one of their citizens. They would take their oil land away from them. And if they didn't have any, they would make 'em go out and get some.

If a bank fails in China, they behead the men at the top of it that are responsible. If one fails over here, we write the men up in the magazines, as how "they started poor, worked hard, took advantage of their opportunities (and depositors)."

If we beheaded all of our that were responsible for failures, we wouldn't have enough people left to bury the heads.

A Chinese wants to get a little piece of land, live on it, die on it, and be let alone. He wants to trade you; he don't want to fight you.

Now a Japanese wants to die for his country, but the Chinese, he ain't going to let patriotism run away with his life. He wants to live; he loves life, he enjoys it. Life ain't serious with him like it is with the Japanese. The Japanese feel they were put on earth for a purpose, but the Chinese, he feels he was put here by mistake.

Well, here I am in Nippon. I have to start right away explaining the meaning of things. "Nippon" means "Sun." I have had very little trouble with the language. 'Course I don't know all the words yet, but I can carry on a pretty fair conversation with the three words I have: Nippon, Banzai, and then they got a word "Ohio" which means Hello, or Good Morning.

Over home, Ohio means the difference between being elected President and being just another ex-candidate.

No matter what you do in Japan, you must first have tea; then, after you do what you was going to do, you have tea again.

Well, Japan won't have her world supremacy in business long. I saw a lot of golf courses being put in. That's the beginning of a nation's decline. When we traded a spade for a putter that's the way we started in the red.

An English capitalist with me on this trip to the orient was telling me about the Japanese manufacturing so many different things now, even in the chemical and medicine business. He seemed to think that there was nothing that they wasn't doing, and doing pretty good.

Well, what can you do about it? You got to give 'em credit. We used to do it. Now we can't, so we got no right to holler.

Don't ever call a Japanese a "Jap." This "Jap" business is a serious matter with 'em. The word "Jap" is short and they are very sensitive about their size, anyhow, and "Jap" makes 'em sound shorter still.

And it's the same with a Chinaman, too. Don't go calling him a Chinaman; he is always a Chinese! never a Chinaman. Course, you don't have to worry about the Chinese, for they have no navy and don't go to conferences. So you don't have to worry whether they are proud, or not.

Japan has got two parties, too. I don't remember their names any more than they could remember ours. But they keep things in a turmoil, just like ours.

Japan has had three wars, all off from her own country, claiming she had to do it for protection. That would be like us saying we had to take Canada to protect us against England.

Why don't they just up and say: "We are naturally ambitious and we are going in and get it?"

The Japanese run their wars just like they do their trains—right on time. All their soldiers are trained between wars, not after one starts.

You see, we have been lucky that way; all of our wars have waited on us till we could get ready. But these Japanese figure that they may have one where the enemy won't wait. So when it is booked all the preliminaries have already been arranged; each soldier knows not only where he is to go, but knows practically who he is to shoot.

The disarmament conference was held up for an hour while we all went to the League of Nations meeting to demand of Japan that she quit shooting while the opening session was in conference.

Will Rogers viewed the militant Japanese of the thirties with fore-boding. He had observed them at close range at so-called disarmament conferences, and he had seen them at war on the Chinese mainland. A most prophetic reference came on a round-the-world trip with Betty and their two sons, Will, Jr., and Jim. Their first stop was Hawaii. At the same time, President Franklin D. Roosevelt was vacationing on Oahu and he invited Will and his family to dinner.

Little has been reported of what was discussed by the two men, both so well informed on domestic and world politics. Will must have mentioned that he and his family would visit Japan. Will's daily squib of August 12, 1934, reported:

> The President told me: "Will, don't jump on Japan. Just keep them from jumping on us!"

The Japanese attack on Pearl Harbor was still over seven years away.

LEAGUE OF NATIONS

The League of Nations was a great thing to make the little fellow behave, but when the big fellows want to get away with anything, it has no more power than a Senate investigating committee.

The League of Nations, to perpetuate peace, is in session. On account of Spain not being in the last war, they won't let her in. If you want to help make peace, you have to fight for it.

Well, I have been prowling around over the earth for three months. I have found more countries than the League of Nations. I have located a lot of those little ones President Wilson made out of big ones. I have also been looking for a friend of America, but I just have to give up and report failure.

Poor old League of Nations, on account of her having no policemen, nobody was going to pay much attention to her.

The League of Nations didn't need guns to make the League a real success. An economic boycott against any nation by all the others would have done the trick.

But nations will give up their lives (even cheer about it). They will give up their money in order to give up their lives, but ask one to give up their trade to prevent war, well, that has never been done.

MISCELLANEOUS

It is open season now in Europe for grouse and Americans.
They shoot the grouse and put them out of their miseries.

The thing that really makes any two nations a little more sympathetic towards each other is the fact that they may be able to use each other.

I looked for combinations that were friendly toward each other and have yet to find one—unless it was Latvia up toward the Baltic Sea and Madagascar down on the Indian Ocean. They have no particular grievance against each other, but they will have as soon as they find out where each other are.

Portugal is having a revolution. Good joke on us. We haven't got enough Marines to cover that one.

Now about this Iraq. . . . I thought the League of Nations was to prevent war.
Yes, and you thought the 18th Amendment was to prevent drinking.

Monaco is the only place I have been where everything is running fine. There is no government, there is nothing to interfere with anything or anybody; just that little old wheel rolling for them all the time.

Finland sort of used to be under Russia, for about a hundred years. I don't mean "sort of under Russia," because when you're under Russia, you ain't "sort of"—you're just under.
Anyhow, the Czar had a palace in Helsingfors where he could come and stay, if he wanted to. It was kind of like England's King. He could go to Ireland. He could, but he'd better not.

Poor little Gandhi, he is becoming discouraged with the London conference. He says they only talk.
I wonder if he thought a nation got independence over a conference table and not over a gun barrel? Where would we have been if George Washington had conferred instead of confiscated?

Chapter X

PHILOSOPHY

*N*ationally syndicated scribe Ed Sullivan wrote a column called "Broadway." On Tuesday, October 25, 1932, under the heading of "Celebrities," he began an attack:

> WILL ROGERS, the gum-chewer, who made good in polite society . . . Here was one of the earlier Masters of Ceremonies . . . You recall him from the days at the New Amsterdam . . . When he twirled his lariat, chewed gum and said: "All I know is what I read in the papers" . . . From that he passed on to introductions of celebrities in the Ziegfeld audiences . . . Personally I never liked his type of work . . . Too much bite and bitterness in his observations . . . To suit me . . . But I understand he's one of the great minds of the country . . . And who am I to argue such a point? . . . Yet it seems to me that there was a fellow named Mark Twain . . . Who got laughs without sinking the barb . . . That is real humor . . . Rogers never has been able to discriminate between wit and personalities . . . There is a vast gulf between . . . Whenever I watch Rogers work, I've always thought . . . I could smell flesh burning from a branding iron . . . An old cowboy custom.

When Will Rogers learned about this unprovoked disparagement, he was hurt. He was fully aware that there were people who did not like his type of humor; that was understandable. But to accuse him of intentionally hurting others . . . He felt he had to reply. On November 1, he began a letter:

MY DEAR ED:

That piece you wrote naturally hurt me. There is not a soul in public life that I "got it in for." No, Ed, that's where you got me wrong. My humor is not so hot, my philosophy don't philo, and my jokes are pre-war, but my good feeling toward mankind, politicians included, is 100 percent. Now, if I was, as you wrote, "searing everybody with a hot branding iron," I don't think I could have gone along this long. I couldn't hurt and insult every one I meet and still last. You know, I have been going a good while, Ed, kinder far beyond my alloted span. You only seem to go back to the Ziegfeld days to dig up my "vitrolic" remarks. Why, I started that back at Hammerstein's Victoria in 1905. I told my little jokes about the fathers of the present crop of politicians. All the present Roosevelts I have been intimate with for years. And young John Coolidge knows the admiration I have for his dad. Just in tonight's mail came the nicest letter from John D. Rockefeller, Sr., whom I often joshed.

I know that mine is not exactly the type of humor (if you can call it that) that has appealed to you younger boys who have Broadway at your feet. I couldn't come there and tell my jokes and have anybody laugh at them. But us country columnists—they don't expect much from us. I started this durn letter yesterday when the election results started coming in, and here it is, two nights later, so I've clean forgot what I was "sore" at you about, Ed, but whatever it was, up in the front end of the letter, I apologize. I will meet you on my next trip back there and insult you over some corned beef and cabbage at Dinty Moore's. The returns are just coming in from the Virgin Islands, Ed. Clark Gable is leading Hoover and Roosevelt, both.

WILL ROGERS

It should be noted that columnist Ed Sullivan reached the height of his fame some three decades later on a nationally televised Sunday-evening variety show. His contribution was as master of ceremonies, the function he had faulted Will Rogers for; and his sole active addition to the show was the introduction of celebrities from studio audiences. Imitation has always been the most authentic form of adulation.

As for Mr. Sullivan's statement, "I could smell flesh burning from a branding iron . . ." it can be noted that this particular reference to Will Rogers was not exactly written with compassionate love or unconstrained admiration. Mr. Sullivan, a highly competent journalist, was feared for the power he wielded. There is, however, no individual on record for ever fearing Will Rogers.

The historical fact is that Will Rogers loved people and that that love was returned. Yet what endeared him to others was unstudied, artless, just the natural acts of a caring individual. There may be cynics who might advance the thought that great stars often perform certain acts simply to gain publicity. In answer to such a charge, consider, as merely one example, the fire in Dromcolliher,* Ireland. Chances are that few, if any, Americans ever heard of it.

Will Rogers was in Europe that summer of 1926, traveling with his family. While he appeared at the London Pavilion, a tragedy took place at Dromcolliher, a village about thirty-six miles southwest of Limerick City, on the border of counties Limerick and Cork. Forty-seven villagers were burned to death, yet the inferno was only reported on page 12 of *The Times*. Most American papers did not even carry the basic facts of the story.

The fire occurred at a "cinematograph entertainment," as the newspaper called it—a very special occasion for the tiny community, when motion picture films would be shown. Because the village had no public hall, the films were to be presented in the only large site available—a roomy loft over a wooden garage building owned by a man named William Ford. The sole access to the space under the roof was by means of an ordinary ladder, which led through a trapdoor. A single electric line was strung from the garage below to provide the

---

*Also recorded as Drumcollogher.

power needed for the projector. About two hundred people, including many women and children, were packed into this room, which was poorly aired through two small, thinly barred windows. Illumination was provided by candlelight.

The program had just started when the highly flammable nitrate film lying on the projectionist's table burst into flames—either from a tipped candle or a careless cigarette smoker. The operator, Patrick Downing, a "skilled man from Cork," tried to smother the flames, but the fire was so fierce that it ignited other unprotected films lying on the table. In a moment the room was filled with flames and choking smoke.

> As the projecting machine was placed near the doorway, escape from the room would have been difficult. Only those near the door had a chance in the panic to get away in safety. Many women and children were trampled under foot and it was not long before a ladder which formed the only means of egress collapsed, leaving the people trapped within the loft. The room by this time was a mass of flames.*

Dromcolliher had no fire department, no infirmary service. Messages were sent by telephone to Limerick, and all through the night ambulances made their way between the disaster site and the County of Limerick hospital at Croom.

When Will Rogers heard about the tragedy, he immediately offered his services and flew to Dublin. A minute entry, well hidden in the interior of *The Times*, makes note of it under the heading of "A Relief Fund." "Mr. Will Rogers, the American comedian, has come to Dublin specially to appear this evening at a concert which has been organized at short notice on behalf of the fund . . ."

That is all it says; no pictures, no interviews, no great display of any personal sacrifice, just a simple statement of record, of the heartfelt impulse to help demonstrated by one human being toward others.

During the devastating Mississippi flood of 1927, Will Rogers paid his way on a flying, one-man tour to raise spirits and money.

Again, in 1931, he took time off for a whirlwind tour of fifty-seven

---

The Times, September 7, 1926.

cities in only seventeen days to assist a campaign for relief funds. Sufferers in the drought-stricken Dust Bowl of the mid- and southwest needed help. With Frank Hawkes as his pilot and "co-star," Will collected a quarter of a million dollars. Every dollar was turned over to the Red Cross. "Every cent we raise is going to the poor people who have been hit by the drought. There ain't going to be no deductions nor exceptions," Rogers said. He paid all his own expenses, and many times also those of Frank Hawkes. Texaco supplied Hawkes' services and the fuel and oil, and contributed to the fund. Assistant Secretary of the Navy David S. Ingalls supplied his personal official plane, a two-seater Curtiss Hell Diver biplane.

When Nicaragua's devastating earthquake of 1931 left thousands homeless, Will Rogers flew to Managua and raised much-needed funds for food and supplies. There was no publicity attached, nor sought. In gratitude, posthumously in 1939, Nicaragua issued a commemorative set of five stamps bearing Will's likeness.

Whenever he heard of a great need, Will would be among the first to help. Whether it was an old lady, penniless and in need of a set of teeth (Will wired $250), $1,000 for toys for the Detroit Free Press Christmas Fund, or $6,500 for a boys' summer camp sponsored by Eddie Cantor, there was always one stipulation: no one was to know where the money came from.

At the time of America's entry into World War I in 1917, Will assisted the Red Cross. He had personally seen that organization at work at the disasters he had rushed to aid, and he supported that institution for the rest of his life. When Will signed a new $75,000 contract for a series of radio broadcasts, he stipulated that the sum be divided evenly between the Red Cross and the Salvation Army; he never received a dollar for this work.

His admiration for the Red Cross is indicated by his summation:

> This Red Cross outdid themselves, feeding and housing and caring for as many as six hundred thousand. Lord, what a blessing an organization like that is. I would rather have originated the Red Cross than to have written the Constitution of the U.S.*

---

*Syndicated weekly article, June 19, 1927.

There still exist numerous accounts of Will's philanthropy, though most of those acts will probably remain forever unrecorded. But cancelled checks and letters of appreciation, from New York's Free Synagogue or a stranded circus, all bear witness to the man who could never see his fellow man suffer.

Visiting the veterans' hospital at Arrow Lake, California, Will entertained a ward of seriously wounded patients, telling them about an experience on the way from Los Angeles, when he had been stopped by a most officious motorcycle policeman for speeding. It was, as so often, a routine made up at the moment, and it had the men roaring with laughter. After the performance, when the commanding officer wanted to express his appreciation, he found Rogers in the corridor, crying; the sight of the maimed soldiers had so affected him.

Rogers always had money in his pocket, just to give it away. Sometimes he gave away too much. Hal Mohr, two-time Oscar-winning director of cinematography and husband of Will Rogers' co-star Evelyn Venable, remembered an incident while going on location:

> We drove out to the Mojave Desert, and we stopped for breakfast, the entire motorcade stopped. Mojave was a rail junction with a large complement of hobos. As we stopped, Will wandered over to the freight yards, and there were a bunch of 'bos. And he just sat down with them and talked with these fellows for over an hour, while the whole motorcade waited to proceed on location. He got all the money he could from everybody and he distributed the money amongst those fellows and went on his merry way. He was that kind of fellow.

As an adult, Will Rogers never belonged to a church, nor did he join any congregation. His children attended Beverly Hills's Community Church, which Will and Betty helped found. He certainly was a believer, though he made no ostentatious declaration of it. Will Rogers lived his religion.

Perhaps Senator Alben Barkley summed up best what Will Rogers' beliefs were: "He gave of his wealth, he gave of his time, he gave of his talents, he gave of his great heart to make America a better place in which to live and he carried to every nation which he visited that same spirit of nobility and of comradeship, which made those who could not speak his language understand his heart and appreciate his soul."

PERSONAL

Every gag I tell must be based on truth. No matter how much I may exaggerate it, it must have a certain amount of truth.

I'm just an old country boy in a big town, trying to get along. I've been eating pretty regular and the reason I have is because I've stayed an old country boy.

I am an awful windy old talker and my wife swears I bore more people than I entertain. She says I can do more talking away from home, and less at home than anybody, for then I bog down and get my nose in a paper.

I do lots of paper reading. If I had put all my paper reading into books, I might have been pretty well read, but this book thing I'm so far behind there is no use trying to catch up now.

I was born on election day, but never was able to get elected to anything. I am going to jump out someday and be indefinite enough about everything and they will call me a politician; then run on a platform of question marks, and be elected unanimously, then reach into the Treasury and bring back my district a new bridge, or tunnel, or dam, and I will be a statesman.

The great trouble in writing for the papers is that you are so apt to hit on some subject that does not appeal to a certain class of people. For instance, if I write a learned article on chewing gum, I find that I lose my clientele of readers who are toothless. Then when I write on just strictly politics, I find that the honest people are not interested. Then, if I write solely on some presidential candidate, I find that there are so many of them that few know the one I am writing about.

When I write an article on bathing beaches, I find that I lose the interest of most of my readers what are not interested in bathing, either tub or beach. When I write an editorial for highbrows, I find that a highbrow is a man who wouldn't read anything that was not written by himself.

If we write or say something that agrees with you, why, then we become quite a smart guy in your estimation. But if we should write or say something that don't agree with your idea of the same subject, then we become a "menace" and should be eliminated from the public print. Now you will say: "Well, what did you pop off when you didn't know what you was talking about?"

Well, if you're going to stop that, why, America would be speechless. There is not any of us real sure of what we are yapping about.

No, I don't think I ever hurt any man's feelings by my little gags. I know I never willfully did it. When I have to do that to make a living, I will quit.

I may not have always said just what they would have liked me to say, but they knew it was meant in good nature.

I love a dog, he does nothing for political reasons.

I know nothing in the world about engines, that is, if they stopped this plane and raised the hood and a rabbit jumped out, I would just figure he belonged in there.

Well, I drag out the old blue serge, double-breasted suit that has fooled many a one, if you don't watch it too close, into thinking maybe it's a quarter-breed tuxedo. Course, the soft shirt and collar looks kinder negligee, but the black bow tie and the old blue serge looking black by lamplight, why, it looks within the requirements of "dress: formal."

I would choose to be brought up where I was brought up. But I bet you, there is a lot of things we did that I would know better than to do them again. If I was going to be brought up again, the first thing I would specialize in would be boxing. Then the next time around I would just go through life getting even with a few that kinder hung it on me then.

Well, you actors and politicians can have all the race horses and cigars and perfumes named after you, but I got a clipping from down in South Carolina that was mighty gratifying to me.

Will Rogers, an old pot hound, was voted the best hunting dog in the state, and he took another prize for the finest looking dog. So my regards to the champion of South Carolina.

In the old days, we wasn't sanitary, why, we were strong enough to withstand germs. But nowadays we have to be careful of microbes, for if they get a hold of us, we are goners.

The old-fashioned gourd that the whole family drank out of, from birth till death, would today kill more of the modern population than a war.

I'm no believer in this "hard work, perseverance and taking advantage of your opportunities" that these magazines are fond of writing some fellow up in. The successful don't work any harder than the failures.

I was supposed to dedicate a monument one time. It was down home in Oklahoma; in fact, I think it was on the capitol grounds in Oklahoma City. There was a big tarpaulin spread over this statue of a cowboy, just waiting for my unveiling.

Well, one of those Oklahoma cyclones come along. (Chamber of Commerce of Oklahoma kicks on that last statement.) Well, this wind hit the statue and the old tarp wouldn't hold; and away she blew. They wired me immediately: "Don't come; another big wind has beat you to the unveiling and did it in one-tenth of the time it would have taken you to blow it off."

If I am broad-minded in any way (and I hope I am in many), I do know that I am broad-minded in a religious way.

I never like to pick on anybody when they are down.

Yesterday was my wife's and my twenty-fifth wedding anniversary. I got her an awful pretty silver thimble, you know, it was our silver anniversary. She had the old one just about worn out.

I also contributed quite a few silver hairs to the occasion. But you know, my wife hasn't got a single gray hair—she ain't got a one.

You see, I've never worried her!

Mr. Coolidge said that newspaper men should stand by the administration's foreign policy.

Now I will admit there has been times when he and I differed on Nicaragua, Mexico and China, but when I read his angle of it all, it sounded plausible.

They say a smart man changes his mind, but an editorial writer never does; so I have been convinced that I would rather be wrong with the administration, than right against it.

I was just wondering what I would have to do if I was to start out to help out my old school, "Drumgoole," which was a little, one-room log cabin, four miles east of Chelsea, Indian Territory.

It was all Indian kids went there, and I, being part Cherokee, had enough white in me to make my honesty questionable.

I have seen Caruso twice, once when I took my wife to hear him as a wedding present, and once on a bet.

All of us, in any line of business, are like that. We are always yapping about the "Good Old Days" and how we look away back and enjoy it, but I tell you there is a lot of hooey to it.

There is a whole lot of all our past lives that wasn't so hot.

I got a telegram from Amarillo, Texas, and they want me to say something about mothers-in-law. They say they are having a mother-in-law day.

I had a wonderful mother-in-law, and I always felt—after looking at mothers-in-law and seeing sons-in-law, I always felt that the jokes were on the wrong ones.

No sir, you can look through everything I ever did write or say, and you never did hear me tell a joke about any mother-in-law, or any creed, color or religion, either.

I am the first acknowledged comedian to receive a vote for the Presidency—not the first comedian, mind you, but the first acknowledged one.

RELIGION

God is a lot more broad-minded than we think He is.

The trouble with our praying is, we just do it as a means of last resort.

Church people all over the country are divided and arguing over where we come from. Never mind where we come from, neighbor! Just let the preachers make it their business where you are going when you leave here.

Say, I just saw the movie *The King of Kings*. This is not an ad. It's a duty to let you know of it. The only way you could make a greater

picture would be to have a better subject, and I doubt if there will
ever be a better subject than the story of Christ.

Some old boys that's claimed they been dead and then come back to
life, they seem to be getting all the play in the papers. One fellow
claimed he got to Heaven and that it was great and he is sorry they
revived him. Well, it's not much trouble to get dead again; a little
street crossing without being alert will do the job.

Then we got an old boy out here in Hollywood that claimed he was
dead for 22 minutes, and he says he was glad to get back alive again.
Sounds like a Chamber of Commerce ad for Hollywood to me.
'Course, coming from where he does, he might have got in the wrong
place.

Southern Methodist Conference out here in California passed a resolution asking Congress to exempt them from war. Don't know what
claim they have over other denominations unless it's that they are
always fighting so much among themselves that two wars at once would
be a hardship on 'em.

Right near New York City, there is an apostle of doom and he says
that tonight is the night that the world is coming to an end. The papers
here are full of it. So everybody says to me, "Will, you ought to get
a lot of fun out of this world ending business." Say, you ain't going
to get me telling no jokes on that. Suppose it happens? Look where I
would be.

It is happening at a very inopportune time for me, because I have
a payment to meet on some land out in California. I have tried all
day to have the payment postponed until tomorrow. I don't know
which would be a greater disappointment to me—having to pay—or
having to die.

But if they bring the world to an end tonight, I think personally
they will make a big mistake. This country has possibilities.

Speaking of not believing, I don't believe that Noah took a pair of
every kind of animal into the Ark, for I have seen men since Prohibition
changed their drink who claim that they saw animals that Noah never
even heard of. But just because I don't believe in Noah's adventures,
maybe others do, and besides my small experience with animals I don't
believe Noah could round up all the animals without the skunk causing
a stampede.

That is no reason why I should go around shouting about it and be arrested for heresy. I can enjoy a good zoo as well as anyone. Whether the animals come here by Ark or subway, makes no difference to me. If they are going to argue religion in the church instead of teaching it, it is no wonder that you can see more people at a circus than at a church.

A candidate is always dragged into a religious controversy. If one side can prove that the other candidate was connected with a Sunday school, it will lose him the Catholic and Jewish vote, and if they can prove it was a Methodist Sunday school, it will lose him the Baptists.

All religions in a campaign seem such handicaps that I think it's better to claim you are an atheist.

This year, being an election year, churches are hit harder by politics than usual. It has been the text of more sermons than the Lord's Supper. A minister can't pray without asking divine guidance in this election. Before they say "amen" he takes a poll vote. Half the contributions go into the campaign funds. The Savior was never asked more imploringly to enter politics than He is this year.

After finishing listening to a baseball game on radio, I figured on account of it being Sunday, I could leave it turned on and not have to listen to some politician—but what do I get? Four preachers, all at different places, and what was they doing—saving sinners? No! Two of 'em was saving Republicans, and the other two was saving the Democrats.

The old sinner won't get much consideration till after election day.

There never was a nation founded and maintained without some kind of belief in something. Nobody knows what the outcome in Russia will be, or how long the government will last. But even if they do get by for quite a while on everything else, they picked the one thing I know of to suppress that is absolutely necessary to run a country on, and that is religion.

Never mind what kind; it's got to be something or you will fall in the end.

To get down to religion in Russia, they will tell you that the worship of Lenin is their religion. Lenin preached revolution, blood and murder in everything I ever read of his. Now you may dig 'em up a religion out of that, but it's too soon.

You know, there is a lot of big men die, but most of them are not so big that they won't all be buried.

Judge Benjamin Lindsay is for free love and Bishop William Manning is holding out for the usual clergyman's fee for the marriage ceremony. It looks like church laws, or civil laws or even universal customs don't mean anything to anybody anymore. Everybody is doing just as they like, regardless of everything.

Every man, every denomination and every organization wants things their way. It's just one of those things we got to pass through; and we will look back and feel ashamed of ourselves afterwards.

That's one wonderful thing about the Bible. There was no censorship in those days. Of course now some of our churches hold conferences and cut out certain parts that they think don't belong in there, or change them according to what they think should be said, instead of what was said. In other words, we are having somebody improving on the words of the Lord!

That's even worse than a film scenario writer brightening up Shakespeare.

All our preachers are doing our principal legislation for us now. We pick up a paper and it says: "We can't get this bill through, because Bishop So-and-so is against it," and "We have to pass this as the Federated Parsons of Ossawatomie are behind it." A preacher just can't save anybody nowadays. He is too busy saving the nation. He can't monkey with individual salvation. In the old days those fellows read their Bibles. Now they read the Congressional Record.

During all this campaigning, a dozen Presidential candidates couldn't make any more headway than a preacher that didn't talk politics.

The Church is in politics more than the politicians. If Congress met on Sundays, why, there would be no services anywhere, all the ministers would have their eyes on Congress.

MISSIONARIES

Something ought to be done about these "primitive" people who live in various parts of the world and don't know a thing but to live off what nature provides.

You would think they would get civilized and learn to live off each other, like us civilized folks do.

Aboard the SS. *Empress of Russia,* on our way to the orient, we got some missionaries on here, going out to make the world good and pure, like us.

The other day I visited one of our California missions. One should never pass any of these missions without stopping and going in. They are among the great historical spots of our country. This one was built in 1776. That's the year our World Series was over with England. An old priest had come into the country, Father Junipero Serra, and he built missions and schools and he taught the Indians. He was a greater humanitarian than all the Pilgrims combined, including the three million that came on the Mayflower. He civilized with a Bible, and the old Pilgrim boys did it with a blunderbuss. My motto is: Save America first, and then, when you get 'em all saved, then go out and save the Portuguese. The Chinese don't need saving!

EVOLUTION

On July 10, 1925, the trial of John Thomas Scopes began. It lasted just eleven days, but it divided the nation immediately. Scopes was a high school science teacher in Dayton, Tennessee, who stood accused of having violated the Tennessee state law prohibiting the teaching in public schools of any theories denying the divine creation of man, as taught in the Bible. In plain words, Scopes, a biologist, had taught evolution. The Tennessee legislature had passed the anti-evolution law by an embarrassing majority of 95 to 11, and it was signed by the governor on March 13, 1925. The American Civil Liberties Union (ACLU) immediately maintained that the law was unconstitutional and offered free legal defense to any teacher who would wish to test the law. John T. Scopes offered to assist, and after having taught his class was formally indicted.

The two opposing lawyers in the hot, sticky courtroom that July were two of the foremost names in America. To "assist" the local prosecutor came Fundamentalist William Jennings Bryan, three times Democratic candidate for the presidency. He was an honored man of high standards, respected even by those of opposing views. For the defense, the ACLU obtained the services of the preeminent trial lawyer of his day, Clarence S. Darrow.

The ruling of the presiding judge prevented any testing of the civil liberties aspect of the constitutionality of the law or any testimony as to the validity of Darwin's theory of evolution.

With not just the United States but also Europe watching, Scopes was convicted and fined one hundred dollars. On appeal the Tennessee Supreme Court upheld the constitutionality of the law in 1927, but cleared Scopes on a technicality.

Keeping his eye on the "monkey" trial, Will Rogers reported:

> If a man is a gentleman, he don't have to announce it; all he has to do is to act like one and let the world decide. No man should have to prove in court what he is, or what he come from. As far as Scopes teaching children evolution, nobody is going to change the belief of Tennessee children as to their ancestry. It is from the action of their parents that they will form their opinions.
>
> No great religious revival will ever be started from an argument over where we come from. The religious revival of the future, when it is started, will be people's fear over where we are going.*

Will approached the argument from a different side:

> Some people certainly are making a fight against the ape. It seems the truth kinder hurts. Now, if a man didn't act like a monkey, he wouldn't have to be proving that he didn't come from one. Personally I like monkeys. If we were half as original as they are, we would never be suspected of coming from something else. They never accuse monkeys of coming from anybody else.

Not until his daily squib, published June 1, 1934, did Will Rogers present proof of his own derivation:

> Among all the big news and headlines of today's news, there was a little item that sure give me great encourage-

---

*Weekly article, July 19, 1925.

ment. It said that some great professor of the Smithsonian Institution had discovered that persons with a "cowlick" was human, and not like the person who had none, as they descended from the ape. No ape ever had a cowlick!

So now, instead of having M.D. and Ph.D. after your name that publicly advertise your supposed knowledge, why, we just take off our hats and show you the old cowlick, and say: "There, you apes, take a look at a human!"

You hang an ape and a political ancestry over me, and you will see me taking it into the Supreme Court, to prove that the ape part is O.K., but that the political end of it is base libel.

William Jennings Bryan tried to prove that we did not descend from the monkey, but he unfortunately picked a time in our history when the actions of the American people proved that we did.

William Jennings Bryan was a fundamentalist, and he was against Darwin's theory of evolution, and I always felt he was wrong in trying to carry it into laws. He was ridiculed a lot, but you can't get far ridiculing a man for upholding the Bible, or even a dictionary, if it is his sincere belief.

The Supreme Court of Tennessee has just ruled that you other states can come from whoever or whatever you want to, but they want it on record that they come from mud only!

I don't know why some of these states want to have their ancestry established by law. There must be some suspicion of doubt somewhere.

The fight over evolution will settle some day, for nobody knows where they come from. Everybody looks at their enemies and hopes and prays they didn't come from the same place.

When some of them say that they will make this anti-evolution thing their life's issue, and take it up through all the various courts and finally get it into the Constitution of the United States, they are wrong.

As for changing the Constitution—that's done every day. They have juggled it around until it looks like a moving picture of a popular book—it's so different from the original. But when those Boys that blue-printed the first Constitution decided that a man can believe what he likes in regard to religion—that's one line that is going to stay put.

These fellows who honestly believe that their great, great grandfathers were as proficient with their toes as with their fingers, they have that right. Most people are proud of their ancestry and it is a touchy thing to cast reflections on a man's forefathers, even if he did arrive here on all fours.

There is a terrible lot of us who don't think that we come from a monkey, but if there are some people who think that they do, why, it's not our business to rob them of what little pleasure they might get out of imagining it.

CIVILIZATION

We Americans had begun to believe that the height of civilization was a good road, a bath tub, radio and an automobile.

I challenge Billy Sunday to a debate on the problem, "Are people harder to fool now than they used to be?" We both been at it so long. I think they are. They are not getting any wiser; it's just that they are getting more cautious.

I guess there has never been a time in our history when as many fools are making money as now. Just to be rich and nothing else is practically a disgrace nowadays.

All our highly civilized nations are great humanitarians, but if two countries are going to kill each other off, neutrals at least would like the privilege of furnishing the ammunition.
     And when Judgement Day comes, civilization will have an alibi: "I never took a human life; I only sold the gun to take it with."

Association has nothing to do with Culture. I know Englishmen that have had the same well-bred butler all their lives and they are just as rude as they ever were. Why, do you know, one of the most cultured men I ever saw come from Texas, and where he learned it, the Lord only knows.

There is nothing that a rich man can do nowadays that a poor one can't follow and make a sucker out of him.
     Up to three years ago the poor thought it was against the law to gamble. Now they can tell you what General Motors closed at just as quick as the man that don't work for a living.

The whole thing, as I see it all over the world, is that the little nations have got no business being little.

A man can make a million dollars overnight and he is on every front page in the morning, but it never tells who gave up the million that he got. What you got tonight that you didn't have last night must have come from somebody. They don't just issue new money.

We have dozens of magazines that print success stories, but you go broke and see what you can do to get your life story published. We love to read in big figures. The old man that didn't get the breaks and couldn't make the grade, him we don't care much for.

We are just stepping too fast. In the old days we figured the world owed us a living, now we figure it owes us an automobile, a player piano, and a radio, Frigidaire, and Clara Bow. The automobile is to take you places you would be better off if you didn't go to. The player piano is to discourage you from trying to play your own simple tunes that your folks spent so much on your learning. The radio is for picking out the right toothpaste. The Frigidaire is to give you ice water when you would be better off if you didn't load up on it, and Clara Bow will just lead you plum astray. She will give a country boy the wrong impression.

But it's all coming under the heading of higher civilization.

You must never disagree with a man while you are facing him. Go around behind him and look the same way he is looking and you will see that things look different from what they do when you're facing him.

Look over his shoulder and get his viewpoint, then go back and face him and you will have a different idea.

Individually and nationally we are just living in a time when none of us are in any shape to be telling somebody else what to do. That's why your League of Nations won't hold water; because the big ones run it and the little ones know that the big ones only turned moral since they got all they can hold. I can come in with a full stomach and advise the rest of the gang not to rob the fruit stand. That ain't right.

Life is a "racket," so get a few laughs, do the best you can, take nothing serious, for nothing is certainly depending on this generation. Each one lives in spite of the previous one and not because of it.

Believe in something for another world, but don't be too set on what

August 16, 1935. American editors selected the Will Rogers-Wiley Post crash as the top American news story for the year 1935. World-wide it ranked only behind Mussolini's war against Abyssinia.

it is, and then you won't start out that life with a disappointment. Live your life so that whenever you lose, you are ahead.

MISCELLANEOUS

Retroactive. That means you can go back and get something that you forgot to get at the time.

Nothing makes a man, or a body of men, as mad as the truth. If there is no truth in it, they laugh it off.

It's great to be great, but it's greater to be human.

There is no chance for personal initiative anymore. We are all just a cog in a big machine that's controlled from New York or Chicago.

That would be a wonderful thing, wouldn't it, if a man could pick his own biographer. Trouble with a lot of these biographers is they go and lower the moral of the character with a lot of facts. Nothing will spoil a big man's life like too much truth.

Have you ever noticed that there is more bad ideas that will work than there is good ones?

We all know the Good Book says, "The Lord loveth the poor and down and out." But at the same time, it looks like the poor don't get much besides "love." They are being loved all the time, but they are also being poor all the time.

Did you ever notice the fellow at a party who is always getting insulted the quickest and oftenest is really, if you know him, a guy that you would think it wouldn't be possible to insult at all?

Nothing will make a reader yawn any quicker than good English.

Was our folks dumb and didn't know anything? Say, don't kid yourself! Those old boys in their youth could take a silver dollar and go out and corral more hot times than we ever thought of. They did a lot of prowling in their time. A horse and buggy would take you so far that it wasn't impossible to walk home, but it was inconvenient.
    Even back in my time, when I was going good, I have come dragging

in from a dance horseback by daylight. We wasn't making payment on as many things, but we was making some mighty nifty whoopee. Your mothers get mighty shocked at you girls nowadays, but in her day, her mother was just on the verge of sending her to a reformatory.

Some criticize today's youth, but I think that that criticism is unwarranted. Youth must have its fling, and because we are too old to fling, we must be tolerant with those that are flinging.

Youth today is no worse than we were, only the publicity is greater today. Long skirts hid more in your mother's day, but the provocation was there. We had no automobiles by the roadside in those days, but horses would stop, too. We covered more space in our dances and didn't use the huddle system.

Youth must sow its wild oats, and oat seed hasn't changed since the day Eve planted the first crop. The manner of sowing is different, but the seed and the harvest are the same.

The kiss was shorter, but there were more of them.

It don't take much to see that something is wrong, but it does take some eyesight to see what will put it right again.

Our optimism is all at a banquet table, where everybody has more than they can eat.

I just wonder if it ain't just cowardice instead of generosity that makes us give most of our tips.

Just give anything enough publicity and we would pay admission to see folks guillotined.

I never go into another fellow's country with what the guy that is always wanting to snoop into somebody else's business calls "An Open Mind." His mind is not open. If it was he wouldn't have to announce it. It's because his mind is narrow that he is suspicious that someone won't think it's open, unless he announces it.

So always be leery of these babies with OPEN MINDS. They are open, all right—they are open at both ends.

Chapter XI

POSTSCRIPT

*I*n 1935, Betty Rogers noticed for the first time that her husband appeared to tire more easily. To the world at large, Will, who was approaching his fifty-sixth birthday, did not seem to cut down on his activities.

There were still the columns, the daily squibs, and the weekly articles; there were still the Sunday broadcasts and the motion pictures; and in between, whenever possible, there were still the speeches. Will not only traveled all over the country to deliver those talks but each one had to be fashioned for the occasion. There were still his favorite pastimes, the polo games, the riding, and the roping. All seemed as before, but if the constant demands on Will's energy had begun to take their toll, a loving wife would be the first to see it.

His crowded calendar can best be illustrated by a brief glimpse at a week on Rogers' speech-making schedule. On Monday, January 15, 1935, he delivered a broadcast speech at Notre Dame University in South Bend, Indiana. The next evening, at the personal invitation of Helen Keller, Will Rogers was in Washington, D.C., speaking at a benefit for the blind. The next night, Wednesday, Will appeared before the Poor Richard Club in Philadelphia. The following day, Thursday, saw Rogers in Indianapolis at a benefit for the James Whitcomb Riley Hospital. One day later, Friday, Rogers addressed the Alfalfa Club in

Washington, D.C. Saturday Will spent in New York City. Then he took off for a benefit for crippled children in Austin, Texas, on Monday, January 22.

In the next few months Will completed three more motion pictures for Fox Film Corporation to fulfill his contractual requirements for the balance of 1935. There was *Doubting Thomas*, directed by David Butler and co-starring Billie Burke, Florenz Ziegfeld's widow. Others in the cast were Broadway's Alison Skipworth, Sterling Holloway, and Frank Albertson. Immediately following, on April 15, Will began filming *In Old Kentucky*, directed by George Marshall. It featured Dorothy Wilson, Russell Hardie, and the famous dancer Bill "Bojangles" Robinson. Next, Will moved on to the third film, *Steamboat Round the Bend*, directed by John Ford. It also starred Anne Shirley, Irvin S. Cobb, Eugene Pallette, and Stepin Fetchit.

Months earlier Rogers had agreed to make one more motion picture in 1935: *Ah! Wilderness*, Eugene O'Neill's only comedy. Metro-Goldwyn-Mayer owned the rights and had wanted Will Rogers to play the lead. After lengthy negotiations for Rogers' services, MGM had come to terms with Will's home studio, Fox Film Corporation. It had all been arranged.

It started in 1934, when Will Rogers appeared in his only legitimate stage play. George M. Cohan had created the role of Nat Miller in O'Neill's play *Ah! Wilderness* on Broadway. Producer Henry Duffy persuaded Will Rogers to star in a limited run of the play in the West Coast production. The play was scheduled for three weeks in San Francisco and then for three weeks in Los Angeles. On April 30, 1934, Will Rogers opened at the Curran Theatre in San Francisco. The chance to see Will Rogers in a legitimate play was such an important occasion that even the distant *New York Times* sent a reporter to cover the opening. The reviewers and the audiences loved Will's characterization.

As agreed, after a sold-out three-week run in San Francisco, the play, co-starring Anne Shoemaker, moved to the El Capitan Theatre in Los Angeles. Here, too, the advance sale had been astonishingly heavy. The 1,571-seat theater was sold out every night and the demand for tickets was steady. During the third—and supposedly last—week of the limited run, Will agreed to an additional matinee show, thus presenting nine performances. He then agreed to a fourth week, with yet one more performance—a tenth—on Sunday. And still there was a clamor to see Will Rogers. A fifth week was added, and then a sixth. Despite an unabated demand for tickets, the show closed abruptly on Saturday night, June 30. The official news release sounded reasonable:

> Engagement was terminated only because picture work of Rogers' at Fox prevented his continuing doubling for screen and stage.

On July 3, 1934, on page 63, *Variety*, the show business Bible, wrote: "[This show] could have continued indefinitely."

Something had happened. The "official" announcement was obviously not the truth, for Will had completed his year's work at Fox. This is easy to prove as he was in Texas ten days later, visiting old friends; and by the twenty-second of the month he was aboard the SS *Malolo*, on a trip around the world.

The truth seems to be that Will had refused to extend the run of the play and had informed his studio that he would make any other film they wanted, but not *Ah! Wilderness*.

The explanation for Rogers' action is documented by several sources. Will's long-time friend Eddie Cantor, the famous entertainer, explained it best:

> Will received a letter from a clergyman: "Relying on you to give the public nothing that could bring the blush of shame to the cheeks of a Christian, I attended your performance with my 14-year-old daughter. But when you did the scene in which the father lectures the son on the subject of his relations with an immoral woman, I took my daughter by the hand and we left the theater. I have not been able to look her in the eye since."

Rogers must have been terribly disturbed by this note. He had seen nothing wrong with that particular scene, or he would never have accepted the role. Critics and audiences had especially lauded this particular father-and-son scene as one which "he played with simple sincerity that brought out handkerchiefs and made tears and smiles mingle." Obviously it was open to misinterpretation. While a play would only be seen by a few thousand, a film would be seen by millions. Will Rogers had never wanted to be connected with any motion picture that could not be seen by the entire family, including all the children. Will decided that he wanted no part of any film that could cause even one parent anguish—whether that parent's objection was valid or not.

That had been in the summer of 1934. MGM went ahead with its preproduction details for *Ah! Wilderness.* Finally, a year later, in early August 1935, MGM revealed the cast for the O'Neill film. Will Rogers' part of Nat Miller was now to be played by Lionel Barrymore, with Wallace Beery as the drinking uncle. The studio also announced that the cast had left for New England, where the exterior shots would be filmed. Had Rogers not received the clergyman's letter, he would have been on his way to New England.

Instead, Will Rogers was at home on his ranch in Pacific Palisades. He considered taking a dirigible trip around South America. Then there had been an invitation from producer Hal Roach, Sr., his old friend, to come to Hawaii on a polo-playing tour. It had sounded tempting.

Director John Ford, another old friend, had invited him to come to Hawaii and perhaps make a film in the islands.

And then there had been aviation pioneer Wiley Post, who had suggested a trip to Alaska and perhaps around the world. Will had weighed them all in his mind. Sooner or later he would have to make a decision.

In his syndicated weekly article, published July 14, 1935, Will wrote:

> Well, after I finish a long siege of work, I sorter begin looking up in the air and see what is flying over, and Mrs. Rogers, in her wise way will say, "Well, I think you better get on one. You are getting sorter nervous."

And so on August 5, Will Rogers left Los Angeles to join Wiley Post on a flight to Alaska.

Ten days later both men were dead when their small plane crashed near Barrow, Alaska.

Index

235